The Spiritual Legacy of
Henri Nouwen

The Spiritual Legacy of Henri Nouwen

DEIRDRE LaNOUE

Continuum

New York ✧ London

2001

The Continuum International Publishing Group Inc
370 Lexington Avenue, New York, NY 10017

The Continuum International Publishing Group Ltd
The Tower Building, 11 York Road, London SE1 7NX

Printed in the United States of America

Library of Congress Cataloging-in-Publication Data

LaNoue, Deirdre.
    The spiritual legacy of Henri Nouwen / Deirdre LaNoue.
      p. cm.
    Includes bibliographical references and index.
    ISBN 0-8264-1283-1 (hardcover)
      1. Nouwen, Henri J. M.—Contributions in spirituality.
    2. Spirituality—Catholic Church—History—20th century.   I. Title.

BX4705.N87 L36 2000
282'.092—dc21
    [B]   00-043118

To Mom and Dad
and
To John

Contents

Acknowledgments

I am grateful for the relationships with which my life has been blessed in the years that I have worked on this project. So many have helped me along the journey and I would like to mention at least a few of them. I would like to thank my colleagues at Baylor University. Your guidance and instruction regarding this project, when it was in the form of a dissertation, helped to make it worth further developing as a general-interest book. I am most grateful for your investment in my life.

I would also like to thank those who assisted in helping me to gain access to research materials concerning Henri Nouwen. Martha Smalley and her staff in the Archives at Yale Divinity School Library offered me complete access to Nouwen's papers as well as the space and time to sift through them.

Special thanks is due to Sue Mosteller and her staff at the Henri Nouwen Literary Center in Richmond Hill, Ontario, for allowing me the opportunity to visit the L'Arche Daybreak community where Nouwen lived and worked for the last ten years of his life. I am most grateful for your gracious hospitality and cooperation so that I might conduct interviews with some of those who knew Nouwen best and gain a personal perspective on why the community at Daybreak was so special to him. You welcomed me in the Spirit of Christ and I am grateful for the friendship born of our time together. Thank you, Sue, for reading the manuscript and offering your own thoughtful insights and suggestions.

I must also thank my colleagues at Dallas Baptist University, especially Dr. Gail Linam and Dr. Mike Williams, for their support and encouragement. Writing a book while teaching full time is not an easy task. Thank you for reading many revisions, making suggestions, and encouraging me to seek a publisher.

I want to thank friends and family for loving me through it all. Thank you Kay, Carolyn, Denise and Tom, Barbara, Pat, Minette, Cindy, Marti, Kaywin, John Sr., Mom and Dad, and especially John—husband, friend, proofreader, research assistant, and the best source for loving hugs this side of heaven. I could not have persevered without your unwavering suppport and encouragement. Your love and care carried me through the discouraging and stressful moments and celebrated with me through the exciting moments in seeing this work come to completion.

Finally, thank you to Frank Oveis, my editor at Continuum, for seeing the value in this work and being willing to publish it. Thank you for your gracious spirit and thoughtful creativity.

To God alone be the glory.

Deirdre LaNoue

The Spiritual Legacy of Henri Nouwen

CHAPTER ONE

⬧

An Introduction to Spirituality and Henri Nouwen

S everal significant writers in the twentieth century—including Eve-
lyn Underhill, Pierre Teilhard de Chardin, Simone Weil, and
Thomas Merton—have served as spiritual guides for modern Americans.
None of these except Merton, however, lived and worked in the United
States with particular insight into the American spiritual milieu. Ironically, the year following Thomas Merton's death in 1968, another Catholic writer, who would soon join this illustrious group of spiritual guides,
began his career. His name was Henri Nouwen.

Nouwen was not first known as an author but rather as a speaker and
professor. His classes were popular everywhere he taught, and he was in
great demand internationally as a keynote speaker for conferences, retreats, and other events. His popularity stemmed from his unique ability
to describe his own spiritual struggles in such a way that many people
easily related their experiences to his. He thereby emerged as an accessible spiritual guide and mentor, challenging modern seekers to find their
own path "into the Holy."[1]

The purpose of this book is to explore the spirituality of Henri
Nouwen within the context of American spirituality in the late twentieth century. What was the key ingredient in Nouwen's life and work
that attracted so many to him? What were the compelling themes in his
writing that attracted such a diverse audience of readers? What was it
about the microcosm of Nouwen's own spiritual journey that enabled
him to communicate so effectively within the spiritual macrocosm of
modern America? Let's begin by attempting to define what is meant by
spirituality.

---

[1] Betty W. Talbert, "The Way of the Heart," *Mission Journal* 16 (August 1982): 19–20.

Spirituality Defined

What is *spirituality*? Is it just another word for religion? And what distinguishes *Christian* spirituality from other types of spirituality?

There are as many definitions of spirituality today as there are authors who write about it. Phyllis Tickle, offering a general or philosphical definition, defines it as "an attitude about the sacred" and a "set of personal choices and disciplines for living in accord with it."[2] Michael Downey defines it as "the human quest for ultimate value, or the human person's striving to attain the highest ideal or goal."[3] Sandra Schneiders takes a more relational approach and defines it as "the actualization of the human capacity for self-transcendence, in and through the establishment of personal relationships."[4]

Schneiders defines *Christian* spirituality as "that particular actualization of the capacity for self-transcendence that is constituted by the substantial gift of the Holy Spirit establishing a life-giving relationship with God in Christ within the believing community."[5] The comparison of Schneiders's general definition with her Christian definition helps us to see the relationship between the two. But a simpler expression is found in the definition by Elizabeth Dreyer in the opening sentence of her article on Christian spirituality in the *HarperCollins Encyclopedia of Catholicism*:

> Christian spirituality is the daily, communal, lived expression of one's ultimate beliefs characterized by openness to the self-transcending love of God, self, neighbor, and world through Jesus Christ and in the power of the Spirit.[6]

This definition certainly harmonizes with Henri Nouwen's view of Christian spirituality, since the majority of his writings address in some fashion how one can nurture one's relationship with God, with self, and with others through the love of Jesus and the power of the Holy Spirit.

Now that we have some kind of idea of what is meant by the term *spirituality*, a brief of history of spirituality in America over the last fifty

---

[2] Phyllis A. Tickle, *Re-Discovering the Sacred: Spirituality in America* (New York: Crossroad Publishing Company, 1995), 16.

[3] Michael Downey, *Understanding Christian Spirituality* (New York: Paulist Press, 1997), 14.

[4] Sandra Schneiders, "Theology and Spirituality: Strangers, Rivals, or Partners?" *Horizons* 13 (Fall 1986): 266.

[5] Ibid.

[6] *HarperCollins Encyclopedia of Catholicism*, s.v. "Christian Spirituality," 1216.

years will help provide a historical context for the life and work of Henri Nouwen.

Five Decades of American Spirituality

The spiritual scene in America has changed drastically over the last fifty years. If the years 1949 and 1999 could be placed side by side, the contrast would certainly be a striking one. What are the events and trends that led to such a contrast? How has American spirituality changed? What was the spiritual milieu in which Henri Nouwen lived and worked?

Religious Vitality in the Postwar Years, 1946–1960

The post–World War II years in America were years of growth and optimism in many respects. The Allied forces returned victorious over Hitler and the Axis powers. Truman and Eisenhower brought a sense of stability to the White House. The United States was the leading power in the free world and patriotism was at an all-time high. Yet the postwar years were also a time of anxiety and strife. The haunting specter of the Cold War gave rise to the witch-hunting tactics of McCarthy and Nixon, who were determined to rout the Reds from American society. The possibility of nuclear war had become reality with the bombing of Hiroshima. African Americans, who had also sacrificed for the idea of democratic freedom in World War II, were more determined than ever to experience that ideal at home, where racism and prejudice were still strong and formidable foes for minorities and the poor.

The economy faltered just after the war, but by 1950 it was thriving. The middle-class population expanded and Americans experienced a higher standard of living. Consumerism skyrocketed and convenience began to be valued more than cost-effectiveness. The American population increased as well. The baby boom exploded and the suburbs skirted the cities in ever widening bands. Life was family centered and community centered. Although mobility was increasing, people tended to stay in familiar geographic areas, close to extended family and within familiar cultural havens.

Christianity also flourished during this era of a booming population, an expanding economy, and a swelling national pride. The majority of the population attended a church of some kind, and Protestant evangelical revivalism added thousands of converts every year. As in the years before the war, Christianity was an integral part of life in America.

The spirituality of the 1950s was therefore strongly dictated by institutional or organized religion. Robert Wuthnow, in his work *After Heaven: Spirituality in America Since the 1950s*, called the spirituality of the 1950s a "dwelling-oriented" spirituality.[7] Spirituality was strongly associated with places of belonging such as home, community, and country. Spirituality was more of a natural response to a natural habitation where the sacred was fairly fixed and easily defined. Such a spirituality was secure and relatively stable. No seeking was required. One simply had to participate in or conform to the prescribed order. Yet in reality life was not perfect at home, in the community, or in the country as a whole, and American spirituality eventually experienced a significant crisis as the changes in society and culture dealt severe blows to the traditional spiritual "dwelling places" of home, community, and country in the 1960s.[8]

The Tumultuous Struggle for Freedom, 1961–1975

Sydney Ahlstrom describes the decade of the 1960s as "a time, in short, when old foundations of national confidence, patriotic idealism, moral traditionalism and even Judeo-Christian theism, were awash. . . . Presuppositions that had held firm for centuries—even millennia—were being widely questioned."[9] What led to this kind of "watershed decade?" The baby-boomer generation began to detect in their parents' generation a moral hypocrisy that was unacceptable to them. Technological marvels, vast production, great ideals, expanding education, and flourishing churches seemed to have only resulted in bigotry, fear, violence, racism, and war. Rampant urbanization and industrial growth left the poor disenfranchised. Pluralism was spawning violence and militancy. Nuclear man now had the potential for more pollution and even self-destruction. The escalating military action in Vietnam seemed pointless, and nobody could trust those in authority to tell the truth. Those who were trusted, public leaders, who symbolized hope, were murdered: John F. Kennedy in 1963 and Martin Luther King Jr. in 1968. Thus a youth movement arose that was antiestablishment.[10]

[7] Robert Wuthnow, *After Heaven: Spirituality in America Since the 1950s* (Berkeley: University of California Press, 1998), 19.

[8] Ibid., 1–18.

[9] Sydney E. Ahlstrom, *A Religious History of the American People* (New Haven: Yale University Press, 1972), 1080.

[10] George Gallup Jr. and Jim Castelli, *The People's Religion: American Faith in the 90s* (New York: Macmillan Publishing Company, 1989), 4.

Spirituality by no means disappeared but went "underground and took expression outside of the religious establishment."[11] Besides the communal disaffections of the beatniks and the flower children, many young people began to turn inward through the occult and Eastern religions. Radical theologians said that God was dead. Existentialism looked for meaning in the present moment. The role of the church and its clergy began to shift toward social issues, and "therapeutic Christianity" began its development as psychology came ever more into vogue.

Wuthnow summarizes this time period well in his claim that spirituality did not decrease in the light of the secularism of the 1960s and early 1970s. Instead it changed courses. American spirituality shifted from a dwelling-oriented spirituality to a seeking-oriented spirituality. Although he admits that this tumultuous time was filled with radical ideas and shocking behaviors, the spirituality of this era did correct some of the aberrations of the postwar years.

> Americans in the fifties chose largely to remain where they were, opting for security rather than risking their faith in a genuine search for spiritual depth; however, in the 1960s many Americans, having learned that they could move around, think through their options, and select a faith that truly captured what they believed to be the truth, took the choice seriously, bargaining with their souls, seeking new spiritual guides, and rediscovering that God dwells not only in homes but also in the byways trod by pilgrims and sojourners.[12]

In this scene where Americans, especially young people, were searching with a new fervency for spiritual meaning, Henri Nouwen came to teach at Notre Dame in 1966 and later, beginning in 1971, at Yale Divinity School. He did not exemplify the typical status quo as far as American Christianity was concerned. He was not Protestant and he was not "old school." He was a psychologist as well as a Dutch Roman Catholic priest, and he was committed to many of the changes that Vatican II had instigated. He longed to help college students see the relevance of authentic Christianity as a source of truth in the midst of much questioning and searching.

A Conservative Reaction, 1976–1990

By the mid-1970s, the pendulum had fully begun to swing in another direction as the secularism of the 1960s gave way to the influence of

---

[11] Wade Clark Roof, *A Generation of Seekers: The Spiritual Journeys of the Baby Boom Generation* (San Francisco: HarperSanFrancisco, 1993), 242.

[12] Wuthnow, *After Heaven*, 57.

neoevangelicalism. *Newsweek* proclaimed 1976 the "year of the evangelical."[13] The United States had a "born again" president in Jimmy Carter. Charles Colson of the Watergate scandals was converted and wrote a book about his experience. Evangelical publishers flourished with magazines like *Christianity Today*, as did parachurch student organizations like Intervarsity Christian Fellowship and Campus Crusade.[14]

Yet gone were the days when most American Christians were content to rely on those in authority to tell them what they believed. Experience was also an important ingredient for discerning the truth, and the new field of psychology was attempting to explain the human experience as very individualized and unique. Bradley Holt writes in his brief history of Christian spirituality, *Thirsty for God*, that spirituality in North America was influenced by the field of psychology perhaps more than on any other continent as Americans sought self-fulfillment, self-realization, and mental health. Holt views this influence as positive in that the theme of healing is a very important one for Christian spirituality and psychology seeks to heal people's emotional wounds. On the other hand, Holt writes that the influence of psychology also had a negative influence by producing a self-absorption that ignored the community and social issues.[15]

By the 1980s Americans were becoming more optimistic about their future and more conservative in their opinions. All three of the presidential candidates in 1980 professed to be "born again" and used that identity in their campaigns to reach a large and influential segment of the population that professed a commitment to Jesus Christ (66 percent by 1988). Decline continued among the more liberal mainline denominations, but the evangelical churches continued to experience a moderate revival.[16] Gallup also described the eighties as a time of "renewed search for spiritual moorings" as well as a "new activism on the part of church leaders."[17]

A major outcome of the evangelical leadership getting more involved in social and political issues was a movement sometimes referred to as the "New Christian Right," a leading example being the organization led by Jerry Falwell called the Moral Majority. These evangelical and politi-

[13] Kenneth L. Woodard, "Born Again!" *Newsweek* 25 October 1976, 68–70, 75–76, 78.

[14] *Encyclopedia of American Religious Experience*, s.v. "Conservative and Charismatic Developments of the Later Twentieth Century," 972.

[15] Bradley P. Holt, *Thirsty for God: A Brief History of Christian Spirituality* (Minneapolis: Augsburg Fortress, 1993), 115–16.

[16] Gallup, *People's Religion*, 15–16, 19.

[17] Ibid., 4.

cally conservative organizations called upon Christians to use their voice at the polls to instill Christian morals in every level of government. Catalysts in society that prompted their involvement were sexual promiscuity, gay rights, abortion, feminism, repudiation of prayer in schools, harassment of Christian private education by the government, and a general disapproval of American culture.[18]

The Moral Majority is also an example of a trend evident in American spirituality after World War II that gained momentum into the 1980s: the growth of special interest groups. Special interest groups had existed in America for more than a century and they certainly are not unique to the United States. But in the years since World War II, religious special interest groups have multiplied in such a way that they have greatly affected the way some American Christians express their faith.[19]

Churches provided access to a wide variety of groups to keep the interest of their members. In keeping with a highly specialized and pragmatic society, the Christian religion adapted itself through these groups in order to sustain commitment. A few examples are prison ministries, Bible study groups, charismatic groups, groups concerned about world hunger, antinuclear coalitions, therapy groups like twelve-step programs,[20] and international mission enterprises. This kind of networking tapped into the desire of many Americans for contact, personal relationships, and sharing caused by the "nagging loneliness that plagues much of their lives."[21]

By the 1980s, while special interest groups were on the rise, denominationalism was on the decline. In earlier decades, denominational affiliation communicated a general sense of what people believed, how they worshipped, and how they generally expressed that faith in daily life. It also tended to identify their cultural and socioeconomic status, perhaps even their geographical region. The barriers of denominational tradition were somewhat immutable. It was unusual for people to switch.[22] In the latter half of this century, however, several factors contributed to the declining significance of denominationalism in America.

[18] "Conservative and Charismatic Developments," 974.

[19] Robert Wuthnow, *Restructuring of American Religion* (Princeton: Princeton University Press, 1988), 100–1.

[20] See a helpful section on the twelve-step program and its relationship to American spirituality in Holt, *Thirsty for God*, 117–19.

[21] Craig Kennet Miller, *Baby Boomer Spirituality: Ten Essential Values of a Generation* (Nashville: Discipleship Resources, 1992), 155.

[22] Wuthnow, *Restructuring of American Religion*, 71–80.

Wuthnow suggests that the reason for the shift is that since Christian denominations now have more social and cultural similarity, they do not differ as substantially on a number of social issues. To the degree that some portions of the American public have fewer educational, social, and cultural differences, so also the reduction of these differences causes the social significance of denominations to decline.[23] Another reason for the declining significance of denominationalism, according to Craig Miller in his work *Baby Boomer Spirituality*, is that boomers have been taught by their consumeristic culture to be smart shoppers who can spot fakes or flaws. They tend to take the time to explore all options and then choose what they like best or what best fits their needs.[24]

Another factor that has contributed to a decline in the significance of denominationalism is the fact that many churches have made it easy for people to switch, downplaying the distinctive elements that present barriers to cross-attendance and changing membership. Some churches even call themselves nondenominational in order to get past barriers that might prevent people from attending. Other churches that are associated with a particular denomination do not use the denomination's name in their church's name.[25] Denominationalism still carries weight in that the vast majority of American Christians still use their denominational label to identify themselves, but it is less significant as a basis for division and there is a considerably higher degree of acceptance of one another.[26]

Alongside the discussion of Christians' participation in a new social activism as well as a growth of community across denominational lines, the issue of the tendency toward spiritual individualism must also be addressed. Many American Christians continued an ever deepening interest in the spiritual journey inward after the tumultuous years of the sixties and early seventies. Perhaps this trend is a result of the tendency, especially within the baby-boomer generation, to be more narcissistic and infatuated with psychology and self-help methods for dealing with the realities of life. Perhaps Vatican II energized the flowering of spirituality in the midst of a culture that was ready to gaze inward. Whatever the cause, as Americans renewed their search for spiritual moorings, this quest changed the landscape of Christian spirituality in America.[27]

[23] Wuthnow, *Restructuring of American Religion*, 87.

[24] Miller, *Baby Boomer Spirituality*, 123–24.

[25] One example is a Southern Baptist church in Grapevine, Texas, that targets the young professionals in the Dallas area. The name of the church is Fellowship Church.

[26] Wuthnow, *Restructuring of American Religion*, 97.

[27] Gallup, *People's Religion*, 4.

The Inner Search for Meaning in the 1990s

The difference between the spirituality of the 1980s and the 1990s is that the word *self* seemed to be replaced by the word *soul*. Psychological language took on much more spiritual tones.[28] Trends of the 1980s remain and have even increased, but the language has become more metaphysical. Americans are more fascinated with the mystery of the sacred and the human soul. Examples of this fascination can be seen in the emphasis on the existence of angels, afterlife experiences, and the frequent appearance of the word *soul* in the titles of books on the bestseller lists, Thomas Moore's *Care of the Soul* being just one of many examples. This focus on the soul indicates a spiritual hunger for that which is beyond career successes and material wealth. Americans are paying much more attention to their inner spirit, and they are willing to read about it and talk about it as never before.

Another aspect of American life in the 1990s that affected spirituality is the fact that the oldest of the boomer generation began to turn fifty in the 1990s. Most of them have children and perhaps a few grandchildren by now. They are at the peak of their careers and their influence on society and culture. But midlife brings new questions. Wade Clark Roof describes the new life passages that the baby-boomer generation is facing as they are rearing children and beginning to face midlife in the 1990s. Their life quests are taking on new dimensions, spiritual dimensions.[29] Boomers are beginning to reexamine their lives. They are "at a critical juncture of affirming life's meanings and fundamental values and of dealing with spiritual voids."[30] Phyllis Tickle adds, "Boomers are seeking purpose, meaning. They want to love and be loved as they sense the inevitability of aging closing in."[31]

Consumerism, religious pluralism, and the decline of denominationalism created a "deli" atmosphere in which Americans mixed and matched spiritual practices and beliefs in order to create their own unique faith. The choice of a church was based not on doctrinal compliance but on whether that particular church met particular social, emotional, and spiritual needs. Such ignoring of doctrinal confessions has necessarily led to the danger of losing perspective on what is authentic Christian spirituality. The lines blurred in the 1990s, not only between the various

[28] Wuthnow, *After Heaven*, 157.
[29] Roof, *Generation of Seekers*, 242–43.
[30] Ibid., 6.
[31] Tickle, *Re-Discovering the Sacred*, 51–57.

traditions within Christianity, but also between the world religions and a plethora of cults and ideas related to the sacred and the concept of spirituality. Such a lack of clarity in recent years created a slightly different concern from that of the 1960s or 1970s. The concern was not that Americans were ignoring their spirituality or denying their spirituality. Most were very willing to talk about it. Nor was the concern that the churches were declining in membership. The conservative, evangelical churches continue to grow. The concern for the 1990s was that authentic Christian spirituality might be lost in the shuffle of a plethora of options now promoted that have a language kin to Christianity but lack the exclusive commitment to the foundational truth of Scripture and orthodox Christian doctrine, which provides the framework for a truly Christian faith.

The Christian philosopher Dallas Willard in his newest work, *The Divine Conspiracy*, assesses the problem with contemporary Christian spirituality in that he points to a postmodern society where Christianity can be professed without the expectation that the practice of and commitment to true Christianity must radically transform one's life. Willard writes that "the most telling thing about the contemporary Christian is that he or she simply has no compelling sense that understanding of and conformity with the clear teachings of Christ is of any vital importance to his or her life, and certainly not that it is in any way essential."[32]

From this brief sketch of the history of American spirituality it is easy to surmise that America held great opportunity for Henri Nouwen to express the gifts and the interests that were uniquely his. He was a psychologist and so spoke the language of typical late-twentieth-century Americans. He was also a deeply committed Christian and a pastor who longed to make a difference in the lives of those who were asking spiritual questions. As the spiritual quest of Americans grew in intensity, the simple accessibility of Nouwen's spiritual writings quenched the thirst of many a soul.

Chapter Overview

Before we begin the exploration of Nouwen's own spirituality, chapter 2 provides a brief literary biography of Nouwen. A review of all of Nouwen's major writings is given in the context of the major phases of his life so that when the themes of his writings are dealt with in later

[32] Dallas Willard, *The Divine Conspiracy* (San Francisco: HarperSanFrancisco, 1998), xv.

chapters, the reader has the biographical and literary context in which to understand them.

Chapters 3, 4, and 5 specifically examine the various themes of Nouwen's writing based on his overarching idea of spirituality as *relationship* with God, self, and others. The development of his ideas is traced, pointing out changes in his thought as well as those ideas that remained unchanged throughout his more than twenty-five years of writing.

Chapter 3 specifically addresses the content of Nouwen's spirituality in regard to *relationship with God*. Nouwen pointed his readers again and again to the important foundation of an ever deepening relationship with God through prayer as supported by other spiritual disciplines such as silence, solitude, contemplation, meditation on Scripture, spiritual direction, and worship.

Chapter 4 addresses the content of Nouwen's spirituality in regard to *relationship with the self*. Nouwen wrote a great deal about the importance of being able to accept one's self as truly loved by God. This acceptance sets one free to love and serve others as well as God.

Chapter 5 addresses the content of Nouwen's spirituality in regard to *relationship with others*. Nouwen wrote about the ministry of every Christian in community with others through compassion, caring, social justice, solidarity, forgiveness, gratitude, and celebration. Nouwen also focused some of his writing on the spirituality of the professional minister. He addressed the importance of the spiritual formation of the minister, the education of the minister, and the roles of a minister in bridging the gap between others and God.

Chapter 6 offers a summary of Nouwen's spirituality and some analysis of what his place and significance might be for modern American spirituality.

CHAPTER TWO

◈

A Literary Biography of Henri Nouwen

Referring to Ignatius of Loyola, Philip Sheldrake writes in *Spirituality and History* that "he could not be a stained-glass figure abstracted from his environment and its influences." The same is true of Henri Nouwen, for it is indeed true that "spirituality is neither disincarnate nor on some ideal plane beyond the limitations of history."[1] To understand the spirituality of Nouwen, one must understand something of his personal history.

Shaping of the Man (1932–1963)

Henri Jozef Machiel Nouwen was born on January 24, 1932, in the small village of Nijkerk, about 28 miles southeast of Amsterdam in the Netherlands.[2] His father, Laurent Jean Marie Nouwen, was a tax lawyer and a professor of law.[3] His mother, Maria Huberta Helena Ramselaar Nouwen, was head bookkeeper for her mother's department store. Maria was also a deeply religious woman with a great interest in literature

---

[1] Philip Sheldrake, *Spirituality and History* (London: SPCK, 1995), 92.

[2] Robert Durback, ed., *Seeds of Hope: A Henri Nouwen Reader* (New York: Bantam Books, 1989), xxi.

[3] Jurjen Beumer, *Henri Nouwen: A Restless Seeking for God*, trans. David E. Schlaver and Nancy Forest-Flier (New York: Crossroad Publishing Company, 1997), 16. This work is the first biography to be published about Nouwen. Beumer was a friend of Nouwen's and it was almost ready for publication when Nouwen died. Beumer added some material concerning his death and published it the next year. The work puts forth some useful information concerning Nouwen's family background and other biographical details but it is still only a sketch. Beumer also comments on a few of the obvious themes in Nouwen's writing but he does not propose to do a detailed study. The source was helpful for this study since it was the only one of its kind but it is not extensive or thorough.

and mysticism.[4] Both parents were devoted to their four children, of whom Henri was the oldest. Two brothers, Paul and Wim, and one sister, Laurine, came along after.[5] Laurent and Maria brought up their children with a strong emphasis on independence and critical thinking. The family was also affluent, which meant that the children had many opportunities to develop materially, socially, and spiritually.[6] Nouwen said his mother and father "created the space where [he] could hear and follow God's call."[7]

Two things characterized Henri Nouwen from the time he was a small boy; they would remain constant themes throughout his life. First, from the time he was a baby he longed for affection, constantly reaching out to be held, to be loved.[8] Second, he never wanted to be anything other than a priest.[9] God was very important to him and this never changed.

The love that young Henri had for God was nurtured especially by his mother and his maternal grandmother. His mother taught him the prayer, "All for you, dear Jesus,"[10] and encouraged Henri throughout his life to be faithful to the intimate relationship between Jesus and himself. When his grandmother, Sarah de Munk Ramselaar, recognized Henri's growing interest in the priesthood, she had her store's carpenter make a child-size altar and she had her seamstress make all the vestments. By the time he was eight, Henri had converted the attic of the family home into a children's chapel where he pretended to hold mass, gave sermons to friends and relatives, and designated a whole hierarchy of bishops, priests, deacons, and altar servers among his friends and siblings. But most important, his grandmother, to use Nouwen's own words, "helped to intro-

[4] Ibid., 17.

[5] Henri Nouwen, *In Memoriam* (Notre Dame: Ave Maria Press, 1980), 53.

[6] Beumer, *Henri Nouwen: A Restless Seeking for God*, 19.

[7] Henri Nouwen, *The Genesee Diary: Report from a Trappist Monastery* (New York: Doubleday, 1976), 10.

[8] Chris Glaser, "Nouwen's Journey," *Christian Century* 114 (19–26 March 1997): 305. Nouwen told a friend that his mother apologized to him just before her death for raising him according to a severe regimen of a German "Dr. Spock" who taught that young children's wills should be broken by restrictions on food and physical touch. Nouwen wondered whether he had been chronically anxious as a child because he was simply hungry. See Robert Jonas's introduction in *Henri Nouwen: Writings Selected with an Introduction by Robert A. Jonas* (Maryknoll, N.Y.: Orbis Books, 1998), xxii.

[9] Arthur Boers, "From the House of Fear to the House of Love: An Encounter with Henri Nouwen" (unpublished, n.d.), 2. This document is located in the Nouwen Archives at Yale Divinity School Library.

[10] Nouwen, *Genesee Diary*, 211.

duce Henri to a life of prayer and encouraged him in a personal relationship with Jesus."[11]

Henri's father was proud of his interest in the priesthood but his encouragement had a different tone from that of his mother and grandmother. His father said, "Show me that you can make it in this world, be an independent person, and compete with others. Show me that you can accomplish something." In contrast, his mother's constant admonition was, "Whatever you do in this life, don't lose contact with Jesus. Being known or having a big job is unimportant. It is important that you continue to carry Jesus in your heart and that you don't lose his light."[12] For the first thirty years of Henri's adult life after his ordination, he responded mostly to the voice of his father. For the last ten years of his life, it was the voice of his mother that spoke louder in the decisions he made.

Nouwen described his years at home as safe, sheltered, a "time in which all the boundaries were clear."[13] Even while his family endured the German occupation of World War II, his parents worked hard to provide a protected but normal life for the family. His mother made sure that his elementary education was not interrupted, by convincing a small group of priests to start a school for boys in the neighboring village of Bussum. Henri went to mass every morning, was an altar boy and studied hard. The family prayed much together, not only because it was a time of war, but because they were very devout in their Catholic faith. They prayed the rosary at night and listened to sermons on the radio.[14] His father also tried to provide cultural experiences by gathering family and neighbors for poetry reading and discussions about art.[15] Thus it was not surprising that Henri had a strong faith, a love for learning, and an appreciation of beauty as an adult.

When Nouwen was twelve, he wanted to attend the minor seminary.[16] But his father told him he was too young to make a decision about

---

[11] Henri Nouwen, *Can You Drink the Cup?* (Notre Dame: Ave Maria Press, 1996), 14.

[12] Boers, "From the House of Fear to the House of Love," 3.

[13] Henri Nouwen, Syllabus for Communion, Community, Ministry course at Regis College, Toronto, September 1994 (Nouwen Archives, Yale Divinity School Library), 1.

[14] Boers, "From the House of Fear to the House of Love," 2–3.

[15] Durback, *Seeds of Hope*, xxii.

[16] A minor seminary was an institution with a four- or six-year program of studies in the humanities and the sciences, established for the education and spiritual formation of candidates for the ordained priesthood. The first four years (comparable to high school), the students could live at home. Following completion of the minor seminary, the candidates

the priesthood. He would have to wait until he was eighteen. After the war, the family moved to The Hague, where Nouwen finished his secondary education at Aloysius College. In 1950, at the age of eighteen, he entered the minor seminary at Apeldoorn, for one year, where his maternal uncle, Monsignor Anton Ramselaar, was president.[17] Nouwen then went on to the major seminary at Rijsenburg, the program for the archdiocese of Utrecht, to study philosophy and theology and to prepare himself for ordination.[18]

Nouwen attributed his good grades not to brilliance but to hard work. He was popular with his fellow students and admitted that scholarship in itself held little appeal for him. He was definitely people oriented, more of a pastor than a scholar from the beginning.[19] He wrote, "All my studies never seemed fruitful for me unless they led me to a deeper understanding of the questions of the spiritual life."[20] But this does not mean his love for learning was diminished. Nouwen described his seminary years as the "garden of his youth":

> Life in the garden of my youth was quite beautiful and offered me invaluable gifts for the rest of my life: a joyful spirit, a deep devotion for Jesus and Mary, a true desire to pray, a great love for theology and spirituality, a good knowledge of contemporary languages, a serious interest in scripture and the early Christian writers, an enthusiasm about preaching, and a very strong sense of vocation.[21]

On Sunday, July 21, 1957, Henri Nouwen was ordained as a priest. As a gift for his ordination, his uncle Anton gave young Henri the chalice that had been given to Anton at his own ordination as a sign of gratitude that another priest had come into the family. The chalice was made by a famous Dutch goldsmith and was adorned with Henri's grandmother's diamonds. "I want you to have it," Anton said. "It comes from your

---

entered a major seminary for the remainder of their education and spiritual formation. See *HarperCollins Encyclopedia of Catholicism*, s.v. "Seminary, minor," 1182.

[17] Durback, *Seeds of Hope*, xxii.

[18] Nouwen, *Can You Drink the Cup?* 15. The major seminary is an institution with a six-year program of studies in philosophy (two years) and theology (four years) established for the educational, pastoral, and spiritual formation of the candidates. The final year is usually a pastoral assignment away from the seminary. See *HarperCollins Encyclopedia of Catholicism*, s.v. "Seminary, major," 1182.

[19] Durback, *Seeds of Hope*, xxii.

[20] Nouwen, *Genesee Diary*, 207.

[21] Nouwen, *Can You Drink the Cup?* 16.

grandmother, who died too soon to see you as a priest but whose love for you, her oldest grandchild, is with you today."[22]

After his ordination, Nouwen requested permission from his archbishop to study psychology and resumed studies at the University of Nijmegen from 1957 until 1964.[23] This request was somewhat unusual because the relationship between psychology and religion was not yet a well-accepted combination. Many Christians at that time perceived psychology to be an enemy of faith. Nouwen, however, believed that the discipline of psychology dealt with issues that were important for the church and pastoral theology. He hoped that psychology would help him in the more practical application of religion.[24]

During this time of graduate work, Nouwen also worked in the mines of South Limburg and Rotterdam and trained as a reserve army chaplain. Nouwen wanted "to know and experience what faith meant in the harsh reality of everyday life."[25] Nouwen also arranged for a position as a chaplain for the Catholic Emigration Service with the Holland-America ship line. Thus Nouwen made his first of many trips to the United States.[26]

While studying psychology in Nijmegen, Nouwen explored the possibility of studying in the United States, particularly at Harvard under Dr. Gordon Allport. But Allport encouraged him to finish at Nijmegen and then to try for a fellowship in a program for psychiatry and religion at the Menninger Clinic in Topeka, Kansas. This program was the birthplace of pastoral psychology and programs for clinical pastoral education (CPE). Nouwen followed Allport's advice. After finishing at Nijmegen, he was accepted as a fellow at the Menninger Clinic from 1964 to 1966, working in clinical pastoral education, research, and writing. These were important years for Nouwen because the combination of psychology and theology was not being offered in the Netherlands. His hope was to introduce what he was learning at the Menninger Clinic into the program for religious education back in the Netherlands. It was also during this

[22] Ibid., 13, 16–17.

[23] The sources are somewhat conflicting on this issue. Some say that Nouwen's archbishop requested that he study psychology. See Douglas Todd, "In Weakness There Is Strength," *The Weekend Sun*, 16 April 1994, D15, and Brett Grainger, "Henri: A Heart's Desire," *Sojourners* 25 (November–December 1996): 26–30. But the major biographical works on Nouwen describe Nouwen himself as being the one to request this educational direction. This author chooses the latter as authoritative because both of these authors knew Nouwen personally. See Beumer, *Henri Nouwen: A Restless Seeking for God*, 23, and Durback, *Seeds of Hope*, xxiii.

[24] Nouwen, *Genesee Diary*, 172.

[25] Beumer, *Henri Nouwen: A Restless Seeking for God*, 23–24.

[26] Ibid., 24.

period that Nouwen gained some measure of political "awakening" to issues of social justice through the movement of Martin Luther King Jr. Nouwen himself participated in the famous march from Selma to Montgomery in 1965.[27]

Notre Dame and the Netherlands (1964–1970)

A colleague with whom Nouwen had worked at the Menninger Clinic, Dr. John Santos, invited Nouwen to teach for a year at the University of Notre Dame in the new psychology department that Santos had begun.[28] Nouwen agreed to teach two semesters, but he actually stayed for two years, 1966 to 1968. Most Catholic universities had rejected the study of psychology because of the atheism of Freud. Nouwen was the first to teach abnormal psychology at Notre Dame and he even brought in Protestant psychology professors for lectures.[29]

Nouwen worked with psychology students but he also taught a noncredit course for the priests who were ministering to students in the Notre Dame community.[30] Nouwen also served as a priest to the academic community, celebrating the Eucharist with students and professors and offering counseling. The combined aspects of his work at Notre Dame, helping students connect insights from psychology with faith and its practice, provided him with the initial professional experiences that would eventually enable him to make significant contributions to the field of pastoral care.[31]

Nouwen liked Notre Dame and made many lasting friendships. But Nouwen also struggled with something that would remain a constant theme in his life as one who had made a commitment to be a celibate priest—his own loneliness and need for affection and community. Knowing that his students dealt with similar problems, Nouwen began lecturing on themes of depression, confusion, intimacy, and love. Students and friends asked for copies of his lectures.[32] One of his listeners was a journalist from the *National Catholic Reporter* who asked

[27] Ibid., 28.

[28] Durback, *Seeds of Hope*, xxiii.

[29] Jonas, *Henri Nouwen*, xxv.

[30] Seward Hiltner, "Henri J. M. Nouwen: Pastoral Theologian of the Year," *Pastoral Psychology* 27 (Fall 1978): 5.

[31] Jonas, *Henri Nouwen*, xxv–xxvi.

[32] Mary Frances Coady, "Nouwen Finds Rest at Daybreak," *Catholic New Times*, 23 November 1986, 3.

for permission to put one of them into print. The response to the article was so positive that Nouwen was asked to submit more articles from his lectures. Nouwen complied and from this collection of articles grew his first book, *Intimacy: Essays in Pastoral Psychology*, published in 1969. Henri Nouwen did not think of himself as an author. He perceived himself as a speaker, a teacher. But the impact of his words upon those who heard him gave impetus to the launch of a writing career as well.[33]

A second book that came from Nouwen's work at Notre Dame was *Creative Ministry*. The theme of the book was "the relationship between professionalism and spirituality in the ministry."[34] The book made a strong contribution to the field of pastoral care,[35] integrating psychology and pastoral theology while touching on five main areas of ministry—teaching, preaching, individual pastoral care, organizing, and celebrating.[36]

Notre Dame offered Nouwen his first teaching experience and he enjoyed his work there. But he also realized that general psychology would never be central to his interests. He was more interested in priestly formation and ministry, and he was strongly influenced by the work of Carl Jung, one of the prominent figures in the field of psychology and religion, and Anton Boisen, the founder of the clinical pastoral education movement.[37] Nouwen was convinced that there was a useful connection between psychology and religion and he wanted to put his knowledge of psychology to work in the context of ministry. "I had such a desire to speak about God and to announce the Word," he said. "I felt that if I ever stayed in the university I should do theology, even though psychology would be a great help."[38]

[33] Durback, *Seeds of Hope, xxviii*.

[34] Henri Nouwen, *Creative Ministry* (New York: Doubleday Image Books, 1971), xv.

[35] Carl J. Armbruster, "Creative Ministry," a book review in *Commonweal*, 3 March 1972, 528.

[36] Nouwen, *Creative Ministry*, xxii.

[37] Because of his personal experiences with psychotic episodes and the need to be hospitalized for them, the American Anton Boisen (1876–1965) began to see the need for the training of pastors to work as chaplains in mental hospitals. In 1930 the Council for the Clinical Training of Theological Students was incorporated. See *Baker Encyclopedia of Psychology*, s.v. "Anton Boisen," 132. An extensive amount of material regarding Anton Boisen can be found among Nouwen's papers in the Archives of Yale Divinity School Library. Nouwen also collected materials regarding Seward Hiltner and Thomas Merton, which can be found in the Archives as well.

[38] Boers, "From the House of Fear to the House of Love," 4.

After completing his second year at Notre Dame, Nouwen returned to the Netherlands in 1968 with the intention of staying. For the first two years he taught pastoral psychology and spirituality to students preparing for ministry. He taught first at the Amsterdam Joint Pastoral Institute and then at the Catholic Theological Institute of Utrecht. During his third year he worked on a degree in theology at the University of Nijmegen with the intention of getting a master's degree. He continued further and completed the doctoral exams as well in 1971[39] but did not write a dissertation.[40]

During this time in the Netherlands, Nouwen wrote two more manuscripts, both in Dutch. *With Open Hands* was the culmination of an experiment with twenty-five theology students who formed a group in 1970 in order to develop a common understanding of what comprised genuine prayer.[41] Translated into English and published in February of 1972, *With Open Hands* became one of Nouwen's most popular works. It was also the work in which Nouwen stated for the first time why he chose to share so much of his own spiritual journey with others through his writing. He wrote, "What is most personal is also the most universal."[42] Nouwen chose to be unusually transparent in his writing about spiritual issues because he believed that others struggled with the same questions as he did. *With Open Hands* was eventually published in several different languages and in 1995 the English version was revised and released again by Ave Maria Press with added text and more contemporary photographs. In this work and the rest of the books that followed, Nouwen had already begun to use less academic language, directing his writing to ordinary Christians, both Catholic and Protestant.

The second manuscript that Nouwen completed addressed the life and thought of Thomas Merton, perhaps the most influential twentieth-century author in the United States reflecting on Christian spirituality. The original manuscript was entitled *Bidden om het leven*. Nouwen translated the manuscript, with assistance, into English and then published it under the title *Pray to Live* with Fides Publishers at Notre Dame in 1972. In 1981 the work appeared again as *Thomas Merton: Contemplative Critic*, published by Liguori Publications.[43] Nouwen met Merton only once, at

[39] Hiltner, "Henri J. M. Nouwen: Pastoral Theologian of the Year," 5.

[40] Beumer, *Henri Nouwen: A Restless Seeking for God*, 30–31.

[41] Henri Nouwen, *With Open Hands*, from an original manuscript in Dutch, *Mit Open Handen*, trans. Patrick Gaffney (Notre Dame: Ave Maria Press, 1972), 7–8.

[42] Nouwen, *With Open Hands*, 7.

[43] Henri Nouwen, *Thomas Merton: Contemplative Critic* (Liguori, Mo.: Triumph Books, an imprint of Liguori Publications, 1981), iv.

the Abbey of Our Lady of Gethsemani in Kentucky, but Merton's life and work greatly influenced him. The first part of the book was a short biography and a commentary on the life and work of Merton. The second part was a collection of excerpts from Merton's writings for the purpose of meditation.

Thomas Merton probably had the most profound influence on Nouwen's work as both a contemplative and an activist. Other writers that Nouwen seemed to favor were Mother Teresa of Calcutta, Jean Vanier, Gustavo Gutiérrez, and Dietrich Bonhoeffer. Nouwen was especially fond of the writings of the Desert Fathers and Mothers and other sources from the Christian East. He often quoted from their stories in his own work. Nouwen had a wide command of the classic works in Christian history, partly gained from the courses he taught in spirituality. Yet Nouwen did not confine his reading to Christian authors. He read many non-Christian authors and had a keen passion for books concerning the art of Van Gogh and Rembrandt.

Yale, Genesee, and Sabbaticals (1971–1981)

A new phase of Nouwen's career began in 1971 when Colin Williams, the new Dean at Yale University Divinity School, invited Nouwen to visit the school. He had read Nouwen's book *Intimacy* and was determined to recruit him. While Nouwen was visiting the campus, the dean invited him to join the faculty.[44] Nouwen refused the offer because of his commitment to the Roman Catholic Church in the Netherlands. But six months later Williams asked him to reconsider the invitation. Nouwen's ecclesiastical superiors left him free to decide. He visited the school again and was impressed by the caliber and healthy mix of students from many different denominations. He decided to accept the position and began teaching in the fall of 1971.[45]

Nouwen does not clarify his reasons for leaving his homeland except for his observation that he was impressed with Yale after he visited the second time for the express purpose of deciding whether to take the position that had been offered. Jurjen Beumer, a personal friend and the first to publish a book about Nouwen, intimates that the areas that Nouwen was interested in could only be pursued in a limited way in the Netherlands.[46] Perhaps once Nouwen returned to his homeland and re-

---

[44] Hiltner, "Henri J. M. Nouwen: Pastoral Theologian of the Year," 5–6.
[45] Durback, *Seeds of Hope*, xxiii–xxiv.
[46] Beumer, *Henri Nouwen: A Restless Seeking for God*, 30–31.

alized that his interests, the combination of psychology and theology, were less suited to the Dutch academic environment, he gradually warmed to the idea of returning to the United States.

The conditions under which Nouwen accepted the position at Yale reflect either a rather large ego on Nouwen's part or a business savvy that took advantage of Yale's invitation to write his own ticket—perhaps both! The conditions were (1) that he would not be expected to write a dissertation; (2) within three years he wanted a permanent appointment; (3) within five years he wanted to become a full professor; and (4) his writing would meet only his own criteria and would not be measured "according to some scientific yardstick." Yale agreed to every condition.[47] Nouwen began as associate professor of pastoral theology. By 1974 he was associate professor with tenure and had been granted permanent resident status in the United States. In 1977 he became a full professor.[48]

There were several positive aspects to the ten years that Nouwen spent at Yale from 1971 to 1981. He was a popular teacher and many students responded to him with enthusiasm. His classes were often filled to capacity. He made many friends and his professional career flourished. He also became more and more popular as a speaker and a writer. Nouwen became more assured of what he felt God had called him to do. He wanted to write books and teach ministers, and he wanted to make North America his home. Nouwen published twelve books during the ten years at Yale.[49]

[47] Ibid., 32.

[48] Hiltner, "Henri J. M. Nouwen: Pastoral Theologian of the Year," 6.

[49] Most of Nouwen's books were published by HarperCollins, Doubleday, Ave Maria Press, Crossroad, and Orbis. An interview with one of his associates revealed that Nouwen probably never approached a publisher on his own with no previously existing relationship or connection of some kind. Ave Maria Press is connected with Notre Dame, where he taught for two years. Orbis Books is connected to the Maryknoll missionaries with whom he worked in South America. People within the publishing business introduced him to others in the business, and so on. Relationships were very important to Nouwen. He wanted a strong and involved relationship with his editors, who became friends and advisors for his writing. Therefore Nouwen usually had a contact for any book he wanted to work on and the publishers sometimes suggested projects that he accepted. Sue Mosteller, interview by author, tape recording, Richmond Hill, Ontario, 9 March 1998. A conversation between this author and Frank Cunningham, who works for Ave Maria Press, at a meeting for the Henri Nouwen Society in Toronto, 19 September 1998, added the insight that Nouwen had a strong sense of business when it came to negotiating a book contract. He had definite ideas about what certain publishers could and could not sell and he chose them accordingly for each manuscript that he published.

Nouwen published one of his most significant books in the field of pastoral care, *The Wounded Healer*, in 1972.[50] Many seminaries and churches used the book as a textbook for ministry. Some observers even called it "a modern classic."[51] In this book, Nouwen attempted to answer the question, "What does it mean to be a minister in our contemporary society?" Nouwen utilized the theme of suffering in each section: a suffering world, a suffering generation, a suffering man, and a suffering minister. His goal was to address the relevance and effectiveness of the contemporary minister who was willing to "make his own wounds available as a source of healing."[52]

In 1974 two more of Nouwen's works went to the press. *Out of Solitude: Three Meditations on the Christian Life* came from three sermons Nouwen preached at Battell, the United Church of Christ at Yale. The sermons were based on Mark 1:35, which spoke of Jesus withdrawing to a solitary place. Nouwen's thought on solitude began as a seedling in this work, which developed into a major branch in his later work. This book also sold very well.[53]

The second work released in 1974, called *Aging: The Fulfillment of Life*, was a psychology text that grew out of some ideas that Nouwen and Walter J. Gaffney, a Yale colleague and coauthor of the book, presented at a conference at the University of Notre Dame. The book emphasized how to make the later years a time of hope rather than a time of loneliness, a time of gradual maturing that is to be embraced, with death understood as the final gift. Nouwen believed that the elderly could also be teachers to those who took care of them, enabling the caretakers to embrace their own aging.[54]

During his tenure at Yale, Nouwen took two sabbaticals, which bore the fruit of more publication. Both were spent at the Abbey of the Genesee, a Trappist monastery in Pifford, New York. Nouwen requested of his close friend, Dom John Eudes Bamberger, the abbot of the

[50] Henri Nouwen, *The Wounded Healer: Ministry in Contemporary Society* (New York: Doubleday Image Books, 1972). This particular work has gone through nineteen printings and the title phrase has entered the vocabulary of the pastoral care field as well as the recovery movement. See Todd, "In Weakness There Is Strength," D15.

[51] See Gerald Renner, "Modern-day 'Saint' Reflects on Works, Life," *The Hartford Courant*, 14 October 1993, B11.

[52] Nouwen, *Wounded Healer*, xv–xvi.

[53] A telephone conversation with Bob Hamma, editor for Ave Maria Press, 24 October 1997, confirmed that over 295,000 copies of the book had been sold.

[54] Henri Nouwen, *Aging: The Fulfillment of Life* (New York: Doubleday Image Books, 1974), 13–20.

monastery, the opportunity to live as a temporary member of the community.[55]

Nouwen had met Bamberger in 1964 while on his way to Topeka, Kansas, to work as a fellow at the Menninger Clinic. He had stopped at the Abbey of Our Lady of Gethsemani in Kentucky, hoping to find someone that he could talk to who could perhaps give him some spiritual guidance. Because of Nouwen's background in psychology, he was introduced to Bamberger, who was a psychiatrist as well as a theologian and monk. Their relationship took on special meaning and Bamberger became a spiritual director for Nouwen.[56]

Bamberger later became the abbot of the Abbey of Genesee in upstate New York. Nouwen visited him and nurtured the hope that perhaps one day he could break away for a retreat at the abbey and live under Bamberger's guidance for a lengthier time. Nouwen was hesitant to ask, knowing that the request to live as a temporary member of a closed monastic community was unusual. But Bamberger consulted the monks and they were willing to make an exception. After receiving a letter bringing the news that he had been voted in, Nouwen cleared the time on his calendar and the papers on his desk and arrived at the Genesee June 1, 1974. He shaved his head, dressed, worked, and worshiped as if he were a monk for seven months.[57]

Nouwen's desire to live in the monastery was the result of what he called "years of restless searching."[58] The thought even lingered in the back of his mind whether the Trappists could become his family, his home, his community.[59] While teaching about solitude, inner freedom, and serenity, Nouwen struggled to find freedom from his own compulsions and illusions, which kept him working, speaking, writing, and teaching to the point that he was anything but serene. He was tired. Yet his own insecurities would not allow him simply to quit. He knew he had to face his "restless self," which meant he had to retreat from his life at Yale and address the difficult questions through prayer and solitude:

> Maybe I spoke more about God than with him. Maybe my writing about prayer kept me from a prayerful life. Maybe I was more concerned about

[55] Durback, *Seeds of Hope*, xxiv.
[56] Nouwen, *Genesee Diary*, 14–15.
[57] Ibid., 15–16.
[58] Ibid., 13.
[59] Ibid., 64. Nouwen never directly explained his interest in the Trappists specifically. One could presume that it was because of his interest in Merton and the fact that Bamberger had become his spiritual director, which is why he took his sabbatical at the Abbey of the Genesee.

the praise of men and women than the love of God. Maybe I was slowly
becoming a prisoner of people's expectations instead of a man liberated by
divine promises. Maybe . . . It was not all that clear, but I realized that I
would only know by stepping back and allowing the hard questions to
touch me even if they hurt.[60]

This struggle, so evident within Nouwen's first few years of professional life, was one that plagued him throughout his adult life. Nouwen
apparently lived in a constant "cycle of long, hectic days of teaching and
service, followed by periods of nervous exhaustion, depression, and in-
somnia."[61] A friend of his in later years who was also a psychologist,
Robert Jonas, wrote, "His vision of a warm and regular monastic life
foundered on the rocks of his predisposition to restlessness, the desire for
fresh intellectual stimulation, a hunger for new friends and experiences,
and a nagging, sometimes self-defeating inability to say no."[62] Jonas believed this was partly a result of the desire Nouwen had to live his life for
others as Jesus did. Yet Jonas admitted that his choices were probably also
motivated in some sense by his "habitual, almost neurotic need to be
needed."[63] Jonas went on to explain, "To me, Henri's presence and ministry obviously tapped into a spiritual power that transcends the conditioning of childhood. And yet, it is also obvious to me that he carried a
pattern of emotional conditioning which both animated his work and
fueled his inner conflicts."[64]

One publication that came out of this first retreat at the Genesee was
the diary that he kept, later published as *The Genesee Diary: Report from a
Trappist Monastery*.[65] While describing the daily events of his months at
the monastery, Nouwen's journal also provides insight into the honest
spiritual questions with which he struggled and the understanding he
gleaned from the experience. Nouwen was known for his sometimes
painful transparency in his writing. This seemed to be the key that drew
many to read his work. In Nouwen, one had an honest spiritual guide
who was not afraid to ask difficult questions, personal questions, univer-

[60] Ibid., 13.
[61] Jonas, *Henri Nouwen*, xxxiii.
[62] Ibid., xxxiv.
[63] Ibid., xxxiv.
[64] Ibid., xxxvi.
[65] According to Sue Mosteller, Nouwen's literary executrix and work associate at the
L'Arche Daybreak community in Toronto, Nouwen did not keep a journal all the time, but
he did at least utilize the habit at several significant points of personal searching during his life
while taking major trips away from his usual routine. Four of his books are excerpts from his
journal writing: *The Genesee Diary, Gracias, The Road to Daybreak*, and *The Inner Voice of Love*.

sal questions that almost anyone could relate to in some way. His acknowledgment of his own weaknesses and spiritual struggles gave many people "permission to search their own hearts more honestly and more deeply."[66]

Another book that came out of the sabbatical at the Genesee in 1974 was the work *Reaching Out: The Three Movements of the Spiritual Life.* The idea for the book first came from a seminar on Christian spirituality at Yale, but the sabbatical at the Genesee gave him the opportunity to finish it. Nouwen described it as the book in which he tried to articulate his "most personal thoughts and feelings about being a Christian."[67] This work was his first attempt to set out a concise description of Christian spirituality, making it a pivotal work in his bibliography. *Reaching Out* was also the first work where Nouwen described the spiritual life as encompassing three relationships—the relationship to self, to others, and to God. This basic definition of spirituality became the foundational framework for much of the rest of his life work.[68] Nouwen did not stray from his practice of transparent self-revelation, believing that "what is experienced as most unique often proves to be most solidly embedded in the common condition of being human."[69]

Nouwen decided, at the end of his stay at the abbey, that he wanted to write more and speak less. He wanted to study more and counsel people less. He wanted to pray more and spend less time in social gatherings.[70] But once Nouwen left the cocoon of the abbey, his life was quickly fragmented and he did not follow through on his decisions.

Nouwen spent his next sabbatical in 1976 as a fellow at the Institute for Ecumenical and Cultural Research in Collegeville, Minnesota, where he prepared three lectures that were presented at the International Conference of the Association for Clinical Pastoral Education and the Canadian Association for Pastoral Education. Nouwen later published the lectures under the title *The Living Reminder: Service and Prayer in Memory of Jesus Christ.* In this work Nouwen attempted to answer the question, "What are the spiritual resources of ministers?" by exploring the connections between spirituality (attention to the life of the spirit) and ministry (service in the name of the Lord). He was concerned about the

---

[66] Ed Wojcicki, "Dear Henri: About Those Feelings," *Catholic Times,* 30 November 1986, 4.

[67] Henri Nouwen, *Reaching Out: The Three Movements of the Spiritual Life* (New York: Doubleday, 1975), 9.

[68] Durback, *Seeds of Hope,* xxx.

[69] Nouwen, *Reaching Out,* 14.

[70] Nouwen, *Genesee Diary,* 207.

temptation to separate service from prayer, resulting in ministers feeling they were too busy serving to pray. Nouwen insisted that service was prayer and prayer was service, and ministers could not afford to separate the two.[71] The common thread with which Nouwen chose to link each point to the other was the concept of remembrance in that ministers remind believers of what they should know or believe. They are to connect the personal histories or stories of others to the story of God. Nouwen utilized this definition of ministry to emphasize what kind of reminders ministers should be, thereby communicating his deep commitment to the inseparable nature of service and prayer in the life of the minister.

Nouwen spent the spring semester of 1978 as the scholar-in-residence at the North American College in Rome, Italy, in order to present some lectures on celibacy and contemplation.[72] During these five months, Nouwen had the opportunity to meet and speak to many English-speaking ministers—nuns, seminarians, and priests. Four of these lectures formed the contents for a book published in 1979, *Clowning in Rome: Reflections on Solitude, Celibacy, Prayer, and Contemplation*. In the circuslike atmosphere of the city of Rome, Nouwen saw these Christian ministers as the clowns, the ones who "by their humble, saintly lives evoke a smile and awaken a hope."[73] In keeping with the theme he often used in talking with ministers, he reminded these men and women of the importance of nurturing the spirit through prayer, contemplation, and solitude.

In the fall of 1978, Nouwen faced a major tragedy—the death of his mother. Nouwen's parents had come to the United States to visit him but she arrived very tired and unable to eat. A doctor discovered a tumor and she returned to the Netherlands for more tests and surgery. The cancer proved to be widespread. She regained consciousness after the surgery but complications developed in her lungs. She died six days later on the evening of October 9, 1978.[74]

This sacred experience in the life of Nouwen found expression in two books. Nouwen told the touching story of his last days with his mother in the work *In Memoriam*, published in 1980. Again Nouwen took one

[71] Henri Nouwen, *The Living Reminder: Service and Prayer in Memory of Jesus Christ* (San Francisco: HarperSanFrancisco, 1981), 11–13.

[72] "Dutch Theologian Nouwen to Teach at Divinity School," *Harvard Gazette*, 28 January 1983, 3.

[73] Henri Nouwen, *Clowning in Rome: Reflections on Solitude, Celibacy, Prayer and Contemplation* (Westminster, Md.: Christian Classics, 1979), 3.

[74] Nouwen, *In Memoriam*, 7–9.

of the most common of human experiences and attempted to speak to the spiritual mystery of life as he perceived it. In the introduction to the book Nouwen wrote, "It is precisely in the moments when we are most human, most in touch with what binds us together, that we discover the hidden depths of life."[75] It was after this experience with his mother's death, as well as a brush with death himself in 1990, that death became a more prominent theme in Nouwen's writing. Nouwen knew that his mother had given him much during her life, but what he discovered was that even her death became a gift that revealed more of the mystery of God. "I saw my own mother entering into that moment in which we are totally alone with God, in which the final decision of life must be made: the decision of faith."[76]

In February of 1979, just four months after his mother's death, Nouwen returned to the Abbey of the Genesee for another sabbatical. His schedule in the United States following his mother's funeral had not allowed much time for him to grieve. The time spent in the quiet of the Genesee gave him the opportunity to feel his loss. Nouwen realized that his mother was the one person who loved him unconditionally.[77] In her death, he was forced to be led closer to God as the one who loved him most.[78]

As a way to process his own grief, he decided to write a letter of consolation to his father, sharing memories of his mother, his love for his father, and his reflections on her death. Nouwen found in its completion that it was as much for himself as for his father that he wrote it. As the thought persisted that perhaps others could learn from this grief experience as well, Nouwen asked his father two and a half years later how he felt about the possibility of the letter being published. His father said, "If you think that your writing about your mother's death and about our grief can be a source of hope and consolation to more people than just ourselves, do not be afraid to have it printed."[79] In 1982, Nouwen published *A Letter of Consolation*, creating a second work on the spiritual aspects of death.

Nouwen also kept a journal during his second stay at the Genesee, but this time it was not a journal of his experiences in the monastery. It was a journal of prayers, sensing that his whole purpose for being there was

[75] Ibid., 10.

[76] Ibid., 32.

[77] Ibid., 60–62.

[78] Henri Nouwen, *A Letter of Consolation* (San Francisco: HarperSanFrancisco, 1982), 53.

[79] Ibid., 5–10.

"to be with God in prayer."[80] By this time, Nouwen was no longer considering the possibility of becoming a monk. His time at the abbey was simply for the purpose of spiritual formation.[81] In 1981 *A Cry for Mercy* appeared, containing selections from his prayer journal and some introductory comments that helped the reader understand the context. Touching what was most universal in the lives of Christians was again his motive:

> I do this not because they teach anyone how to pray, or because they offer a method of prayer, but because they point in their awkward powerlessness to the real and very powerful presence of the Divine Spirit who is promised to us by our Lord as a never-failing guide. It is my hope, therefore, that those who recognize in these prayers the cries of their own hearts will also recognize the quiet prayer of God's Spirit in the midst of their own halting and stuttering words.[82]

Nouwen completed three more books by 1981, his last year at Yale Divinity School. *The Way of the Heart* resulted from a seminar that Nouwen taught on desert spirituality at Yale in which the participants attempted to discover what the Desert Fathers and Mothers of the fourth century had to say to ministers in the twentieth century.[83] Nouwen used the phrases *flee, be silent*, and *pray* as the outline for the text, encouraging ministers to practice the spiritual disciplines that transform the mind and empower them to be "light in the darkness."[84]

The second book that Nouwen completed during his last year at Yale was *Making All Things New: An Invitation to the Spiritual Life*. In response to people who continued to ask him to define the spiritual life, Nouwen wanted to create a small book that one could read easily and quickly, one that not only explained the spiritual life but also encouraged people to live it. He targeted not only those who knew and practiced the Christian faith, but also those who might not be Christian but were on a personal spiritual quest. Nouwen used as a touch point for all humans the experience of worry. Applying the words of Jesus in Matthew 6, "Do not worry," Nouwen compared the destructive effects of worry to what Je-

---

[80] Henri Nouwen, *A Cry for Mercy: Prayers from the Genesee* (Maryknoll, N.Y.: Orbis Books, 1981), xii.

[81] Ibid., xi.

[82] Ibid,, xiii.

[83] Henri Nouwen, *The Way of the Heart: Desert Spirituality and Contemporary Ministry* (New York: Ballantine Books, 1981), vii.

[84] Ibid., 1–4.

sus offers through a life in the Spirit, which makes all things new. Nouwen also discussed some spiritual disciplines that enable this re-creative work of the Spirit to take place and force worry to lose its hold.[85]

The final book that Nouwen worked on during his tenure at Yale was *Compassion: A Reflection on the Christian Life*, a collaboration between Nouwen, Donald McNeill, and Douglas Morrison. The idea began with a conversation among them at a Greek restaurant in Washington, D.C., as they expressed discontent with the individualism and spiritual dryness of their academic lives at Notre Dame, Catholic University, and Yale. They decided to meet on nine subsequent Thursdays in Washington to study and pray together. The most urgent question that presented itself in their discussions was how to live compassionately in the world.[86] The thesis of their book, which grew out of these discussions, was that human beings are more competitive than compassionate, but Jesus called his followers to be compassionate as the Father is compassionate (Luke 6:36). This was a radical call that required both prayer and action, disciplines that guide one's relationship with God and with other fellow human beings.[87] This work reflected Nouwen's growing interest in social issues and the challenge for Christians to be light in the midst of darkness.

As mentioned previously, in the conversations with his colleagues in the Greek restaurant, Nouwen struggled with life in the academic world. Nouwen felt torn between his career and his vocation. The competitive nature of the academic setting at Yale promoted mostly rivalry and isolation. While he was teaching about the spiritual life of prayer, meditation, contemplation, humility, intimacy, vulnerability, and gentleness, the milieu around him seemingly emphasized only the intellectual life with its competition for success and prestige.[88] Nouwen felt he was not rooted deeply enough in Christ to stay in the environment of Yale.[89] He wanted to go back to a more basic kind of ministry but he was not sure exactly what that ministry would be.

Nouwen submitted his resignation from his tenured position at Yale in July 1981. He moved to the Abbey of the Genesee and was given the

[85] Henri Nouwen, *Making All Things New: An Invitation to the Spiritual Life* (San Francisco: HarperSanFrancisco, 1981), 15–17.

[86] Henri Nouwen, Donald P. MacNeill, and Douglas A. Morrison, *Compassion: A Reflection on the Christian Life* (New York: Doubleday Image Books, 1982), xi–xii.

[87] Ibid., 7–9.

[88] Mary C. Uhler, "From Harvard to L'Arche: Henri Nouwen Shares His Journey," *Catholic Herald*, 23 July 1987, 1.

[89] Boers, "From the House of Fear to the House of Love," 5.

status of a "family brother" with rooms in the Nazareth guest house of the abbey. He used this temporary setting as the base of operations for his travel and speaking engagements for the next fifteen months.[90]

Harvard and Latin America (1982–1985)

Nouwen had been interested for a long time in the affairs of Latin America and had at times wondered if God might be calling him to a life among the poor as a missionary. While visiting the Sojourners[91] community in Washington, D.C., on one occasion, he had the opportunity to meet Brazilian archbishop Dom Helder Camara. Nouwen probed him relentlessly with his questions. He was obviously fascinated by the work of the church in the third world.[92] From the beginning of his time at Yale, Nouwen had thought a great deal about the relationship between North and South America. Nouwen believed God was using the undeniable link between the two to reveal more of himself through each continent to the other. Nouwen made short visits to Mexico, Chile, and Paraguay and studied Spanish in Bolivia. All of these excursions only strengthened his belief in the potential spiritual unity between North and South America.[93] Was God calling him to be a part of the building of a bridge between the two?

Nouwen decided to confront the question directly after resigning from Yale. Through some contacts with Maryknoll missionaries,[94] Nouwen made plans to spend six months in Bolivia and Peru.[95] In October 1981, Nouwen flew to Peru to meet his Maryknoll hosts and then trav-

[90] Bob Bickel, "Priest's Prolific Prose 'An Afterthought,' " *Rochester* (N.Y.) *Democrat and Chronicle*, 2 February 1983, B5.

[91] The Sojourners organization was founded in 1971 and has its headquarters in Washington, D.C. The organization seeks to raise critical issues confronting Christians in America. Until 1980 it was known as the People's Christian Coalition. The *Sojourners* magazine promotes human rights, racial justice, and peacemaking and has a circulation of approximately 24,000. See *Encyclopedia of Associations*, s.v. "Sojourners," 1930.

[92] Jim Wallis, "The Deepest Questions of Life and Faith," *Sojourners* 25 (November-December 1996): 29.

[93] Henri Nouwen, ¡*Gracias! A Latin American Journal* (San Francisco: Harper and Row, Publishers, 1983), xiii–xiv.

[94] Maryknoll is the Catholic Foreign Mission Society of America, established in 1911; Maryknoll established missions in South America in 1942. See the *HarperCollins Encyclopedia of Catholicism*, s.v. "Maryknoll," 831.

[95] Durback, *Seeds of Hope*, xiv–xv.

eled to Cochabamba, Bolivia, for a three-month course designed to improve his Spanish. In January 1982 he returned to Peru for three months of orientation with the missionaries in the Maryknoll Center house in Lima, living with a Peruvian family in the parish.[96]

Nouwen had a great admiration for Gustavo Gutiérrez, the father of liberation theology, and met with him regularly in Lima.[97] Nouwen's spirituality definitely began to take on more social involvement as a result of these experiences. But he was also critical of liberation theology. He wondered if it was too much a copy of other worldly social theories. He was critical of any system that focused on political and social issues and ignored the spiritual dimension.[98] In Gutiérrez, he found a unity of prayer and action that he saw in few other liberation theologians,[99] but many of the Maryknoll missionaries made him uncomfortable because of their intense attention to the issues of social justice at the expense of personal spirituality.

As was his custom, Nouwen kept a journal of his experiences, later published as *¡Gracias! A Latin American Journal*.[100] The purpose of the journal was not to keep a record of the sights and experiences of Latin America but rather to focus his thoughts on discerning whether God was calling him to live and work in Latin America in the years to come.[101] *¡Gracias!* provided a glimpse of the struggle that many Christians experience—how to discern the will of God. The reader is unsure from one page to the next whether Nouwen believed he should stay or return to the United States. This reflects the reality that discernment of God's will was not always clear or easily known to him.

Nouwen decided at the end of the six-month experience that God was not calling him to live and work in Latin America. He did not seem to have what it took for such a work. The missionaries in Peru were "intensely individualistic in their struggle for justice and peace."[102] Nouwen's longing for a community of prayer was not compatible with their lifestyle and, as mentioned earlier, he was uneasy with "the militant lib-

---

[96] Nouwen, *¡Gracias!* xi, xiv.

[97] Beumer, *Henri Nouwen: A Restless Seeking for God*, 49.

[98] Nouwen, *¡Gracias!* 40.

[99] Beumer, *Henri Nouwen: A Restless Seeking for God*, 50.

[100] Nouwen's original journals from the Latin America trip are located in the Nouwen archives at Yale Divinity School Library. Nouwen typically used small books of lined paper and his handwriting is a challenge to read!

[101] Nouwen, *¡Gracias!* xiv.

[102] Coady, "Nouwen Finds Rest at Daybreak," 3.

erational mood."[103] People also told him that his gifts would be better
used by going back to North America to lecture and write about the
situations in Latin America.[104] Nouwen accepted their guidance with
difficulty because he was emotionally attached to the Latin American
people and had hoped to find a home among them, but he knew his
advisors were right. In March 1982, Nouwen returned to his temporary
quarters at the Genesee.[105]

After his return to the United States, Nouwen received an invitation
to teach at Harvard Divinity School. He refused, saying that he no longer
wanted to teach full-time at the university level. A compromise seemingly settled the dilemma temporarily when Nouwen agreed to teach
only one semester each year. This arrangement left him free to pursue
his other interests, including Latin America, the rest of the year. Nouwen
was to teach Christian spirituality with a special emphasis on the spiritual
aspects of liberation theology. Nouwen thought perhaps this was to be
his way of serving the church in Latin America—by helping students in
the North understand it more fully.[106] He moved to Cambridge, Massa-
chusetts, in the late fall of 1982 to prepare for his first semester, which
began in January of 1983.[107]

Nouwen was given the position of Lentz Lecturer during the spring
of 1983, which entailed public lectures, retreats, and speaking informally
with students, staff, and faculty. In the fall of 1983 he was appointed as
professor of divinity.[108] Harvard recruited Nouwen because of his "unusual ability to enable persons to enter into the Scriptures, theological
reflection, and prayer, so as to discover their own deepest spirituality and
its relationship to the needs of the modern world."[109] With a mission to
train religious leaders, the Harvard Divinity School faculty believed
Nouwen could bring depth not only to the study, but the practice, of
spirituality among the ministry students.[110]

When the spring semester of 1983 was over, Nouwen left for another
tour in Latin America, beginning this time in Mexico. Some critics were

[103] Glen Argan, "Nouwen Finds a Home," *Western Catholic Reporter*, 21 March 1994, 6.

[104] Coady, "Nouwen Finds Rest at Daybreak," 3.

[105] Durback, *Seeds of Hope*, xxv.

[106] Henri Nouwen, *The Road to Daybreak: A Spiritual Journey* (New York: Doubleday Image Books, 1988), 3.

[107] Durback, *Seeds of Hope*, xxv.

[108] *Harvard Gazette*, 28 January 1983, 3.

[109] Ibid.

[110] "Henri Nouwen Receives Appointment at HDS," *Harvard Divinity Bulletin*, February–
March 1983, 2.

skeptical about Nouwen's reasons for continued involvement in Latin America, wondering if it was "just another opportunity to write a book and become an instant expert on Latin American affairs."[111] When asked about his purpose or motives in going, Nouwen explained that he simply wanted to contribute to the mission of the Catholic Church and serve in whatever way his gifts allowed. He did not go with preconceived ideas about what he would accomplish. He left with only the intention to listen closely—to the native people, to the missionaries, and to God.[112]

Nouwen began his journey by going to Mexico City, where he became a student at the Center for Economic and Social Studies, concentrating on Central America. After a month Nouwen went to Nicaragua at the invitation of a Maryknoll missionary, with the hope of gaining a better understanding of the painful situations caused by war.[113] In the highly dangerous militarized zone on the border between Nicaragua and Honduras, Nouwen met for several weeks with peasants, listened to their stories, and prayed with them.[114] After seeing with his own eyes the devastation brought by the war between the leftist Sandinista government and the U.S.-trained contra rebels, Nouwen became convinced that the United States should stay out of the affairs of the country. Upon his return to the United States he launched a two-month lecture tour of the United States seeking to connect the spiritual life of his listeners to their responsibility towards Nicaragua. He believed an authentic Christian response to the situation was to stay out of Nicaragua's affairs, not only to avoid violence, but also out of respect for the development of the country.[115] He wanted to "call Christians to consciousness" about what was happening. He directed his listeners to tell their president to stop sending guns to Central America, not for the sake of politics, but for the sake of "the Christ who suffers anew in a suffering people."[116] One listener described Nouwen's passionate plea with these words:

> I saw a simple man, a man of prayer—so different from the night before when the President spoke on television in such an array of power. But that night I saw a man who had only his own witness, no charts, no CIA white papers, just a report of how he asked a Nicaraguan mother for forgiveness

---

[111] John E. Vesey, "Nouwen's Difficult Journey," *The Tablet*, 19 May 1983, 1.

[112] Ibid.

[113] Ibid.

[114] Durback, *Seeds of Hope*, xxv.

[115] Coady, "Nouwen Finds Rest at Daybreak," 3.

[116] Francis X. Meehan, "He Pleads, Knowing the Charge to Come," *The Philadelphia Inquirer*, 13 August 1983, A9.

that her son had been killed by U.S.-trained *contras* and of how she gave
him that forgiveness openly and compassionately.[117]

Exhausted and spiritually depleted after his tour, Nouwen accepted
the invitation of Jean Vanier, founder of L'Arche, to visit him in France
in the fall of 1983. Vanier had been a professor of philosophy at St. Michael's College in Toronto when, in 1964, he made the decision to leave
the academic world and invited two men with mental disabilities to
move into his home in Trosly, France. It was not long before others asked
to join Vanier in his work. More households were formed and in time
L'Arche became an international federation of communities scattered
throughout the world.[118] Vanier believed that people with mental disabilities, just like all other human beings, needed a home—a place to belong. Only when they belonged could they truly become all they were
meant to be.[119] Every person in the community, disabled or not, had a
"unique and mysterious value" with the right to life, care, education,
work, friendship, communion, and spiritual development.[120] Yet the
value of L'Arche was not limited to what it offered those within the community. The mission of L'Arche was also to "change society by choosing
to live relationships in community as a sign of love and hope."[121]

Nouwen's contact with Vanier began in the late 1970s with a peculiar
greeting. One afternoon a young woman by the name of Jan Risse rang
Nouwen's doorbell. When he answered she smiled and said that she
brought greetings to him from Jean Vanier. Nouwen had never met Vanier but knew about him. Nouwen expressed his gratitude but was skeptical that the woman came only to deliver the greeting. He thought
perhaps she also wanted to ask something of him. When he asked, she
said that there was nothing she wanted except to bring the greeting, yet
she continued to stand at his door. Nouwen finally invited her in but
explained that he had appointments to meet at his office. She said, "Oh,
you go ahead. I'll just spend some quiet time here until you return."
When Nouwen returned, she had a beautiful evening meal prepared.
Surprisingly, the young woman stayed in town several days and did many
acts of kindness and service for Nouwen. When she finally left, she sim-

[117] Ibid.

[118] Durback, *Seeds of Hope*, xxvi.

[119] Jean Vanier, "The Healing Community," *Compass*, September 1989, 6–8.

[120] Conal Mullen, "A Lesson in Love," *The Edmonton Journal*, 26 March 1994, B4.

[121] Martha Crean, "L'Arche Celebrates 25 Years in Canada," *Catholic New Times*, 22 January 1995, 18.

ply said, "Just remember, Jean Vanier sends his greetings to you." Though certainly unusual, the visit seemed inconsequential to Nouwen at the time.[122]

Then in 1981 Vanier phoned Nouwen and invited him to a silent retreat in Chicago. Nouwen thought that perhaps Vanier was asking him to speak. But Vanier replied, "Henri, it is a *silent* retreat. We can just be together and pray." The two soon became good friends.[123]

Nouwen did not realize it, but this friendship with Vanier, which had its beginning back in the 1970s, would eventually reveal the path that Nouwen had been searching for in relation to his sense that God was calling him to serve the poor. In 1983, following his tour of speaking concerning Latin America, Nouwen stayed six weeks with Vanier at his home in France. Vanier did not ask Nouwen to give a lecture or write a book. He sensed that Nouwen was "a man without a home."[124] He simply said, "We have a home for you and we really don't want you to do very much. Just waste some time with us!"[125] The people of L'Arche encouraged him to pray, to go to the chapel alone, to sleep in or have dinner with some of the disabled people in their homes.[126] When it was time to return to Harvard for the spring semester of 1984, Nouwen made the commitment to come again the next fall for a thirty-day retreat. Nouwen's encounter with Vanier created a turning point in Nouwen's spiritual journey to be realized more clearly later.[127]

After teaching the spring semester of 1984 at Harvard, Nouwen made another trip to Latin America at the invitation of another friend, John Vesey, who had just been appointed by his archbishop to a parish in Guatemala. Vesey took the place of Father Stan Rother, who was murdered in 1981. Nouwen and Peter Weiskel, a friend and gifted photographer, stayed with Vesey in Guatemala for only ten days, from August 27 to September 5, in order to pray with him and the Guatemalan people. Nouwen and Weiskel later put together a book that told the story of Stan Rother and John Vesey and included photographs Weiskel had taken of the Guatemalan people and landscapes. Nouwen believed that the story of Rother's martyrdom needed to be told be-

[122] Nouwen, *Road to Daybreak*, 1–2.
[123] Ibid., 2.
[124] Argan, "Nouwen Finds a Home," 6.
[125] Coady, "Nouwen Finds Rest at Daybreak," 3.
[126] Boers, "From the House of Fear to the House of Love," 6.
[127] Durback, *Seeds of Hope*, xxvi.

cause "martyrs are blood witnesses of God's inexhaustible love for his people."[128] Nouwen published *Love in a Fearful Land: A Guatemalan Story* in 1985.

Nouwen was not happy with his life at Harvard. He loved to teach and his classes and evening lectures were always full, but he found it to be the most difficult place to live of any in his experience. Nouwen continued to long for community, but he perceived Harvard as an ambitious place, even more so than Yale.[129] Nouwen could not abide the academic pretentiousness that he sensed from some of the faculty, who expressed a particular distaste for scholars whose reputation and popularity reached beyond the academy and whispered condescending remarks about Nouwen's "crowd," referring to the large crowds that came to hear him lecture.[130] Robert Jonas, a student of Nouwen's at Harvard and a personal friend, wrote, "Henri's shameless declaration of Christ's living presence among us was probably an embarrassment to some of his Harvard colleagues and students who were used to the fine, dispassionate art of theological reasoning."[131] The discrepancy between the praise that Nouwen received when he accepted the Harvard position and the ridicule, as perceived by Nouwen, that he received later is difficult to explain. Perhaps a mutual respect never developed between him and some of the faculty. Perhaps Nouwen would not have been comfortable at Harvard regardless of his reception by colleagues because of his own doubt about whether he wanted to remain in the academic arena.

Nouwen also realized quickly that the students had a greater need for spiritual formation than for information about the burning issues of the Latin American church. Thus his teaching moved to more general areas of the spiritual life and his "reverse mission" from South to North was not realized.[132] Nouwen taught in the spring semester of 1985 and then resigned. He wrote later:

> After twenty-five years of priesthood, I found myself praying poorly, living somewhat isolated from other people, and very much preoccupied with burning issues . . . I woke up one day with the realization that I was living

[128] Henri Nouwen, *Love in a Fearful Land: A Guatemalan Story* (Notre Dame: Ave Maria Press, 1985), 10–13.

[129] Boers, "From the House of Fear to the House of Love," 7.

[130] Dan Wakefield, "Spiritual Impact: Encounters with Henri Nouwen," *Christian Century* 114 (19–26 March 1997): 301.

[131] Jonas, *Henri Nouwen*, xlviii.

[132] Nouwen, *Road to Daybreak*, 3.

in a very dark place and that the term "burnout" was a convenient psychological translation for a spiritual death.[133]

Finding a Home with L'Arche (1986–1996)

Nouwen began to pray for direction, acknowledging that he would follow God wherever he wanted him to go, but that the instructions would have to be "clear and unambiguous."[134] After resigning from Harvard, Nouwen was invited once again to return to L'Arche in Trosly, France, this time to stay for a year. Nouwen considered the invitation a gift from God in order to help him discern what God's will was for this time in his life.[135] According to one observer, Mary Uhler, the voice of Jean Vanier had become the "other voice" of Nouwen's mother, which had remained dormant in him for most of his career.[136] Vanier and life at L'Arche called Nouwen back to a life of prayer and the nurturing of his relationship with Jesus above all else. "When people asked him how he was doing, they did not mean have you written any articles or books lately? Did you take a trip or give a speech somewhere? They meant, How are you and God doing? Have you spent enough time in prayer?"[137] The demand of L'Arche was to keep in touch with his heart through solitude and prayer and to love the people around him. It was more a matter of "sharing your being with others than that you're accomplishing a lot of things."[138]

Nouwen wrote the manuscripts for two more books during his visits with Vanier in France between 1983 and 1986. *Lifesigns: Intimacy, Fecundity, and Ecstasy in Christian Perspective* was based on the conviction that people often live life and make decisions out of fear. But love is stronger than fear. Nouwen sought to demonstrate the movement from fear into love based on John 15 and the truth that people do not have to live and react out of fear if their lives are abiding in the love of Jesus.[139]

The second book that Nouwen wrote as a result of experiences in France was *Behold the Beauty of the Lord: Praying with Icons*. Each time that

[133] Henri Nouwen, *In the Name of Jesus: Reflections on Christian Leadership* (New York: Crossroad Publishing Company, 1989), 10–11.

[134] Ibid., 11.

[135] Durback, *Seeds of Hope*, xxvii.

[136] Uhler, "From Harvard to L'Arche," 1.

[137] Bert Witvoet, "Profile," *Calvinist Contact*, 23 October 1987, 10.

[138] Coady, "Nouwen Finds Rest at Daybreak," 3.

[139] Henri Nouwen, *Lifesigns: Intimacy, Fecundity, and Ecstasy in Christian Perspective* (New York: Doubleday Image Books, 1986), 15–23.

Nouwen came to France, in 1983, 1984, and 1985, Vanier's assistant placed a different icon in his room for Nouwen to enjoy. After gazing at each one for many weeks, Nouwen wrote down his thoughts. Nouwen believed icons, as Eastern spirituality taught, were "for the sole purpose of offering access through the gate of the visible to the mystery of the invisible." Nouwen intended that the text he had written be used as a meditation along with pictures of the icons in order that the reader might learn to pray with icons as "faithful guides" on the journey.[140]

From August 1985 to August 1986 Nouwen became enmeshed in the world of the disabled. He ate with them, played with them, worked with them, and learned from them. He visited several of the L'Arche communities. And as usual, Nouwen kept a journal of his experience, which he later published as *The Road to Daybreak: A Spiritual Journey* in 1988.[141]

Daybreak is the oldest and one of the largest L'Arche communities in North America,[142] founded in 1969 in Toronto, Canada.[143] Nouwen visited the community briefly for the first time in October 1985 while in North America for other engagements. This particular trip gave Nouwen the opportunity to learn more of L'Arche's purpose and programs. The whole community consisted of about eighty people. Three of the community's homes were located on a farm thirty minutes from downtown Toronto; three more homes were in the suburban town of Richmond Hill and two more were in Toronto. Nouwen prayed with members and assistants, went on outings with them, and listened to the assistants talk about why they were there. The Daybreak community received Nouwen warmly, and at the end of his nine-day stay, he felt he was an intimate part of the lives there. Nouwen knew that this visit was significant and would somehow affect his future decisions.[144]

On December 12, 1985, a letter arrived which confirmed Nouwen's feelings about Daybreak's significance. The letter was an invitation from the Daybreak Community Council for Nouwen to join the Daybreak community:

> We truly feel that you have a gift to bring us. At the same time, our sense is that Daybreak would be a good place for you, too. We would want to

---

[140] Henri Nouwen, *Behold the Beauty of the Lord: Praying with Icons* (Notre Dame: Ave Maria Press, 1987), 9–16.

[141] Durback, *Seeds of Hope*, xxvii.

[142] Grainger, "Henri: A Heart's Desire," 26.

[143] Durback, *Seeds of Hope*, xxvii.

[144] Nouwen, *Road to Daybreak*, 33–43.

support you in your important vocation of writing and speaking by providing you with a community that will love you and call you to grow.[145]

Nouwen had been praying specifically for direction regarding what to
do next. He knew this letter was as explicit direction as one could ask
for. He asked for advice from Vanier and others in the community and
he knew he needed his bishop's approval of the change as well. He
prayed for courage and strength to be obedient no matter what the outcome.[146]

Nouwen traveled to the Netherlands the day after Christmas in 1985
to visit his family and to meet with his bishop. He met with Cardinal
Simonis, who listened carefully, asked many practical questions, and then
said his first inclination was to approve the request but he wanted time
to pray about it and study the matter. On January 4, 1986, Nouwen
received the final word. The cardinal told him to go to Daybreak for
three years. After such time, the option should be left open for Nouwen
to return to the Netherlands if he wanted to. Nouwen was glad to have
the cardinal's blessing and he was excited about his new future.[147] The
spirituality of L'Arche offered a dimension for him that had been lacking
in his other positions—living and working in a believing community.[148]

While back in the Netherlands, Nouwen was struck by the new prosperity and secularity of his homeland. In his journal Nouwen wrote,
"The country feels very self-satisfied. There is not much space left, inside
or outside, to be with God and God alone. . . . The Dutch have become
a distracted people—very good and kind, and good-natured but caught
in too much of everything."[149] Nouwen felt the effects even in his own
family. As he attempted to involve the family in celebrating the Eucharist
and share words about Jesus and his healing presence, few were receptive.
Even the news of his decision to go to Daybreak had little effect on
them.[150]

A Dutch publisher had once asked Nouwen when he would write
another book in Dutch. Nouwen saw himself as an American writer after
so many years in America. He sensed a secularization, a defensive, for-
tresslike mentality in the Dutch church, and a lack of interest in Christian
spirituality and his work.[151] Nouwen felt he had little to say to his home-

[145] Ibid., 94–95.
[146] Ibid., 95.
[147] Ibid., 117.
[148] Beumer, *Henri Nouwen: A Restless Seeking for God*, 58.
[149] Nouwen, *Road to Daybreak*, 108.
[150] Ibid., 115.
[151] Jonas, *Henri Nouwen*, lii.

land which had become so strange to him. The nudge from the publisher, however, eventually led to a book called *Letters to Marc About Jesus*. The letters were written to Nouwen's nephew, Marc. Nouwen told Marc that he wanted to write a book in Dutch about what it meant to live a spiritual life. He wanted to write it in the form of letters to Marc and receive Marc's thoughtful input as a young man who had been born into a comfortable life but was nonetheless sensing a certain void in his life. Marc was most willing to cooperate and gave helpful, clarifying responses which Nouwen integrated into the book.[152]

In May of 1986 Nouwen made another trip to Canada in order to meet with the Daybreak council. The council invited him to tell them more about his spiritual journey and his reasons for accepting their call to come to Canada and be their pastor. It was acknowledged that Nouwen had a lot to learn about life with the disabled and he would need a significant period of adjustment. It was also agreed that Nouwen would help to start a small spiritual center called Dayspring as a source of spiritual renewal for the English-speaking L'Arche members and their friends. The community sensed the need to develop a rich spiritual life that celebrated the liturgical year, broadened their knowledge of the Scriptures, and deepened their prayer life. However, the community also made the commitment to honor, protect, and support Nouwen's vocation to write as well as fulfill speaking engagements. Nouwen hired a secretary to help with correspondence and phone calls. He realized that life at Daybreak would not be easy but would teach him something new about God's love.[153]

As Nouwen began his life at Daybreak in August of 1986, it was a community of people with different religions, backgrounds, and lifestyles. Not everyone was a Christian and living in such a place called Nouwen to be a witness to God in a completely new way.[154] He was no longer living in the limelight. The emphasis was not on accomplishments but on faithfulness—to God, to the people with disabilities, and to a life of wholeness.[155]

Nouwen also encountered changes in the everyday business of living. Nouwen lived for the first fourteen months in one of Daybreak's homes, called New House, with core members (those with disabilities) and their

[152] Henri Nouwen, *Letters to Marc About Jesus* (San Francisco: HarperSanFrancisco, 1988), vii–viii. Originally published in Dutch by Lannoo in 1987 with the title *Brieven aan Marc*.

[153] Nouwen, *Road to Daybreak*, 191–92.

[154] Nouwen, Regis College Syllabus, 1.

[155] Witvoet, "Profile," 10.

assistants. Here was a man who had spent more than thirty years living by himself around universities that provided all the services he needed for daily life. Yet now he was required to be a full participant in the family life of a home in Richmond Hill.[156] Everyone at Daybreak was interested in this fifty-five-year-old priest of such brilliance who seemed unable to make a sandwich![157] When he asked for the first time whom to give his laundry to, he received a lesson in "modern laundry technology."[158]

Christian spirituality became central to the community after Nouwen's arrival. Nouwen loved to celebrate the Eucharist and did so every weekday in the chapel. For those core members who could not as easily come to the chapel, Nouwen visited their homes. Before long Nouwen conducted some kind of worship service or activity at least every day and often twice a day. During the ten years that Nouwen lived at Daybreak, thousands came to hear him teach the Word. As more people came to know him through his writings, they longed to meet him, to be in the presence of this man who had the unusual ability to touch the heart and soul with his words. Robert Jonas, one of Nouwen's closest friends, writes:

> Over the years, the clear glass chalice has reflected the faces of many thousands who have come to hear the Word: handicapped people lying across bean-bag chairs, lay care-givers, Catholic priests and Protestant ministers, Latin American peasants, professors, middle-class Catholics, wealthy philanthropists, seminary students, and United States Senators. They come to hear the Word, but also to be in the presence of the radiance that seems to stream from this man. They come because they hope to receive, into their own shadows of doubt, despair, and hopelessness, a bit of his reflected, dancing light. And perhaps to discover their own. They come because this man, more than anyone else they know, seems not only to speak the Word, but actually to *become* it. Some say that when Henri Nouwen presides at a Eucharist, one not only hears but *sees* the Word, right here, right now.[159]

Nouwen tried to provide creatively for the spiritual needs of both Catholic and Protestant members of the Daybreak community and sought to make sure that those of other religions were provided for as

[156] Gunar Kravalis, "At Home with Henri Nouwen—A Visit to Daybreak," *The Presbyterian Record*, April 1989, 24.

[157] Carolyn Whitney-Brown, "Safe in God's Heart," *Sojourners* 25 (November–December 1996): 32.

[158] Grainger, "Henri: A Heart's Desire," 27.

[159] Jonas, *Henri Nouwen*, xiii–xiv.

well. On Sunday, all members who desired to do so attended their own churches in the Toronto area.[160]

Another aspect of the community's spiritual life was Dayspring, a house on Daybreak's property that was converted in 1987, at Nouwen's initiative, into a retreat center, not only for those working in the Daybreak community, but for other L'Arche friends and visitors. The upper level of the house provided several bedrooms for guests, a sitting area with a library, and a kitchen. The lower level of the house had an office and a large room decorated as a chapel that was used for the community's worship experiences. Sue Mosteller, a sister of St. Joseph, who came to work with the Daybreak community in 1972, worked with Nouwen after his arrival in creating programs and providing pastoral care for the community. She took responsibility for the Dayspring retreat center for almost five years and filled the pastoral role when Nouwen was away.[161]

Nouwen was very passionate and creative. When he talked, he used his entire body and few could move fast enough to keep up with the ideas that he wanted to make realities. Those who worked with him were exasperated with this at times, but fully acknowledged the immense significance of his presence at Daybreak for their own lives and the life of the community. Sue Mosteller described him as a colleague and as a friend:

> The community just shook when Henri was around. He was so creative and so energetic that you sometimes had to remind him to slow down. But his passion for God and for people deepened me immensely and I loved the way he was so free and open to see beyond the walls of our Roman Catholic tradition which had kept things very black and white for me from the time I was a young girl. He helped me to broaden my vision and to see a bigger world. I loved being his friend but it was sometimes difficult. Being his friend was complicated, desperate, it was horrible and it was marvelous all at the same time! I helped him to remain sensitive to the community and he helped me to broaden my ideas of spirituality.[162]

In the home where Nouwen lived there were six people with disabilities—Rose, Adam, Bill, John, Trevor and Raymond—and four assis-

[160] Sue Mosteller, interview by author, tape recording, Richmond Hill, Ontario, 9 March 1998.

[161] This author visited the Daybreak community in Richmond Hill, Ontarion March 9–12, 1998 and stayed in the rooms that had belonged to Nouwen. Sue Mosteller, now the literary executrix for Nouwen and director of the Henri Nouwen Literary Center, granted an interview to the author during this visit.

[162] Sue Mosteller, interview by author, tape recording, Richmond Hill, Ontario, 11 March 1998.

tants.[163] One of the first assignments given to Nouwen was the task of helping Adam in the mornings. Adam was a twenty-five-year-old man who could not speak and seldom smiled. He had epileptic seizures that exhausted him and made him require extra sleep. Dressing, walking, eating, and going to the bathroom all required careful attention. Adam and the lessons that Nouwen learned from him became the subjects of some of Nouwen's articles and a book much later.[164]

Nouwen strived to make friends with all the members of the household and each one loved him in his or her own way—a hug, a smile, flowers, showing him their latest artistic creation, or buying him a beer. All of them had experienced much brokenness and pain. But they gave their love freely and Nouwen developed deep affection for them.[165] Their love was not based on anything that Nouwen had accomplished, and it began to set him free from the bondage of believing that his value as a person and his worthiness to be loved should be based on his accomplishments.[166] This did not mean that Nouwen stopped writing or speaking, so one might be tempted to wonder whether Daybreak made any difference in his need to publish and be recognized. But as will be seen in later chapters, the themes found in the later years of his writing demonstrate that Nouwen began to resist using his accomplishments to validate his worth as a person.

In truth, life at Daybreak caused Nouwen to begin to see many of his own handicaps. Not only was he extraordinarily weak in the ordinary tasks of a household, but he also discovered that he was also most weak where he thought he was strong—in his ability to nurture intimacy. He did not always respond well to those with whom he shared a home. Living in such close community demanded that he learn to love as genuinely and as honestly as they did. The men and women with disabilities could tell when he was not sincere and they did not let him get away with his dishonesty. Nouwen could no longer function as he had before, using appropriate facades despite what he genuinely felt.[167]

The lessons on intimacy, however, did not end there. Nouwen began to realize that he not only depended on his own accomplishments to prove his self-worth, but he also depended too much on the affection

---

[163] Nouwen, *Road to Daybreak*, 219.

[164] See "Adam's Peace," *World Vision*, August–September 1988, 4–7 and *Adam: God's Beloved* (Maryknoll, N.Y.: Orbis Books, 1997).

[165] Nouwen, *Road to Daybreak*, 220.

[166] Uhler, "From Harvard to L'Arche," 1, 3.

[167] Catherine Odell, "Father Nouwen Sees the Light at Daybreak," *Our Sunday Visitor*, 12 July 1992, 5.

and approval of others. After finding the community for which he had longed most of his life, Nouwen had to face the deepest struggle of his soul. He wrote that no human friendship, no community, could meet the deepest longings of his heart. Only God could. Nouwen had to choose again to follow Jesus alone in order to live in community as he had been called to do. Nouwen had to ask himself, "Is Jesus truly enough for you, or do you keep looking for others to give you your sense of worth?"[168]

During the first fourteen months of Nouwen's life at Daybreak, he was convinced he was in the right place and he was happy with his work. By the end of 1987, however, he encountered a "dark night of the soul" that shook him to his emotional foundations.[169] Nouwen called this time of emotional crisis the most difficult period of his life. He was extremely depressed. He wrote, "Here I was, a writer about the spiritual life, known as someone who loves God and gives hope to people, flat on the ground and in total darkness."[170] The ironic part of it was that Nouwen had finally found the home he had always longed for. He said it was "as if he needed a safe place to hit bottom!"[171] As Nouwen began to deal with this deep, inner anguish, he became exhausted mentally and physically.[172] With the support of Daybreak, he went to a retreat center in Winnipeg, Manitoba, from January to July of 1988 and lived under the care of two spiritual directors.[173]

The crisis was triggered by the sudden interruption of a friendship[174] that Nouwen had come to depend on. No other friend had made him feel as loved and cared for. No other friend had he trusted with such confidence. But this friendship could not fill the void that began to open up within him. He knew this was true intellectually, but emotionally he became possessive and needy, to the point that the friendship had to be interrupted. Nouwen fell into a great abyss of depression and knew he could not climb out without guidance. In his retreat, he found two spir-

[168] Nouwen, *Road to Daybreak*, 220–24.

[169] Amy Greene, "An Interview with Catholic Priest Writer Henri Nouwen," *SBC Today*, September 1990, 10.

[170] Henri Nouwen, *The Inner Voice of Love: A Journey Through Anguish to Freedom* (New York: Doubleday, 1996), xiii.

[171] Nouwen, *Inner Voice of Love*, xiv.

[172] Boers, "From the House of Fear to the House of Love," 7–8.

[173] Henri Nouwen, *Heart Speaks to Heart* (Notre Dame: Ave Maria Press, 1989), 12.

[174] Nouwen never revealed in his published journal who this friend was. Perhaps this was for the sake of his friend's privacy as well as his own.

itual directors who met with him daily and gently moved him from one day to the next until he could begin to see the light of hope.

In all of this, Nouwen did not lose his ability to write. Instead he used the exercise of writing to help him put into words what he was learning. This diary was eventually published, but not for eight years. What Nouwen had written seemed too intense and raw to be of use to anyone. He found a place of expression for some of his thoughts from this time in a book that he published four years later called *The Return of the Prodigal Son*. This book was mostly the result of his reflections on a painting of Rembrandt's by the same title.[175] A poster print of the painting was one of Nouwen's treasured possessions and he even had the opportunity to see the original painting in St. Petersburg before coming to live at Daybreak. In his book, Nouwen spoke of how he could relate to each of the main figures in the painting—the prodigal son, the older brother, and the father. In speaking to each role, he shared his journey from teaching about love to allowing himself to be loved by God without condition.[176] Nouwen's "dark night of the soul" was a significant part of that journey.

Eventually, after much convincing by friends and much editing, portions of the actual diary that Nouwen kept during his months of deep depression were published eight years later, in 1996, under the title *The Inner Voice of Love: A Journey Through Anguish to Freedom*.[177] The eight years before its publication allowed Nouwen to gain some distance and perspective on the words he had written. He accomplished a delicate balance in the way he decided which portions of the journal to include. Perhaps for the sake of privacy (Nouwen's as well as those closely involved), some details were not included, but the honesty of Nouwen's spiritual struggle was vividly preserved.

One other book actually had its origin in the time Nouwen spent in France as well as the time Nouwen spent away from Daybreak in 1988. The small work was entitled *Heart Speaks to Heart: Three Prayers to Jesus*. This book began with a conversation between Jean Vanier's mother, Mammie Vanier, and Nouwen while he was in France. She was determined that Nouwen should write a book about the devotion to the Sacred Heart of Jesus. He did not feel comfortable with the idea. But during his six months away from Daybreak in early 1988, Nouwen celebrated Holy Week with a community of Trappists in Holland, Manitoba. While there he decided to read some literature on the devotion to

[175] Nouwen, *Inner Voice of Love*, xv–xviii.
[176] Henri Nouwen, *The Return of the Prodigal Son: A Story of Homecoming* (New York: Doubleday Image Books, 1992), 6–14.
[177] Nouwen, *Inner Voice of Love*, xviii–xix.

the Sacred Heart. The result of his reading plus the time of solitude and meditation on the passion of Christ was three prayers written from his heart to the heart of Jesus.[178] Nouwen gave a copy of them to Mammie Vanier for her ninetieth birthday that year.[179]

A portion of another book also came from the time that Nouwen spent with the Trappists during Holy Week of 1988. He wrote a homily on Mary, the mother of Jesus, which he preached on May 31, 1988 (a Marian year),[180] at St. Michael's Cathedral in Toronto. This homily was later published as the first part of a book called *Jesus and Mary: Finding Our Sacred Center*. The second part of the book was the journal of a spiritual pilgrimage that Nouwen took to Lourdes, France, in January of 1990. Both writings dealt with Nouwen's beliefs about Mary and his relationship with her as the gentle guide who took him by the hand and led him into "deeper union with her son."[181]

Nouwen returned from Winnipeg to his work at Daybreak, not without apprehension, in the early fall of 1988. Nouwen did not move back into New House, but took a room in the Dayspring retreat center. As is often true with those who experience a dark night of the soul, Nouwen came back with more depth of insight into the spiritual life. The tone of Nouwen's entire ministry changed subtly as he emphasized more and more the importance of grounding one's self-identity in the love of God alone. His ministry at Daybreak flourished and so did his speaking and writing.

In 1989 Nouwen completed the text for a book called *In the Name of Jesus: Reflections on Christian Leadership*. The text began as a speech that Nouwen was invited to give to the Center for Human Development in Washington, D.C., in September of 1987 on the subject of Christian leadership in the twenty-first century. Nouwen wrote from his new experiences as a priest at Daybreak. Interestingly, Nouwen did not go to Washington by himself. Bill, one of the disabled members of his community, went with him. Nouwen often took one or several from his

---

[178] Nouwen, *Heart Speaks to Heart*, 7–14.

[179] Ibid., 59–62.

[180] A Marian year is a year marked by special events, prayers, penance, and papal indulgences honoring the Blessed Virgin Mary. John Paul II made the fourteen months ending on the Feast of the Assumption in 1988 as a Marian year in part as a preparation for the third millennium of Christianity. See *The Modern Catholic Encyclopedia*, s.v. "Marian Year," 541.

[181] Henri Nouwen, *Jesus and Mary: Finding Our Sacred Center* (Cincinnati: St. Anthony Messenger Press, 1993), 1–7.

community with him to his engagements. The book ended up being not only a copy of the speech he made, but also the story of Bill's impact on Nouwen and the people they encountered at the conference as they proclaimed the Gospel together.[182]

After Nouwen worked in the Daybreak community for four years, Jean Vanier came with several associates to visit the community and evaluate all that had happened in the community as a result of Nouwen's presence and work. The culmination of the evaluation process brought everyone in the community together to affirm Nouwen as well as to suggest possible directions for the future. One of those suggestions encouraged Nouwen to create a pastoral team and involve more people in the pastoral ministry of the community. Nouwen took this suggestion seriously and immediately began to make changes. The pastoral team was created. Nouwen provided a seminar for those who were identified with gifts for preaching and trained them so that he was not the only one to give the homilies. When an Anglican priest joined the community, Nouwen encouraged her to celebrate the Eucharist on Wednesdays. Core members who desired to help with worship experiences were trained to assist in serving the Eucharist. Thus the spiritual care of the community did not depend solely on Nouwen. The community could function without him when the need arose and the spiritual life of the community flourished as a result of having so many involved. All members of the community (core members, assistants, and staff) who desired to be included were included and everyone was considered an important part of the community's spiritual life.[183]

In the winter of 1990, Nouwen was hit by the right mirror of a van while walking along the side of an icy road in Richmond Hill. He was trying to get from one of Daybreak's houses to another that was just five minutes away by car, but since it was so icy, he decided to walk.[184] In an instant he was faced with a new experience that taught him a new aspect of God's love and the spiritual life. Nouwen had five broken ribs and internal bleeding. He was placed in an intensive care unit and eventually had to have his spleen removed. He very narrowly escaped death.[185] Facing the possibility of his own death for the first time, Nouwen sought to make peace in all of his relationships, and he took a new step of faith and

[182] Nouwen, *In the Name of Jesus*, 1–7.

[183] Sue Mosteller, interview by author, tape recording, Richmond Hill, Ontario, 9 March 1998.

[184] Henri Nouwen, *Beyond the Mirror: Reflections on Death and Life* (New York: Crossroad Publishing Company, 1990), 15–26.

[185] Ibid., 27–47.

trust in God alone. And when the physical crisis passed, Nouwen accepted the calling of God on his life with renewed commitment. Nouwen wrote about his accident and the lessons learned in *Beyond the Mirror: Reflections on Death and Life*. Not to write about it, Nouwen felt, would have been unfaithful to his vocation to "proclaim the presence of God at all times and in all places."[186]

While recovering in the hospital, Nouwen worked on another project as well. Sister Helen David, an artist, had asked him before the accident to write some reflections in response to her drawings of the Stations of the Cross. The pictures were not typical depictions of the biblical narrative of the passion of Christ, but pictures of various scenes of suffering humanity as seen through a window frame, each an opportunity to unite the suffering of humanity with the suffering of Christ, who died and rose for all people. Helen David's drawings and Nouwen's thoughts were published together by Orbis Books in *Walk with Jesus: Stations of the Cross*.[187]

Life of the Beloved: Spiritual Living in a Secular World is a book that Nouwen wrote in 1992 as the result of a friendship that began back in his days at Yale. Fred Bratman was a young, ambitious journalist with no commitment to any religion, though his background was Jewish. As the friendship grew over the years, Bratman began to challenge Nouwen to write a book for him and people like him, people who could not relate to the traditional language of the church and the Bible and yet were searching for meaning and truth. Nouwen finally took him up on the challenge and attempted to describe the spiritual life without using typical religious language.[188] He used the theme of "being the beloved." He wrote that knowing who we are as the beloved children of God empowers us to live with purpose and meaning.

For Fred and his friends, Nouwen was not successful in speaking to their needs. Fred said to him, "You speak from a context and tradition that is alien to us, and your words are based on many presuppositions that we don't share with you. You are not aware of how truly secular we are."[189] Nouwen's life and words were completely pervaded with the knowledge of God's presence. Fred had not even decided that there was

[186] Ibid., 9.

[187] Henri Nouwen, *Walk with Jesus: Stations of the Cross* (Maryknoll, N.Y.: Orbis Books, 1990), ix–x.

[188] Henri Nouwen, *Life of the Beloved: Spiritual Living in a Secular World* (New York: Crossroad Publishing Company, 1992), 16–21.

[189] Ibid., 115.

a God. This particular book had not bridged that gap. And yet this book became one of the clearest expressions of the spiritual truth that Nouwen had been trying to learn for many years—that his own self-identity was based totally upon his relationship to God. Ironically, when the text was read by some Christian friends, they believed Nouwen had been able to say something very profound and meaningful and they encouraged him to publish it.[190]

Nouwen had an unusual acceptance among Protestants from the beginning of his career but his reputation blossomed dramatically after preaching a series of sermons at the Crystal Cathedral for Robert Schuller's televised *Hour of Power* in 1992. By 1994 his popularity among Protestants seemed even more apparent. One survey in a Vancouver newspaper asked 3,400 Protestant leaders who most influenced them. The results ranked Nouwen second, with Lyle Schaller, a church growth specialist, being first and Billy Graham third.[191]

In 1994 Nouwen wrote the texts for three more books. The first was an expanded expression of the theme of death and dying that he briefly mentioned in *Beyond the Mirror*. The book was entitled *Our Greatest Gift: A Meditation on Dying and Caring*. As usual this work was born out of Nouwen's own experiences. His sister-in-law died in May of 1993 of cancer. (Nouwen dedicated the book to her.) His father was turning ninety and the death of his mother was still a vivid memory. Nouwen sat on the bedside of a friend who was dying of AIDS in November of 1993. One of the older disabled members of the Daybreak community, Moe, died in December of 1993. All of these experiences encouraged conversation with friends about death and the questions arose, "Are we preparing ourselves for death? Are we helping each other to die?"[192] While on a one-month sabbatical in 1994, Nouwen decided to address these questions. He based his thesis on the idea that death can be a gift to others when it is faced with hope—the hope that the fruit of one's life can live beyond the years of one's existence.

As a priest, Nouwen celebrated the Eucharist nearly every day. Another book that he decided to write was a book that expressed some of his thoughts about the Eucharist. He wanted to write about the connection between the daily celebration of the Eucharist and daily human experience. He called it *With Burning Hearts*. He used the biblical story of

---

[190] Ibid., 118–19.

[191] Jonas, *Henri Nouwen*, lviii.

[192] Henri Nouwen, *Our Greatest Gift: A Meditation on Dying and Caring* (San Francisco: HarperSanFrancisco, 1994), xi–xvii.

the two disciples on the road to Emmaus in Luke 24. Nouwen's thesis was that the life of Jesus, which was celebrated in the Eucharist, was also the life that each Christian was called to live on a daily basis.[193]

Nouwen wrote *Here and Now: Living in the Spirit* in 1994, creating a collection of meditations on the important themes in his thoughts on the spiritual life. He drew some of the segments from his other books and articles while adding some new material as well. Nouwen wanted to provide a coherent vision of the spiritual life in the form of a mosaic, each piece significant in itself but also contributing to the picture as a whole.[194]

In 1995 the Crossroad Publishing Company released four booklets of Nouwen's work: *The Path of Peace, The Path of Waiting, The Path of Freedom*, and *The Path of Power.* The booklet on peace reflected some of Nouwen's past writing about the peace found in working with Adam. In the past Nouwen had said much about peacemaking as a result of his involvement in Latin America. Ten years later, Nouwen was still committed to the idea of working for peace, but he was also much more quick to point out that such peace ultimately is not of this world. Human beings cannot make peace a reality, but God can make it a reality in the hearts of those who would receive it regardless of the presence or absence of conflict.[195]

In *The Path of Waiting*, Nouwen's thoughts on waiting were based on the first few chapters of Luke, depicting the idea of people waiting on God, and then on the last few chapters of Luke, which demonstrated the idea of God waiting for us. His thesis was that Christians wait for the promise of God to be fulfilled. This waiting is an active and celebratory waiting. But God is also waiting for us to share fully in his love.[196]

In *The Path of Power* Nouwen wrote of a "theology of weakness." He reviewed the powers of the world, including religion, which could be detrimental to people when they escalated into hatred, violence, and war. He then wrote how God chose the weak things of the world to reveal himself. When Christians were willing to quit playing power games and look to God as the true stronghold of power from above, then

[193] Henri Nouwen, *With Burning Hearts: A Meditation on the Eucharistic Life* (Maryknoll, N.Y.: Orbis Books, 1994), 9–13.

[194] Henri Nouwen, *Here and Now: Living in the Spirit* (New York: Crossroad Publishing Company, 1994), 13–14.

[195] Henri Nouwen, *The Path of Peace* (New York: Crossroad Publishing Company, 1995), 5–46.

[196] Henri Nouwen, *The Path of Waiting* (New York: Crossroad Publishing Company, 1995), 5–46.

healing and blessing were the results.[197] *The Path of Freedom* was simply a condensed version of the story of his accident in *Beyond the Mirror*.[198]

In 1995 Nouwen also brought to fruition another interest of his, not through the publishing of a book, but through the completion of a documentary film called *Angels Over the Net*.[199] Nouwen had always had a fascination with the circus, as did his father.[200] Some of this interest was hinted at in his book *Clowning in Rome*.[201] The film was about Nouwen's interest in a troupe of trapeze artists called The Flying Rodleighs. After seeing them perform several times, Nouwen asked if he could travel with them for a while to learn about their work and the parallels that could be drawn to the spiritual life. The documentary filmed not only the Rodleighs in action but also Nouwen's conversations with them. Nouwen believed the body could teach spiritual lessons through the actions of the trapeze artist. He hoped to write a book about the Rodleighs and looked for a publisher who would support the project. No one initially seemed interested. Nouwen met a publisher later in New Mexico, however, who encouraged him in the project and was willing to publish it.[202]

From September of 1995 through August of 1996 Nouwen was granted a sabbatical from Daybreak in honor of his tenth year of service in the community. He used the time to continue his work on several writing projects. In *Can You Drink the Cup?* Nouwen spoke to the

---

[197] Henri Nouwen, *The Path of Power* (New York: Crossroad Publishing Company, 1995), 5–46.

[198] Henri Nouwen, *The Path of Freedom* (New York: Crossroad Publishing Company, 1995), 5.

[199] Henri Nouwen, *Angels Over the Net*, prod. Isabelle Steyaert and dir. Bart Gavigan, 30 min., Spark Productions, 1995, videocassette.

[200] Grainger, "Henri: A Heart's Desire," 29.

[201] Nouwen refers to ministers as clowns, the ones who come out in between acts and truly relate to the audience through their weaknesses more than their strengths. See *Clowning in Rome*, 1–4.

[202] Wakefield, "Spiritual Impact," 303. Sue Mosteller, Nouwen's literary executrix, revealed during an interview with the author that Nouwen never actually wrote a manuscript about the Rodleighs before he died. He did have several notebooks full of notes from his research and interviews with the Rodleighs. He hoped to write the book during his 1995–1996 sabbatical but wanted to use a whole new style of writing and, perhaps intimidated by the idea of doing something so different from his usual genre, kept putting the project off during his sabbatical. Mosteller has the research notes but they do not contain Nouwen's own thoughts about the material. She hopes to write down some of her own memories of what he said about the Rodleighs and perhaps finish the project at some point when there is opportunity. Sue Mosteller, interview by author, tape recording, Richmond Hill, Ontario, 9 March 1998.

themes of holding, lifting, and drinking, using the chalice of the Eucharist as an object lesson for the Christian life. Nouwen utilized the scriptural text of Matthew 20, where the mother of James and John asked that her sons have the favored positions beside Jesus in his kingdom. Then Jesus asked, "Can you drink the cup that I am going to drink?" Nouwen commented that when he held the chalice for the first time at his ordination, he was very confident he could drink the cup of Jesus. But many years later, sitting around the table with disabled men and women, Nouwen realized that to live a sacrificial life such as Jesus did was indeed a challenge.[203] To answer yes to Jesus' question every day was to live intentionally and sacrificially, and it was the way to everlasting life.[204] The book was dedicated to Adam, who died in February of 1996, just as the book was ready for printing.[205]

Another writing project began in the fall of 1995 when editors with HarperSanFrancisco asked Nouwen about the possibility of using excerpts from some of his writings to create a yearbook with 365 quotations. Nouwen liked the idea but he wanted to write new material for it. Between September of 1995 and the end of the year, Nouwen wrote 387 reflections. He first began to write about Jesus, the center of his faith, and by the time he finished, he realized he had written his own creed.[206] The book, released in 1997 as *Bread for the Journey: A Daybook of Wisdom and Faith*, is his least penetrating work. Perhaps it would have been better if Nouwen had allowed the editors to do what they first intended, using excerpts from his other work.

Perhaps because of the exercise of writing the yearbook, in which he tried to communicate something of his own creed, Nouwen decided to work on a book about the Apostle's Creed. But after the death of Adam in February of 1996, Nouwen changed his mind and decided to write an expression of what Adam's life had taught him about the Christian life. Nouwen completed a rough draft of the manuscript but intended to meet with Adam's family in order to strengthen the chapters on Adam's early life. Nouwen died before he was able to do so. Sue Mosteller finished the work and Orbis Books published it in the fall of 1997.[207]

During this same sabbatical, Nouwen also worked on editing his private journal from the difficult months of 1988 mentioned earlier. Ironi-

[203] Nouwen, *Can You Drink the Cup?*, 13–21.

[204] Ibid., 101.

[205] Ibid., 8.

[206] Henri Nouwen, *Bread for the Journey: A Daybook of Wisdom and Faith* (San Francisco: HarperSanFrancisco, 1997), xxi–xxiv.

[207] Nouwen, *Adam: God's Beloved*, 9.

cally, *The Inner Voice of Love: A Journey Through Anguish to Freedom,* which revealed some of Nouwen's most heartbroken moments, was released on the very day that Nouwen's heart literally broke.[208]

In keeping with his usual habit, Nouwen determined to keep a journal during his sabbatical away from the routine of Daybreak.[209] It was not a sabbatical spent in one place for the entire year. He stayed in several places while he worked on manuscripts and he also traveled some to see family and friends. The first day's entry in his journal revealed his excitement:

> Free at last! Free to think critically, to feel deeply, and to pray as never before. Free to write about the many experiences that I have stored up in my heart and mind during the last nine years. Free to deepen friendships and explore new ways of loving. Free most of all to fight with the Angel of God and ask for a new blessing.[210]

The sabbatical journal contained a description of Nouwen's activities and encounters with all different kinds of people. He also wrote down his thoughts about his relationship with God and his own continuing struggle to know him more fully:

> The year ahead of me must be a year of prayer, even though I say that my prayer is as dead as a rock. My prayer surely is, but not necessarily the Spirit's prayer in me. Maybe the time has come to let go of my prayer, my effort to be close to God, my way of being in communion with the divine, and to allow the Spirit of God to blow freely in me.[211]

After completing his year of writing, Nouwen returned to Daybreak only briefly before traveling to the Netherlands to visit his father and meet a film crew. He was on his way to St. Petersburg, Russia, to make a film about his favorite painting, *The Return of the Prodigal Son.*[212] After checking into a hotel on Sunday evening, September 15, for some rest upon arrival in the Netherlands, Nouwen called the desk asking for medical attention. He was immediately hospitalized and it was determined that he had had a heart attack. He stayed in intensive care for

[208] Glaser, "Nouwen's Journey," 305.

[209] This journal was edited after his death by Sue Mosteller and published as *The Sabbatical Journey* (New York: The Crossroad Publishing Company, 1998). Sue Mosteller allowed this author to see a copy of the journal before it was published.

[210] Nouwen, *Sabbatical Journey,* 3.

[211] Ibid., 6.

[212] Michael O'Laughlin, "Henri Nouwen in Life and Death," *America* 163 (10 May 1997): 18.

several days, critically ill. His family and friends from Daybreak managed
to arrive quickly and spent more time with him once he was removed
from intensive care. He continued to gain strength throughout the week.
He even talked to his assistants in his office several times and walked his
family to the lobby of the hospital on Friday evening. Everyone relaxed.
He was apparently out of danger. But early the next morning, Nouwen
suffered a second heart attack and died alone on Saturday, September 21,
1996, at the age of sixty-four.[213]

Grief-stricken, Nouwen's ninety-three-year-old father prayed the
Our Father at the bedside of his dead son. The Daybreak community
wept in shock. Nouwen's body was taken to a funeral home in Hilver-
sum, and on Tuesday his close friends and family gathered for a wake,
spending an afternoon of quiet and prayer. That same evening there was
another wake in the cathedral church of St. Catherine of Utrecht, his
casket placed on the same steps where he had prostrated himself for ordination to the priesthood thirty-nine years before. On Wednesday
morning, a eucharistic celebration was held in the same cathedral, filled
with mourning family and friends. Nouwen's archbishop, Adrianus Cardinal Simonis, was the celebrant and Jean Vanier gave a meditation. A
farewell was given by Nouwen's brother Paul.[214]

At the decision of Nouwen's family, Nouwen's body was taken back
to Richmond Hill, Toronto, for a full funeral mass and burial on Saturday, September 28.[215] The weather was melancholy as a light drizzle fell,
but the mood was celebratory in the Cathedral of the Transfiguration.
Nouwen's casket was made of simple pine by the Woodery, the carpentry
shop at Daybreak. Many of the members with disabilities made colorful
drawings that were transferred to the lid of the casket by a Daybreak
artist. During the mass, songs were sung, accompanied by guitars, flutes,
and violins. Actors and actresses from the community gave life to the
gospel reading. Dancers also contributed expressions of praise to God on
tiptoe and some even from wheelchairs. Sunflowers and irises, carried in
by dozens of children, surrounded the altar and his body. One observer
said it was not unlike the carnival atmosphere of a circus.[216] Nouwen
certainly would have liked it. Sue Mosteller remarked, "Henri wrote
about everything he experienced and we were sorry he was not going to

---

[213] Ibid., 18.
[214] Beumer, *Henri Nouwen: A Restless Seeking for God*, 174, 176.
[215] Grainger, "Henri: A Heart's Desire," 28.
[216] Ibid., 29.

be able to write about his own funeral because it was a beautiful experience!"[217]

Nouwen's funeral was attended by people from many differing faith traditions. Twenty-two of his friends spoke, which revealed his interest in and support of suffering people everywhere. Nouwen had requested burial in a public cemetery where the core members of Daybreak who were from other faith traditions could also be buried, but at the request of the Catholic bishop, who assured the community of the availability of plots for other family members of Daybreak, the community buried him in a small Catholic cemetery not far from Daybreak. One witness said this seemed fitting—"further testimony of his identification with the marginalized and the church universal."[218]

The obituaries and articles that have followed since his death have all tried in one way or another to give voice to the significance of Nouwen's life. One article which quoted Nouwen's own words about his personal rules for living, summarized his life well: "I say 'yes' to God's love, I live fully in the moment, I care for the weak, and I trust that my life will be fruitful."[219]

To summarize one person's life is an impossibility. Henri Nouwen's influence is seen first and foremost among those who knew him personally.[220] Many of those who had the privilege of knowing Nouwen personally were forever influenced by this unusually gifted, larger-than-life man who welcomed people into his life and gave himself to them. His close friends were not always comfortable with his woundedness or his neediness. He was by no means a perfect saint. Yet the ripple effect of his personal life upon the lives of so many others is extraordinary. To be so well loved and honored by so many of those who knew him is certain demonstration of his significance and value.

Yet for hundreds of thousands more, Nouwen's writings are the fruit that will continue to bear fruit. He had an uncanny way of speaking to

[217] Sue Mosteller, interview with author, tape recording, Richmond Hill, Ontario, 11 March 1998.

[218] Glaser, "Nouwen's Journey," 305.

[219] Mullen, "A Lesson in Love," B4.

[220] This author had the privilege of being invited to a retreat in Toronto, Canada, September 18–20, 1998, which was to be attended by Nouwen's friends and work associates in honor of the second anniversary of his death and the launching of the Henri Nouwen Society in the United States. Casual conversations with those who knew Nouwen so well around the table and in gathered sessions of worship and discussion brought into living color the great capacity that Nouwen had for friendship and sharing his life with others in a unique and intimate way.

the heart of the matter where spirituality was concerned and those who never met him felt they knew him and that he was a spiritual guide for them on a spiritual journey that was joyful, challenging, sorrowful, painful, terrible, enriching, incredible, and grace filled all at the same time. His friend, Robert Jonas, captured a true sense of the value of Nouwen's books for those who loved and admired his work:

> We think about his many books—more than forty in all—in which he courageously stood with one foot in the shadow of self-rejection and one foot in the daylight of God's love. We know that he stood there for all of us, articulating so simply and beautifully what that wild, dangerous territory between the human and the divine looks like. Many of us would have preferred that Henri's human woundedness be less visible. But somehow, we know that his ever-present, acompanying shadow was there only because of the Light in which he walked.[221]

A fruitful life can be measured in many ways. Certainly the memories of the personal experiences that so many had with Henri Nouwen will continue to be written down and the impact of his life will continue to be told. Yet Nouwen's writings[222] are also a witness to Nouwen's fruitful life and the influence of his thought on Christian spirituality. It is to the themes of his own spirituality that we now turn in order to understand better the impact of this man and his work on modern American spirituality.

[221] Jonas, *Henri Nouwen*, xiv.

[222] This study focuses primarily on Nouwen's books because, although Nouwen wrote hundreds of articles for journals, as well as newspapers and magazines, many of those articles were excerpts from his books. Others represent shortened summaries of some of the recurring themes in his books. A student of Nouwen's work can perhaps gain a glimpse here and there of more subtle nuances concerning certain ideas in these articles, but there are no dominant themes in his articles that are not found to some extent in his books as well. One particular article offers an excellent summary of Nouwen's spirituality as a whole. See Henri Nouwen, "Moving from Solitude to Community to Ministry," *Leadership* 16 (Spring 1995): 81–87.

CHAPTER THREE

⬧

To Whom Do I Belong?

The Relationship to God

Introduction

Nouwen was a spiritual guide for many as a speaker, teacher, and friend, personally influencing countless thousands of people. Yet Nouwen touched thousands more through his writing, and this legacy continues. Nouwen's purpose for writing was based on the conviction that his life belonged to others just as much as to himself and what he experienced as most unique and personal often proved to be "solidly embedded in the common condition of being human."[1] Thus Nouwen believed that as he shared his own spiritual journey through his writing, others might find help for their own journeys. Over forty books are the fruit of this conviction, and through these works, written across twenty-seven years of Nouwen's life, one can detect the prominent themes of his spirituality.

Several general characteristics of Nouwen's writing should be mentioned before the exploration of individual themes. First, Nouwen's writing style was experiential, transparent, intimate, and pastoral. Nouwen never offered a manual of techniques. He did not advise or insist. He invited his readers to join him on the journey of knowing God.[2] Nouwen was never judgmental or condemning. He did not teach in terms of "oughts" or "shoulds." He simply used the instruction and stories of Scripture, illustrations from Christian history, and his own life's experience to communicate what he believed to be the truth about the Christian life, inviting his readers to know God and live life in

---

[1] Nouwen, *Reaching Out*, 14.

[2] Annice Callahan, *Spiritual Guides for Today* (New York: Crossroad Publishing Company, 1992), 132.

relationship with him, which in turn transforms every other aspect of life.

Second, Nouwen wrote about the various facets of what it means to live the Christian life. Such writing is necessarily theological; thus, as these next three chapters attempt to describe his thought, they will also be making some observations concerning his theology. It is important to note, however, that Nouwen was not a systematic theologian. Beumer wrote that Nouwen's thinking was never finished. It was too creative, too dynamic, ever developing, and it resisted the typical categories of systematic theology.[3] For Nouwen, theology was for the purpose of serving spirituality. Nouwen viewed theology in the more ancient sense of faith seeking understanding, its central purpose being to know or experience God. Beumer also called Nouwen's theology a mystical theology in that his main goal was to help others to know God and be in communion with him.[4]

Third, Nouwen's thought is overwhelmingly Christological. Although Nouwen speaks often of God, it is the person of Jesus, God incarnate, who most clearly reveals God the Father and demonstrates how to be in relationship with him. Nouwen does refer to the Holy Spirit on a few occasions, but emphasis on the Spirit and its role in Christian spirituality is noticeably absent. Nouwen emphasized not only the importance of the incarnation of Christ as the one who showed human beings how to know and love God, but he also emphasized the kenosis of Christ, the emptying of himself for others through his life and death, as an example for Christians to imitate. Christ was at the center of most of Nouwen's thought about the Christian life, which he once defined as "living with Jesus at the center."[5] Robert Jonas confirmed this characteristic of Nouwen's spirituality when he wrote, "Jesus' life and word ignited powerful centripetal forces in Henri's soul, drawing every ordinary experience into the one archetypal story of Christ. Jesus was Henri's mentor and model of maturity."[6]

Fourth, Nouwen was a psychologist as well as a theologian and both fields of knowledge were prominent in his work. His first few books utilized a more clinical and academic vocabulary, but it was not long before Nouwen adopted a style of communication that was much more conversational and less specialized. Nouwen certainly believed in the usefulness of psychology to understand the human condition. Yet Nou-

[3] Beumer, *Henri Nouwen: A Restless Seeking for God*, 140–42.
[4] Ibid., 143–44.
[5] Nouwen, *Letters to Marc About Jesus*, 7.
[6] Jonas, *Henri Nouwen*, xxii.

wen believed that psychology could only address one side of the coin. Theology had to address the other side. The blending of these two categories was evident throughout Nouwen's work. This is what, in my opinion, contributes to the unique nature of Nouwen's thought. The foundation of Nouwen's thought was theological, but his practical knowledge of the human psyche enabled him to explain Christian spirituality in ways that many contemporary minds could understand.

Finally, Nouwen's style of writing was accessible. He had a knack for creating simple classifications, often in sets of three, through which to communicate his messages. He avoided complicated theological or philosophical arguments, yet he was in no way shallow or trifling. Nouwen was approachable, and this was a key to his popular success as a writer.

Nouwen's overarching definition of the spiritual life was closely connected to the answer that Jesus gave to the Sadducees and Pharisees in Matthew 22:34–40. When asked which was the greatest commandment in the Law, Jesus replied, " 'Love the Lord your God with all your heart and with all your soul and with all your mind.' This is the first and greatest commandment. And the second is like it: 'Love your neighbor as yourself.' " Jesus' answer reflected three love relationships: with God, self, and others.[7]

Nouwen's spirituality is, above all, relational. Nouwen believed that modern people of all ages long for intimacy, for connectedness. He wrote:

> In our highly technological and competitive world, it is hard to avoid completely the forces which fill up our inner and outer space and disconnect us from our innermost selves, our fellow human beings, and our God.[8]

Nouwen wrote his first definitive work on these three aspects of the spiritual life in *Reaching Out*. The spiritual life, according to his definition, was to live life in the Spirit of Jesus Christ by reaching out to the innermost self with courageous honesty, to fellow human beings with relentless care, and to God with increasing prayer.[9] These three relationships, then, are the three topics for this and the next two chapters. This chapter will explore Nouwen's thought on the relationship with God, since he believed this relationship was the foundation for the other two. Next, we will examine Nouwen's thought on the relationship with self,

---

[7] Nouwen himself mentions this particular passage of Scripture in several works. See *The Way of the Heart*, 32; *Letters to Marc About Jesus*, 63; and *The Genesee Diary*, 85.

[8] Nouwen, *Making All Things New*, 36.

[9] Nouwen, *Reaching Out*, 13–14.

or self-identity, which finds its meaning only in relationship to God. Finally, we will investigate Nouwen's thought on one's relationship with other human beings, which depends a great deal on the health and vitality of one's relationship to God and self.

Nouwen pointed out two ideas about the spiritual life that are important to remember here. First of all, the spiritual life is difficult to measure. Americans, in their tendency toward pragmatism, are tempted to measure spiritual progress in a legalistic fashion. Nouwen cautioned against this habit by proposing that relationships often do not move in a linear fashion from imperfection to perfection. Instead, relationships tend to vacillate back and forth, as if held in tension between two poles. Certainly Nouwen desired to grow in his spiritual relationships and he encouraged others to do so as well. Spirituality, however, required a lifetime of perseverance, with the understanding that perfection will not be attained this side of eternity.[10]

The second point about the spiritual life is that these three relationships are rarely neatly separated in the experience of daily life. Nouwen refrained from talking about steps or stages as some earlier spiritual guides have done. He believed that certain themes occur in different relationships in "various tonalities and often flow into one another as the different movements of a symphony."[11]

Keeping both of these points in mind is helpful when trying to distinguish the various themes of Nouwen's spirituality. The written word requires thinking and organizing in a linear fashion, but a better metaphor for the spiritual life is a circle. How do you draw a circle? You have to start at some point and move the pencil around. In the same way, a description of Nouwen's spiritual themes must start somewhere, but it is important to remember that each of these relationships and the themes connected with them blend and meld with one another in a variety of ways.

As soon as one takes the initiative to place Nouwen's thought into categories, interpretation is happening. A structure is being constructed at least one step or one level away from reality. The categories are less real than the individual expressions of thought, but they are helpful for synthesizing and gaining understanding of what Nouwen said about the Christian life. With these cautions in mind, we begin with a human being's relationship with God.

[10] Ibid., 17–18.
[11] Ibid., 20.

To Whom Do I Belong?

For Nouwen, this was the core question of the spiritual life and his answer was a resounding "To God!"[12] At various places throughout Nouwen's writings, he reviewed this most basic question. The answer was the same and yet the contexts and explanations varied:

> To live a spiritual life is to live in the presence of God. . . . The heart must be empty of all other things, because God will possess the heart alone.[13]

> A truly spiritual life is life in which we won't rest until we have found rest in the embrace of the One who is the Father and Mother of all desires.[14]

> If you were to ask me point-blank, "What does it mean to you to live spiritually?" I would have to reply, "Living with Jesus at the center." . . . The gospel is, first and foremost, the story of the death and resurrection of Jesus, and that story constitutes the core of the spiritual life.[15]

In all of these quotes, Nouwen pointed to God alone as the center of the spiritual life, yet this relationship is experienced in the context of daily life. Nouwen emphasized that the spiritual life is "contained in the most ordinary experiences of everyday living."[16] The spiritual life is not beyond or after our everyday existence. "The spiritual life can only be real when it is lived in the midst of the pains and joys of the here and now."[17]

So the answer to Nouwen's core question is that we belong to God in the here and now of daily life. This truth, for Nouwen, is the foundation upon which he builds the rest of his thought on the spiritual life. Nouwen never seemed to doubt the concept intellectually, but he did seem to struggle a great deal with actually living as if it were true. He wrote while at the Abbey of the Genesee, "Why do I always want to read about the spiritual life but not really live it?"[18] This is the definitive struggle for Nouwen throughout his spiritual journey. How do I live out the truth that I belong to God? How do I love God alone?

[12] Nouwen, *Behold the Beauty of the Lord*, 31.
[13] Nouwen, *Genesee Diary*, 174.
[14] Nouwen, *Here and Now*, 44.
[15] Nouwen, *Letters to Marc About Jesus*, 7, 27.
[16] Nouwen, *Genesee Diary*, 41.
[17] Nouwen, *Making All Things New*, 21.
[18] Nouwen, *Genesee Diary*, 27.

People Loving God

"The goal of our life is not people. It is God."[19] Nouwen believed that God must be the center, the foundation, the anchor of all, as opposed to making people or self the center. Nouwen referred often to God the Father, but was more likely to speak of God in the person of Jesus, the Son of God incarnate, as the focus of his thought on relating to and loving God. He wrote:

> Jesus has to be and to become ever more the center of my life. It is not enough that Jesus is my teacher, my guide, my source of inspiration. It is not even enough that he is my companion on the journey, my friend and my brother. Jesus must become the heart of my heart, the fire of my life, the lover of my soul, the bridegroom of my spirit. He must become my only thought, my only concern, my only desire.[20]

But Nouwen was well aware that his heart remained divided. He did not believe so much that one should stop being busy as that one should change the center of attention to the Kingdom of God so that it is in "all we think, say, or do."[21] Yet he realized the difficulty of doing so. He wrote, "I want to love God, but also make a career. I want to be a good Christian, but also have my successes as a teacher, preacher, or speaker. I want to be a saint, but also enjoy the sensations of a sinner."[22] Nouwen left the Abbey of the Genesee with a determination to love God above all else, but when he returned to the abbey in 1978, he knew he was far from all that he had hoped to be. His prayers in *Cry for Mercy* are full of supplications for God to enable him to love God more "freely, boldly, courageously, and generously."[23]

How does one love God? Nouwen's answer was through the classical spiritual disciplines that are modeled by Jesus and the early church fathers. These disciplines are the means by which to accomplish the ends of loving God and being made into his likeness.

Nouwen's ideas about loving God are at the heart of the Christian tradition and are supported by the teachings of Jesus and the rest of Scripture. Nouwen's thought about loving God is also supported by his emphasis on the spiritual disciplines, therefore his instruction to love God has substance as long as one does not divorce this theme from his work

[19] Nouwen, *Cry for Mercy*, 25.
[20] Nouwen, *Jesus and Mary*, 30.
[21] Nouwen, *Making All Things New*, 42–43.
[22] Nouwen, *Genesee Diary*, 76.
[23] Nouwen, *Cry for Mercy*, 46, see also 56 and 77.

concerning the disciplines. For it is in his instruction on the spiritual disciplines that one learns how to love God.

God Loving People

The other side of the paradox in the struggle to love God alone was Nouwen's belief that "we cannot find God. We can only be found by him."[24] In other words, the challenge of a spiritual relationship with God was not figuring out how to initiate a relationship with God but learning how to respond to the relationship that God himself had already initiated in love through Jesus. This changed the focus from how much Nouwen loved God to how much God loved him, and Nouwen had a great deal to say about the unconditional love of God.

Nouwen believed God "embraced all of history with his eternally creative and recreative love."[25] This love was unconditional in that God decided to love people in total freedom and not because they deserved it. Unconditional love, however, did not mean a love without concern:

> What can we say about God's love? We can say that God's love is unconditional. God does not say, "I love you, if . . ." Does that mean that God does not care what we do or say? No, because God's love wouldn't be real if God didn't care. To love without condition does not mean to love without concern. . . . We often confuse unconditional love with unconditional approval. God loves us without conditions but does not approve of every human behavior.[26]

For Nouwen, responding to the unconditional love of God is not first and foremost about keeping the rules or living morally, although he believed God does desire this as well. Responding to God's love means understanding what it means to be the children of God, fully loved.[27] Once one truly trusts him, one will be set free to live as God intended. Nouwen brought all of these ideas together beautifully in one of his last books, *The Return of the Prodigal Son*, as he spoke of the younger son "coming home." Nouwen wrote that "trust is the deep inner conviction that the Father wants me home."[28] Yet one of the greatest challenges of the spiritual life is to receive God's forgiveness so that one might truly stay at home. He wrote, "Receiving forgiveness requires a total willing-

[24] Nouwen, *Genesee Diary*, 136.

[25] Nouwen, *Way of the Heart*, 76.

[26] Nouwen, *Bread for the Journey*, February 5 and 6.

[27] Greene, "Interview with Nouwen," 11.

[28] Nouwen, *Return of the Prodigal Son*, 84.

ness to let God be God and do all the healing, restoring, and renewing. As long as I want to do even part of that myself, I end up with partial solutions. . . ."[29]

Nouwen acknowledged that God's unconditional love also leaves his children free to respond—free to stay home, free to leave home, free to return home. God does not force divine love on them. Although God desires them to step into the light of God's love, they are free to stay in the darkness. Just as the father loved the prodigal son and gave him his freedom, so God gives his children theirs, while longing that they stay safely at home.

> Here is the mystery of my life unveiled. I am loved so much that I am left free to leave home. The blessing is there from the beginning. I have left it and keep on leaving it. But the Father is always looking for me with out-stretched arms to receive me back and whisper again in my ear: "You are my Beloved, on you my favor rests."[30]

It is important to note that Nouwen hardly ever addressed the idea of sin directly. He did often speak of his own weaknesses, his own imperfections, his struggle to choose to be what God intended him to be and to behave as God intended him to behave. One can easily read the idea of sinfulness into these expressions. Yet Nouwen hardly ever spoke directly of sin as the problem that keeps one from a relationship with God. It seems implicit in his thought that Jesus took care of this on the cross. The part of humans is only to receive the love that God has already offered through his Son and allow that love to transform them into the people they were created to be, but Nouwen did not speak of this experience as a onetime act of "conversion" as an evangelical would. Perhaps there was a first time for someone to turn to God and receive his love, but Nouwen used the same language to describe what a Christian must continue to do—receive and respond to the love of God in Christ so that the relationship might continue to grow and deepen.

Spiritual Disciplines

The spiritual life, then, is saying "Yes" to the reality of being the beloved sons and daughters of God bearing forth the fruitful life that this foundational relationship affords.[31] How is this done? If God must find

[29] Ibid., 53.
[30] Ibid., 78.
[31] Nouwen, *Life of the Beloved*, 106.

us, as was discussed earlier, and if God's Spirit is the one that changes and transforms, then what is the human's part in the relationship? For Nouwen, this is where the spiritual disciplines such as prayer, solitude, silence, contemplation, and worship fit into the Christian life. Nouwen taught several courses on various aspects of the spiritual disciplines, including a course on the Desert Fathers and Mothers of the early church. It is evident that his own thought on the disciplines was significantly shaped by the practices of these early saints as well as the spiritual practices of Jesus himself.

Nouwen seemed to expound on two ideas regarding the role of the spiritual disciplines in the Christian's life. The first had to do with creating space. In several of his works, Nouwen described the spiritual disciplines as the means by which to "make available the inner space where God can touch you with an all-transforming love."[32] Nouwen was careful to say that the disciplines are not for the purpose of manipulating God, as if he has to respond in a certain way because of their practice.[33] The disciplines are the doorway through which one receives God, the path by which one draws near to God.[34]

> Discipline in the spiritual life is the concentrated effort to create the space and time where God can become our master and where we can respond freely to God's guidance. Thus, discipline is the creation of boundaries that keep time and space open for God . . . a time and a place where God's gracious presence can be acknowledged and responded to.[35]

The second idea, which is closely related, is that the spiritual disciplines are the means by which believers become obedient as they listen to the inner voice of God's Spirit. Nouwen explained that the Latin word from which the English word *obedience* is derived means "to hear." Nouwen contrasted this obedient life to the absurd life. The Latin word from which the English word *absurd* is derived means "deaf."[36] An obedient life is a life that listens to God. An absurd life is a life that is deaf to the voice of God. Spiritual discipline, then, is the "effort to create some inner and outer space in our lives, where this obedience can be practiced."[37] Just as Jesus lived a life of obedience by giving his undivided attention to

---

[32] Nouwen, *Letters to Marc About Jesus*, 75.
[33] Nouwen, *Reaching Out*, 126.
[34] Nouwen, *Inner Voice of Love*, 23.
[35] Nouwen, *Bread for the Journey*, February 27.
[36] Nouwen, *Making All Things New*, 67.
[37] Ibid., 68.

the voice of his Father, so the Christian is called to a life of obedience.[38] To remain deaf is to remain strangers to God and to our deepest selves, never realizing our true identity or who we were meant to be because we have not listened to him.[39]

Nouwen spoke to some aspect of the spiritual disciplines in almost all of his books, and the overwhelming majority of this writing was dedicated to the discipline of prayer. If prayer is communion with God, then prayer is the fundamental way of nurturing a relationship with God and inviting his presence into one's life. Nouwen sometimes did not distinguish prayer clearly as a separate discipline from the other disciplines about which he taught. Prayer seemed at times to be the encompassing word for the whole idea of nurturing a relationship with God through the spiritual disciplines of the inner life. Certain aspects of prayer, however, can be distinguished in his thought. Prayer will be addressed first within the context of exploring other spiritual disciplines to which Nouwen gave attention in his writing: solitude, silence, contemplation, study, worship, celibacy, waiting, and spiritual direction.

Prayer

One method for defining prayer is saying what it is not. In Nouwen's thought, prayer was not an activity of the mind alone, but was primarily an activity of the heart. Prayer was not just thinking about God or speaking to him. "Our mind may be filled with ideas of God while our heart remains far from him."[40] Prayer is also not a pious decoration for people to see, something like an ornament hung on the Christmas tree.[41] Nor is prayer simply saying the right things to God as in confessing a laundry list of mistakes or requesting a wish list from Santa Claus.[42] Nouwen acknowledged that prayer was difficult to define, which led to it being the victim of trivialities and platitudes. While he perceived it as the "most human of all human acts," he knew that many perceived it as the "most superfluous and superstitious" of activities.[43]

Though Nouwen admitted that defining prayer was as difficult as defining love or art, he insisted that prayer must continue to be talked

[38] Nouwen, MacNeill, and Morrison, *Compassion*, 39–40.
[39] Ibid., 91.
[40] Nouwen, *Way of the Heart*, 57–58.
[41] Nouwen, *With Open Hands*, 17.
[42] Nouwen, *Intimacy*, 51.
[43] Nouwen, *Reaching Out*, 115.

about and defined in as many ways as possible.[44] Nouwen himself defined prayer in the following ways, trying to capture its essence:

Prayer is creating room. In keeping with Nouwen's first definition of a spiritual discipline as a practice that creates room in which God can transform a person, Nouwen saw prayer as creating room for God. "God dwells only where man steps back to give him room."[45]

This is a valid definition. The Desert Fathers and Mothers fled to the desert in order to find a place where they could be alone with God and submit themselves totally to his transforming power. A prominent characteristic of American spirituality, however, is to view prayer as a method for getting what is needed from God, hoping that he will create a little room in his own heart or his own schedule in order to address certain needs or desires. Nouwen counters this idea by saying that prayer is about human transformation, not God persuasion.

Prayer is listening, being obedient. In keeping with Nouwen's second idea about a spiritual discipline being an expression of obedience, or listening to God, Nouwen also defined prayer as "being all ear before God."[46] Without prayer, without listening to God, believers will remain deaf and their lives will grow absurd.[47]

This definition of prayer is also in keeping with classic contemplative Christianity and counter to contemporary views that prayer is about telling God what he needs to do or, if one is more humble, asking him for things. True, there is more emphasis in contemporary American spirituality on meditation, but this is usually for therapeutic purposes so that stress might be reduced or connection made with the inner self. Nouwen countered these ideas with a more God-centered definition that points to the necessity of not only listening to God, but being willing to obey him. Jesus often spoke of his prayer life in the sense of listening to his Father and doing what he commanded.[48]

One could wish, however, that Nouwen had been more succinct on how to listen to God. He does mention the discipline of reading the Bible as a means of knowing God and hearing his instruction. This discipline will be addressed later in this chapter. Otherwise, one might sur-

[44] Ibid., 115.
[45] Nouwen, *Genesee Diary*, 170.
[46] Nouwen, *Making All Things New*, 68.
[47] Nouwen, *Clowning in Rome*, 106.
[48] For example, see John 8:26, 28, 47 and 10:18.

mise that Nouwen believed God speaks through the human conscience, through others in the Christian community, or through circumstances, from the way Nouwen described his own experiences in trying to discern what God was saying to him, but he does not instruct his readers on how to listen to God beyond a few general statements.

Prayer is the most basic movement. For Nouwen, prayer was the "most basic movement of the spiritual life."[49] Prayer is not one of the many things that Christians do but "the basic receptive attitude out of which all of life can receive new vitality."[50]

> The question of when or how to pray is not really the most important one. The crucial question is whether you should pray always and whether your prayer is necessary. . . . Whenever you feel that a little praying can't do any harm, you will find it can't do much good either. . . . Prayer is only prayer when we can say that without it, a man could not live.[51]

In other words, for Nouwen, prayer was not one component of many involved in nurturing a relationship with God. Prayer was the vital link, the vehicle through which one relates to God. Nouwen seems to view prayer as the all-encompassing activity for engaging in a relationship with God. A better illustration of this same idea is his idea of prayer as the breath of life.

Prayer is the breath of life. Nouwen saw prayer as the breath of life, that is, "praying is living."[52] The breath is, however, God's breathing within his children in order to bring them life. It is true that prayer is not about what those praying can cause to happen, but about what happens in those who pray as the Spirit, or breath of God, is set free to transform them.[53] Therefore, prayer is affective more than effective.[54]

Some people tend to view prayer as something that is done is order to elicit a certain result. Nouwen hardly ever spoke of prayer in this manner. For him, prayer was the means through which the Spirit of God shaped the heart and mind of the believer. Perhaps Nouwen tended to emphasize this aspect of prayer in order to accent a relationship and not a result.

[49] Nouwen, *Reaching Out*, 114.
[50] Ibid., 133.
[51] Nouwen, *With Open Hands*, 94.
[52] Ibid., 157.
[53] Nouwen, MacNeill, and Morrison, *Compassion*, 105.
[54] Greene, "Interview with Nouwen," 11.

Prayer is unceasing and all-pervasive. Just as a person does not cease to breathe, so, in Nouwen's thought, prayer should not cease. This does not mean that a person has to think about God all the time or be in a constant posture of the head bowed and eyes closed. Unceasing prayer for Nouwen, in keeping with Paul's admonition to "pray without ceasing" (1 Thess. 5:17), was to think and live in the presence of God. It is giving every part of life to God. It is bringing all of one's thoughts into a loving conversation with God. Such a discipline is indeed difficult, because human beings resist submitting all that they are to God. "Unceasing prayer is indeed an ongoing struggle against idolatry," but bringing the dark as well as the light in our lives to God in an encompassing act of prayer is to be truly obedient.[55]

Prayer is being dependent on God. Prayer, for Nouwen, meant realizing that a human being is helpless and totally dependent on God for all things. Prayer is not a last resort after people have done all that they can do. Prayer involves going to God for everything.

> Prayer requires that we stand in God's presence with open hands, naked and vulnerable, proclaiming to ourselves and to others that without God we can do nothing. This is difficult in a climate where the predominant counsel is, "Do your best and God will do the rest." When life is divided into "our best" and "God's rest," we have turned prayer into a last resort to be used only when all our own resources are depleted. Then even the Lord has become the victim of our impatience. Discipleship does not mean to use God when we can no longer function ourselves. On the contrary, it means to recognize that we can do nothing at all, but that God can do everything through us. As disciples, we find not some but all of our strength, hope, courage, and confidence in God. Therefore, prayer must be our first concern.[56]

These last four definitions of prayer are also useful and within the perimeters of authentic Christianity because they are closely related to Jesus' teaching in John 15 about abiding. A branch must be connected to the vine to receive life and sustenance. Jesus knew that his followers would have to remain closely connected to him in a spiritual manner through the Holy Spirit. His followers would have to realize their most basic dependence upon him for every aspect of what it meant to live fruitful lives.

Americans tend to view prayer as the safety valve, something one resorts to when nothing else is working. Some tend to view prayer as a

[55] Nouwen, *Clowning in Rome*, 70, 75.
[56] Nouwen, MacNeill, and Morrison, *Compassion*, 104.

useful practice that can contribute to a meaningful and more healthy lifestyle, but Nouwen attempted to teach that the vital connection between people and God is through the discipline of prayer and that they could not live as their Creator intended apart from a constant connection with him through prayer.

Prayer is being useless. The fact that believers are totally dependent on God leads Nouwen to a unique way of describing prayer. Since spiritual discipline is for the purpose of creating space for God to act and move, prayer is "a way of being empty and useless in the presence of God and so proclaiming our basic belief that all is grace. . . ."[57] Yet standing empty and useless before God is hard work and a difficult discipline, especially in American culture. American pragmatists might say that "doing things" is more important than prayer, which is a task for times when there is nothing else better to do. Some people might even say that prayer is a waste of time.

> In our utilitarian culture, in which we suffer from a collective compulsion to do something practical, helpful, or useful, and to make a contribution that can give us a sense of worth, contemplative prayer is a form of radical criticism. It is not useful or practical but a way of wasting time for God. It cuts a hole in our busyness and reminds us and others that it is God and not we who creates and sustains the world.[58]

I like this definition very much, although it makes one think twice about what Nouwen is saying. Many American Christians might be shocked at Nouwen's description of prayer as wasting time with God. But if one thinks about it in the sense of a relationship, just being in the presence of someone is valuable. This is the point Nouwen was driving at. Prayer is the communal link in a spiritual relationship with God. Relationships do not always need to accomplish something. Relationships do not always need to be taking or receiving. Relationships are often strengthened just by two persons being present to one another. Nouwen struggled to counter the pragmatic attitude of Americans that insisted everything have a use or an outcome. Nouwen knew his audience well and understood those tendencies in the culture that could result in a withered spiritual life.

Prayer is hospitality. Nouwen also saw prayer as a way to minister to others, not only by praying for them, although he viewed intercession as

[57] Nouwen, *Living Reminder*, 52.
[58] Nouwen, *Clowning in Rome*, 53.

a valuable ministry, but by creating an inner space that is inspiring to others as they get to know one personally. This is in keeping with Nouwen's concept of prayer as affective. In other words, the Spirit of God through prayer shapes the character of a person so that he or she exemplifies those characteristics that are holy and pleasing to God and to others.

> Our inner life is like a holy space that needs to be kept in good order and well decorated. Prayer, in whatever form, is the way to make our inner room a place where we can welcome those people who search for God. . . . Without prayer and contemplation the walls of our inner room will remain barren, and few will be inspired.[59]

This is perhaps Nouwen's most unusual definition of prayer, but the fact that Nouwen would connect the importance of a relationship with God to a relationship with others is not unusual for him at all. Nouwen's spirituality was not an extreme contemplation that was oblivious to the needs of others or the Christian's responsibility to meet them. The idea that one's prayer life had the potential to affect the lives of others was important for Nouwen and an integral part of his entire view of the spiritual life.

The main purpose of prayer, for Nouwen, was intimate communion with God, creating space in which God can move and speak. Nouwen wrote that prayer "invites us to live in ever closer communion with the one who loves us more than any human being ever can."[60] "We must pray not, first of all, because it feels good or helps us, but because God loves us and wants our attention."[61]

Scattered throughout Nouwen's writings, however, one can detect other purposes. Prayer can, second, make one truly whole and holy through the transforming power of the Holy Spirit. Prayer is the bridge between who a person really is and who he or she needs to be. This is not something that the human being accomplishes but something that is accomplished by God as he molds people into his image. "Prayer is 'soul work' because souls are those sacred centers where all is one and where God is present in the most intimate way."[62]

Third, prayer can clarify direction for one's decisions and make the truths of God plain.[63] Nouwen often prayed about the direction his life

[59] Nouwen, *Here and Now*, 94–95.
[60] Nouwen, *Road to Daybreak*, 120.
[61] Ibid., 117.
[62] Nouwen, *Bread for the Journey*, January 15.
[63] Nouwen, *Intimacy*, 47.

should take, which is especially demonstrated in his decision to leave academic life and search for a new place of ministry that was in keeping with God's plan and purpose.

Nouwen also believed prayer reveals how Christians are to be "in the world but not of it" in that prayer compels them to be involved in the lives of others, but it also provides them the necessary distance from which to see the world for what it is.[64] Lastly, prayer does not necessarily protect believers from pain but can actually be a source of more pain.

> To the degree that our prayer has become the prayer of our heart we will love more and suffer more, we will see more light and more darkness, more grace and more sin, more of God and more of humanity. To the degree that we have descended into our heart and reached out to God from there, solitude can speak to solitude, deep to deep and heart to heart. It is there where love and pain are found together.[65]

Perhaps most important for Nouwen in his later years, prayer reminds believers of their true identities as the beloved children of God and reminds them of their true home. This is best expressed in his work *Life of the Beloved*:

> When we are thrown up and down by the little waves on the surface of our existence, we become easy victims of our manipulative world, but, when we continue to hear the deep gentle voice that blesses us, we can walk through life with a stable sense of well-being and true belonging.[66]

It is interesting to notice what Nouwen did not say about prayer. Nouwen did not mention the Roman Catholic practices of praying the rosary or using the memorized prayers such as the Our Father or Hail, Mary. He did not write about the various types of prayer like adoration, confession, petition, or thanksgiving. He rarely mentioned intercession, although in examining his life habits it is clear he prayed for people and led others to do so, especially at Daybreak. Silence on such subjects does not argue that he did not practice them or was opposed to them. Perhaps the emphases that Nouwen expressed point to what Nouwen believed his readers needed to hear most.

Nouwen did not expound much on exactly how to pray. He did not provide a formula or a set of exercises. He did, however, outline a few basic principles. For example, one constant theme throughout his books

---

[64] Nouwen, *Genesee Diary*, 177, and *With Open Hands*, 129.
[65] Nouwen, *Reaching Out*, 150.
[66] Nouwen, *Life of the Beloved*, 60.

was that prayer should be the first priority in a Christian's life. At the Genesee in 1974, Nouwen knew that he talked about prayer more than he actually practiced it. He knew that prayer did not have priority in his life.[67] In fact, he was still struggling into the last year of his life to give prayer the priority that he believed it should have. He wrote in his sabbatical journal:

> I have lived with the expectation that prayer would become easier as I grew older and closer to death. But the opposite seems to be happening. . . . The year ahead of me must be a year of prayer. . . . Maybe the time has come to let go of *my* prayer, *my* effort to be close to God, *my* way of being in communion with the Divine, and allow the Spirit God to blow freely in me.[68]

Nouwen's honesty here has to be appreciated. Nouwen knew that the busier his life became, the less priority he gave to prayer. Why did he not have the discipline to do what he knew to be right? Why is the same true for many people? Nouwen never taught or wrote from the vantage point of one who had "arrived," telling others what they should and ought to do. His readers simply encountered a human being who struggled as they struggled and yet somehow inspired them to keep moving, to keep growing, to keep striving toward a prayerful life.

Without many specific details, Nouwen encouraged his readers to find a consistent time of communion with God alone every day. His suggestions were usually thirty minutes to an hour, but he believed strongly that *any* amount of time consistently dedicated every day would make a difference. Perhaps this instruction was the result of an interview with Mother Teresa of Calcutta. After he told her of his many spiritual struggles for more than ten minutes, she simply said, "Well, when you spend one hour a day adoring your Lord and never do anything which you know is wrong . . . you will be fine!" Nouwen was at first frustrated by her simplistic response, but then he realized she was right. In the most basic discipline, he had been lacking.[69] Nouwen confessed in *The Road to Daybreak* that as he was faithful to spending thirty, sixty, or ninety minutes in prayer, even with all of the mind's confusion and distractions, "a gentle voice was speaking to [him] far beyond [his] noisy place."[70] In a later work he wrote:

[67] Nouwen, *Genesee Diary*, 42.
[68] Nouwen, *Sabbatical Journey*, 5–6.
[69] Nouwen, *Here and Now*, 88.
[70] Nouwen, *Road to Daybreak*, 30.

Still, when we remain faithful to our discipline, even if it is only ten minutes a day, we gradually come to see—by the candlelight of our prayers—that there is a space within us where God dwells and where we are invited to dwell with God. Once we come to know that inner, holy place, a place more beautiful and precious than any place we can travel to, we want to be there and be spiritually fed.[71]

As was pointed out earlier, Nouwen did not provide much instruction on how to spend time in prayer, only that one should do it. On a few occasions he did suggest that one read the Scriptures, perhaps in the Gospels, and then just listen with the mind and heart.[72] Nouwen did not speak much at all about what to *say* in prayer. Perhaps he assumed that people talk too much in prayer, if anything. Perhaps he assumed people knew what to say. Listening was, for Nouwen, the more important aspect of prayer, especially during the time that is set aside to be still and to be quiet. On the few occasions when Nouwen did suggest what to say in prayer, he usually referred to Hesychastic[73] prayer, a method used to pray unceasingly throughout the day in the midst of work and other distractions. Nouwen taught a course on the spirituality of the Desert Fathers and Mothers that influenced his thinking a great deal in this area. He suggested a simple prayer such as the Jesus Prayer[74] or a simple phrase from Scripture to repeat over and over in a contemplative fashion. Such prayer was for the purpose of praying throughout the day and allowing the "mind to descend into the heart in order to stand in the presence of God."[75] Nouwen called this kind of prayer "prayer of the heart" or "simple prayer" in keeping with the desert tradition.[76]

When asked how to handle the distractions of the mind while praying, Nouwen suggested that the distractions should not be fought as enemies

[71] Nouwen, *Here and Now*, 21.

[72] Nouwen, *Reaching Out*, 135.

[73] This term is derived from the Greek word *hesychia* for "quiet" or "one who lives in stillness," which refers to a way of inner prayer taught and practiced in the Christian East from the fourth century onwards; in a narrower sense it denotes the use of the Jesus Prayer (see note 74) accompanied by the physical technique of controlled breathing. See *A Dictionary of Christian Spirituality*, s.v. "Hesychasm," 189–90.

[74] The standard form of this prayer from fourth-century Egyptian spirituality is "Lord Jesus Christ, Son of God, have mercy on me, the sinner." See *A Dictionary of Christian Spirituality*, s.v. "Jesus, Prayer to," 223.

[75] Nouwen, *Way of the Heart*, 64.

[76] Ibid., 64–65.

but should be invited into the prayer experience. Any thought, worry, or distraction should be brought into the conversation so as to integrate the whole of life into communion with God and resist the temptation to compartmentalize, allowing God only into a portion of our lives.[77] Such honesty is difficult, Nouwen admitted, because there are usually attitudes and thoughts deep in our soul that we do not want to admit are present. Much honesty is required for true prayer.[78]

Richard Foster, in his most recent work, *Streams of Living Water*, described six major traditions of Christian spirituality as illustrated throughout the history of the Christian church. One of those traditions he entitled "the contemplative tradition," and Foster placed Nouwen within this tradition. Foster named one of the characteristic strengths of the contemplative tradition as being the centrality of prayer. He wrote, "Contemplatives do not think of prayer as a good thing, or an important thing, but as the *essential* thing."[79] Foster's assessment is accurate; Nouwen fits best into this tradition because prayer was indeed the essential thing in Nouwen's thought. Every other aspect of the spiritual life hinged on prayer. Beumer wrote of Nouwen, "Prayer forms the very pulse of his work. In the midst of everything that he was engaged in, prayer was his constant plumbline."[80] Such an attitude was directly in keeping with the desert spirituality by which Nouwen was so influenced. Theophan the Recluse said, "If prayer is right, everything is right."[81]

Solitude

Discerning what Nouwen had to say about solitude can be difficult in that Nouwen sometimes used the terms *prayer* and *solitude* interchangeably. Therefore, some of his writing about solitude was no different than what he said about prayer. Nouwen did believe that both solitude and silence were the disciplines that most supported the discipline of prayer. Prayer can be an unceasing kind of lifestyle, but Nouwen always emphasized the importance of being with God alone in a quiet and solitary

---

[77] Nouwen, *Reaching Out*, 131; *Genesee Diary*, 39; *Here and Now*, 90; *Bread for the Journey*, January 14; and Pat Poundstone, "The Importance of Prayer," *North Texas Catholic*, 1 April 1994, 14.

[78] Nouwen, *With Open Hands*, 12.

[79] Richard Foster, *Streams of Living Water* (San Francisco: HarperSanFrancisco, 1998), 52.

[80] Beumer, *Henri Nouwen: A Restless Seeking for God*, 92.

[81] *The Art of Prayer*, comp. Igumen Chariton of Valamo, trans. E. Kadloubovsky and E. M. Palmer (London: Faber & Faber, 1966), 51, as cited in Richard Foster, *Streams of Living Water*, 52.

place, pointing to the example of Jesus, who often withdrew to solitary places to pray (Mark 1:35).

Solitude as time. One book reviewer, Betty Talbert, pointed out that Nouwen seemed to use the word *solitude* in three ways: as a time, as an experience, and as an attribute of character.[82] As mentioned above, Nouwen often encouraged Christians to set aside a specific time every day to spend with God alone, away from the world and its distractions. Without solitude, people are likely to become driven, spinning without direction, fragmented, without the integration that communion with God can provide. The discipline of solitude requires making the choice to detach, if only for a few moments, from the world and its busyness:

> Still we do not have to be passive victims of a world that wants to entertain and distract us. We can make some decisions and choices. A spiritual life in the midst of our energy-draining society requires us to take conscious steps to safeguard that inner space where we can keep our eyes fixed on the beauty of the Lord.[83]

Such words must have struck to the very core of Nouwen's American readers. They remain challenging and insightful for contemporary American spirituality. The typical American lifestyle tends to avoid solitude or to plaintively cry that there is no time for such indulgence. Here, again, Nouwen confronted American culture with instruction that pointed out where Christians were allowing their environment to cripple their spiritual vitality. He reminded his readers that they were responsible for their own choices. Nouwen viewed most Americans as busy, driven people, and he reminded them that such a lifestyle was a matter of choice. He suffered from his own hectic pace. He did not always make good choices himself, but that did not keep him from insisting that solitude was vital to one's relationship with God.

Solitude as experience. Nouwen also spoke of solitude as an experience where one can let go of the scaffolding of one's busy life and be forced to face one's inner self and experience the Spirit's transforming power. Nouwen believed that without solitude it was virtually impossible to live a spiritual life, for solitude is "the furnace of transformation in which we are transformed from our false, compulsive self into the new self of Jesus Christ."[84]

[82] Talbert, "Way of the Heart," 3.
[83] Nouwen, *Behold the Beauty of the Lord*, 12.
[84] Nouwen, *Making All Things New*, 69, and *Way of the Heart*, 8.

People are sometimes afraid to face themselves in solitude. They do not want to deal with the many emotions and needs that lurk underneath the surface of their busy lives. In grappling with the many realities that are within, solitude can become the experience that offers the opportunity for the old self to die and the new self to be born in intimate communion with God alone.[85]

Nouwen sounded much more like a psychologist than a pastor or theologian when talking about solitude in these terms. Yet the Desert Fathers and Mothers were ever present in his thought. The monastics who escaped to the desert to find solitude and communion with God in the early centuries of the church, like St. Anthony, often described how their experiences in solitude forced them to face their inner selves and be stripped of anything that hindered unceasing communion with God.

Solitude as an attitude of the heart. While speaking of the importance of solitude, Nouwen never advocated permanent withdrawal from the world but believed that solitude could play a role in the practical nature of daily life even when it was not possible to find physical solitude. Once solitude became a habit in the literal sense of being alone with God for at least a small part of each day, Nouwen believed that solitude could eventually become a habit of the heart regardless of the surroundings throughout the rest of the day. Nouwen explained that such an attitude of the heart made Jesus the center of one's everyday life.

> Once the solitude of time and space has become a solitude of the heart, we will never have to leave that solitude. We will be able to live the spiritual life in any place at any time. Thus the discipline of solitude enables us to live active lives in the world, while remaining always in the presence of the living God.[86]

This is a valid insight supported by the Catholic spiritual tradition. Brother Lawrence, a French Carmelite brother who lived in the seventeenth century and whose classic writings are titled *Practicing the Presence of God*, advocated the practice of being mindful of God's presence throughout the day so that one can create a sanctuary of solitude within the heart in which to converse with God no matter what the outward circumstances may be.[87] A contemporary of Nouwen's also affirms this idea. Richard Foster, in his book *Celebration of Discipline*, wrote, "Soli-

[85] Nouwen, *Way of the Heart*, 15.
[86] Nouwen, *Making All Things New*, 80.
[87] Brother Lawrence, *The Practice of the Presence of God* (Mount Vernon, N.Y.: Peter Pauper Press, 1973), 48. Nouwen mentioned reading this work in *Genesee Diary*, 174.

tude is more a state of mind and heart than it is a place. There is a solitude of the heart that can be maintained at all times."[88]

Solitude makes us fruitful. Another idea that Nouwen associated with solitude was that solitude makes Christians better able to relate to and minister in the community. Solitude is essential for community because solitude teaches believers an inner freedom to be content with themselves and God alone so that they do not feel the compulsion to cling to one another in an unhealthy sort of way.[89] Solitude also results in the critical distance needed to "pay careful attention to the world and search for an honest response."[90] Nouwen saw this principle at work in the life of Thomas Merton, who found in solitude the ability to speak to the needs and questions of the world. Nouwen wrote of Merton:

> Perhaps Merton's most important discovery was the discovery of his fellowman at the depths of his own solitude. He experienced a new solidarity in the depths of his silence and he seemed to find there, where he was most alone, the basis of community.[91]

Thomas Kelly, author of the Christian spiritual classic, *A Testament of Devotion*, affirmed this idea as well when he wrote:

> The final grounds of holy Fellowship are in God. Lives immersed and drowned in God are drowned in love, and know one another in love. God is the medium, the matrix, the focus, the solvent. . . . He who is wholly surrounded by God, enveloped by God, clothed with God, glowing in selfless love toward Him—such a man no one can touch except he touch God also.[92]

It is evident, then, that Nouwen's thought on solitude was very much in keeping with several of the classical writings within Christian spirituality. Nouwen reminded Americans of this important spiritual discipline because their tendency was to avoid solitude at all costs and to view loneliness as an enemy. Nouwen battled such tendencies in himself and yet knew of the rich lessons imparted by the life of Jesus and the saints of the church. In the midst of a society that had become obsessed with

---

[88] Richard Foster, *Celebration of Discipline*, rev. ed. (San Francisco: HarperSanFrancisco, 1988), 96.

[89] Nouwen, *Clowning in Rome*, 15.

[90] Nouwen, *Reaching Out*, 49.

[91] Nouwen, *Contemplative Critic*, 50.

[92] Thomas R. Kelly, *A Testament of Devotion* (San Francisco: HarperSanFrancisco, 1996), 56.

avoiding the path of solitude, Nouwen insisted that this path was a necessary one to a meaningful relationship with God. Beumer affirmed this
assessment:

> With this spiritual vision of human relationships Nouwen was taking a
> stand against the dominant psychological approach of our times. He did
> not want to suppress existential human loneliness, but in the final analysis
> he wanted to see it as a source for every life, a Source where Love dwells.[93]

Silence

Many people cannot stand silence. They need to have a radio, television,
Walkman, magazine, or something that continues the flow of words. Silence often makes people feel more alone. They want the "company" of
the noise around them. Nouwen believed that people who found silence
disturbing usually had great difficulty with prayer.[94] Nouwen went so far
as to say that modern society is a "wordy world" that has contaminated
our thinking to the point where people tend to believe that "our words
are more important than our silence."[95] Nouwen viewed silence as necessary both for the inner life of prayer and the outer life of fruitful ministry in the world.

The inner life of silence. As for the inner life, Nouwen believed that silence was necessary for the purpose of listening to God. Silence "makes
us quiet and deepens our awareness of ourselves and God."[96] Silence also
opens up a space where the Word of God can be heard and received.
Nouwen wrote, "The word leads to silence and silence to the word. The
word is born in silence, and silence is the deepest response to the
word."[97]

The outer life of silence. Nouwen also saw the discipline of silence as the
way to "protect the inner fire" that can be dissipated at times by idle
words spoken to one another.[98] When people are less generous with their
words, however, then the words that are spoken have more creative
power.[99] Nouwen realized the need for balance in his life between words

[93] Beumer, *Henri Nouwen: A Restless Seeking for God*, 88–89.
[94] Nouwen, *With Open Hands*, 36.
[95] Nouwen, *Way of the Heart*, 42.
[96] Nouwen, *Reaching Out*, 136.
[97] Ibid., 136.
[98] Nouwen, *Way of the Heart*, 39.
[99] Ibid., 41.

and silence, especially since he was a speaker and teacher. He wrote, "I realize that the more I speak, the more I will need silence to remain faithful to what I say."[100]

Watching Nouwen speak in person, it was evident that silence probably did not come easily to Nouwen, though he believed it to be very important. He was a man who loved people, who loved affection and interaction, who could be so full of words and expression as he spoke that it seemed he would burst. His temperament was not quiet and serene. He was high-strung and his associates spoke of him as "filling the room" whenever he was present. In light of these natural tendencies, Nouwen probably realized the balance that was needed in his own life compared to the desert spirituality of which he taught and wrote. Nouwen lived in the dichotomy that most modern Christians live in. Silence and solitude are not encouraged or accommodated in modern culture. Nouwen called himself and others back to the example of Jesus and the early church fathers, to a place where there is more serenity, less chaos, more wholeness, less fragmentation, more stillness, less frenetic activity.[101] An intimate relationship with God is best nurtured by the intimate conversation of prayer. Solitude and silence make such intimate conversation possible.

Contemplation

In keeping with the saying of Plato that "an unexamined life is a life not worth living,"[102] Nouwen believed that the unique power of the human person was the ability to reflect on one's life. He believed reflection was essential for growth, development, and change.[103] Reflection is a more basic way of explaining what contemplation or meditation was for Nouwen. Nouwen defined contemplation as "a vision of the nature of things," the ability to see things for what they are.[104]

> Contemplative life is a human response to the fundamental fact that the central things in life, although spiritually perceptible, remain invisible in large measure and can very easily be overlooked by the inattentive, busy, distracted person that each of us can so readily become. The contemplative

[100] Nouwen, *Genesee Diary*, 134.

[101] Nouwen, *Way of the Heart*, 48–49.

[102] Plato, *Dialogues of Plato*, vol. 7 of *Great Books of the Western World*, ed. Robert M. Hutchins (Chicago: Encyclopedia Britannica, Inc., 1952), 210.

[103] Nouwen, *Can You Drink the Cup?*, 26–27.

[104] Nouwen, *Clowning in Rome*, 88.

looks not so much around things but through them into their center. . . .
[T]he contemplative life is like hearing a different drummer.[105]

Nouwen advocated two foci for contemplation that helped the mind to "descend into the heart" in order to discern the nature of reality. The first focus was that of God himself. Nouwen suggested that contemplative prayer is prayer in which believers attentively look at God, "an imaging of Christ, a letting him enter fully into their consciousness so that he becomes the icon always present in their inner room."[106] The second focus that Nouwen mentions is Scripture, especially the Gospels. The Scriptures were, for Nouwen, a tangible way to envision Jesus and learn from his life. In the daily contemplation of the Gospel, Nouwen said, "the life of Jesus becomes more and more alive in me and starts to guide me in my daily activities."[107] Nouwen did not encourage, however, elaborate theological analysis during this contemplative reading, but encouraged his readers to simply read the sentences over and over, focusing on what the passage said. The reason for a more meditative encounter with the Bible was so that its truth could "descend from the mind into the heart." Nouwen saw a distinction between head knowledge of Scripture and heart knowledge that allowed the truths to transform and change the inner wellspring from which life flows.

> Our contemplation should first of all be simple, very simple. Contemplative prayer enables us to allow the Word of God to descend from our mind into our heart, where it can become fruitful. That is why it is so important to avoid all long inner reasoning and inner speeches and to focus quietly on a word or sentence. Then we must ruminate on it, murmur it, chew it, hear it, so that in our innermost self we can really sense its power.[108]

Nouwen was somewhat unusual in his attention to Scripture, especially as a Roman Catholic. He made reference to specific passages of Scripture over seven hundred times in the forty books that he wrote.[109] Perhaps this is one reason why Nouwen was so appealing to evangelicals and widely read by them. Nouwen gave much attention to Scripture and gave direct illustrations from the life of Jesus in the Gospels as rationale for the spiritual practices of the Christian life. Perhaps because evangeli-

---

[105] Nouwen, *Genesee Diary*, 36, 48.
[106] Nouwen, *Clowning in Rome*, 77–78.
[107] Nouwen, *Here and Now*, 93.
[108] Nouwen, *Clowning in Rome*, 105.
[109] See the appendix for an index of Scripture passages Nouwen referenced in his books.

cals hold the Bible as the sole authority for faith and practice, and focus a great deal on the earthly ministry of Jesus as their example, Nouwen's attention to the Bible for the purpose of spiritual formation gave him credibility in their eyes. Nouwen did use stories and illustrations from non-Christian spiritualities at times but these references decreased in his post-Yale years as he relied more and more on the Bible for the support and illustration of his thought. Robert Jonas wrote, "Henri's moving outside the circle of Christian spirituality did trouble some fundamentalist Christians. But his message about Jesus was so clear, powerful, and grounded in the New Testament that they could easily forgive what they considered to be his occasional lapses of judgement."[110]

One must not go overboard, however, in emphasizing his use of Scripture. Nouwen was not a biblical scholar and did not teach from it in an expositional manner, with balanced treatment of all of its books. Nouwen had favorite passages and most of his references were to the Gospels. Nouwen gave honor to the Scripture, however, and clearly took its teachings as the primary instruction for living the Christian life. Such dependence on Scripture prevented Nouwen's spiritual guidance from being totally subjective, dependent on his experiences alone or his understanding and interpretation of the church's teachings. Beumer saw this approach to spirituality as valuable in that it demonstrated a healthy mix of the Protestant tradition, which leans heavily on the authority of Scripture, and the Roman Catholic tradition, which leans toward the more mystical practice of a contemplation of God that is based on silence and ritualism.[111] Nouwen directed his readers to the Bible as a source for contemplating God himself, so that their understanding of God and his ways might strengthen their relationship with him.

Worship in the Eucharist

Worship through the celebration of the Eucharist was a frequent activity in Nouwen's life. He celebrated it every day if possible, either by himself, or with a small group in a private setting, or in chapels and cathedrals. He did not dictate in any of his writings on the Eucharist how often anyone else should celebrate it, but he did believe it was an important part of spiritual formation, and his own life's example confirms this belief. He wrote, "The Eucharist is the center of my life and everything else receives its meaning from that center." Because the Eucharist represented the mystery of Christ's work for salvation, Nouwen believed that

---

[110] Jonas, *Henri Nouwen*, xl, lxi.
[111] Beumer, *Henri Nouwen: A Restless Seeking for God*, 158.

worship through the Eucharist was another way to allow Jesus to shape the heart, deepen faith, strengthen hope, and purify love.[112] At least two themes were evident in Nouwen's writings about the Eucharist—gratitude and sacrifice.

Nouwen dedicated one entire book, *With Burning Hearts*, to a meditation on the Eucharist using the story in Luke 24 of the disciples who encountered Jesus on the road to Emmaus. In this work, Nouwen used the concept of movement from resentment to gratitude to describe the eucharistic life. For Nouwen, the act of worship in the Eucharist was a symbol of what the Christian life is to be, an act of gratitude, a way of saying thank you to him who "joined us on the road."[113]

The theme of sacrifice is most evident in *Can You Drink the Cup?* Nouwen used the chalice of the eucharistic celebation as a metaphor for the Christian life and the importance of full participation in it no matter what the consequences might be. Nouwen believed that the Eucharist was a constant reminder that Christ died so that others might live. He did not promote Christianity as the secret formula for a life without pain or suffering. Nouwen believed the celebration of the Eucharist reminded Jesus' followers that the Christian life was to be "an act of selfless love, an act of immense trust, an act of surrender to a God who will give what we need when we need it."[114] It is a life of unconditional love, a life lived in the spirit of Jesus, who modeled unconditional love to the fullest.

Robert Jonas described the Eucharist as Nouwen's "spiritual center of gravity."[115] The central thrust of the Christian life was embodied in the Eucharist, symbolizing that one's relationship with God is held together by unconditional love—the sacrificial love of God for his child and the child for his or her heavenly Father. The consistent practice of celebrating the Eucharist told the story again and again so that the Christian might not lose perspective on what the Christian life was all about.

It is important to underscore that Nouwen's view of worship through the Eucharist was not that worship was for the purpose of creating an opiate for those participating, that they might feel good and get a charge for the week. Certainly Nouwen affirmed the benefit of the community coming together to express love for God and one another. Yet his emphasis pointed to the importance of worship as a way to "re-center" the community and each participant on the meaning behind the Christian life, which was a cause for both celebration and consecration.

[112] Nouwen, *Jesus and Mary*, 26.
[113] Nouwen, *With Burning Hearts*, 95.
[114] Nouwen, *Can You Drink the Cup?* 106.
[115] Jonas, *Henri Nouwen*, lxvii.

Celibacy

Nouwen gave significant attention to the practice of celibacy in only one book, *Clowning in Rome*, which was a set of lectures given to priests and nuns while on a sabbatical in Rome. Nouwen believed that celibacy provided the opportunity to be free and open to God's presence and available for his service. The celibate also became, in Nouwen's mind, a witness to the necessity of keeping God the priority, a reminder to all people that they belong to God. Nouwen did not advocate, however, that to be empty for God or to give priority to God was the special privilege of celibates. Nouwen believed that the clergy offered merely a living reminder that every Christian should seek the Kingdom of God first.[116]

Nouwen was personally committed to his own vow of celibacy, which was sometimes torturous for him. Because he was a person who was in continuous need of affection and a sense of belonging or family, sexual pleasure was a constant temptation for him. His friend, Robert Jonas, wrote: "In spite of his intellectual commitment to celibacy, he sometimes found it exceedingly painful to avoid special relationships. All his life, Henri hungered to be 'special' in someone's eyes."[117]

Although Nouwen never openly admitted a struggle with homosexuality in his writing or speaking, his close friends knew that he did struggle with it.[118] In the midst of this torturous struggle, however, Nouwen was committed to his vow of celibacy and wanted to be obedient in every way to Christ. He longed for healing and release from desires for relationships that he knew could never fill his innermost need for the intimacy of God. Nouwen accepted those who lived a homosexual lifestyle as people who were still loved by God. He never stated his condemnation or condonement of the lifestyle itself in his writing.[119] His struggle

[116] Nouwen, *Clowning in Rome*, 44–58.

[117] Jonas, *Henri Nouwen*, liv.

[118] Sue Mosteller, interview with author, tape recording, Richmond Hill, Ontario, 11 March 1998.

[119] An exception might be an essay that can be found among his papers in the Archives of the Yale Divinity School Library. This paper is not dated and his reason for writing it is not mentioned. Given the appearance of the font of the manuscript, it seems reasonable to think he wrote the paper sometime during his tenure at Yale, 1971 to 1981. In the essay, Nouwen admitted that he used to view homosexuals as psychologically immature people who needed psychotherapy but should also be treated with understanding and sympathy. After conversations with homosexuals who were offended by this position, Nouwen wrote that he came to understand their feelings to be valid in that there was no option for change or that they did

to recover emotional health after a friendship with a man became too emotionally possessing was revealed in *The Inner Voice of Love*, though homosexuality is never mentioned.

Because of the controversial nature of this issue, it is no wonder that Nouwen was less than transparent about his struggle. He is more transparent, however, than most in admitting his need for affection and intimacy. Nouwen was an open book in many ways, but on this particular subject, he sought to be wise in what he revealed and what he kept private. The bottom line for him always was that he wanted to be faithful and obedient to his vocation and bring all aspects of his life into the purview of his relationship with God with honesty and dependence on him as the source of all that is needed for healing or transformation.

Waiting

Waiting is not usually mentioned in the list of classical spiritual disciplines. Attention must be given to this theme, however, because Nouwen mentioned it briefly in some works but also dedicated a chapter to it in *Out of Solitude* and wrote a small booklet called *The Path of Waiting*. Sometimes he referred to it as "the spirituality of waiting." Nouwen acknowledged the constant demand for instant gratification in the modern world, which, in Nouwen's estimation, sometimes caused Christians to construct their own spiritual experiences instead of just waiting on God to provide for their needs.[120]

Nouwen applied this spiritual discipline especially to times when the Christian is experiencing discouragement or sorrow. Nouwen believed that exercising faith in God and waiting for his promises to be fulfilled during these times accomplished a purpose of its own. He wrote:

> This intimate experience in which every bit of life is touched by a bit of death can point us beyond the limits of our existence . . . allowing our weeping and wailing to become the purifying preparation by which we are made ready to receive the joy which is promised to us.[121]

---

not want to change. He goes on, however, to say that all persons, once they acknowledge what their feelings are, must make a moral choice in how to respond to them. At this point Nouwen is vague about what those choices can be. He concludes the essay by saying that Christ does not ask us to deny our feelings but to "make them available for God's love." See "The Self-Availability of the Homosexual," n.d. This document can be found in the Nouwen Archives at Yale Divinity School Library.

[120] Nouwen, *Reaching Out*, 129.
[121] Nouwen, *Out of Solitude*, 55–56.

Waiting meant hoping in God in an open-ended way that did not try to control the future or God's manner of working in our situation. Yet waiting was not a passive activity, but an active one, in Nouwen's view. Active waiting meant staying alert to God's activity and reading the Bible as well as sharing the experience with others in community.[122]

Nouwen again challenged the typical character of American culture by suggesting that waiting was not something that must always be avoided, nor was it a useless and passive activity. The emphasis on efficiency in American life advocates that all waiting is negative and that if anything can be done to control it or limit it, so much the better. Yet Nouwen correctly argued that relationships require trust and a relinquishment of the need to control. A relationship with God requires a willingness to wait on him in hopeful anticipation that his timing and his response can be trusted.

Spiritual Direction

Nouwen saw spiritual direction as another discipline that could nurture the relationship with God and help to create space in which God could speak and act. He addressed the subject briefly in Reaching Out by indicating several purposes for spiritual direction: (1) it helps believers to distinguish between the many voices that speak to them; (2) it is a source of encouragement not to give up; (3) it discourages rashness or pride; and (4) it can suggest what to do or read for a given situation.[123]

Nouwen also suggested that spiritual direction does not always have to be a one-on-one relationship. Spiritual guides from the past can also be spiritual directors through their writings. Such personalities in church history, he wrote, "don't ask for imitation . . . they invite us into their lives and offer a hospitable space for our own search."[124] Nouwen believed that a spiritual director's purpose, above all else, was to help the believer to listen to God's voice and be obedient.[125]

Nouwen sought spiritual direction himself on many occasions. He sought the direction of John Eudes Bamberger at the Genesee. He sought the direction of Père Thomas and Jean Vanier as he began to explore the possibility of working with L'Arche. He sought spiritual

---

[122] Nouwen, Path of Waiting, 17–18.

[123] Nouwen, Reaching Out, 137.

[124] Ibid., 138–40.

[125] Henri Nouwen, "Spiritual Direction," n.d. This essay is located in the Nouwen Archives of Yale Divinity School Library.

guidance and psychological counseling during his emotional crisis after joining the Daybreak community. He was ever accountable to the leadership of the Daybreak community for guidance in how to fulfill his vocation. He valued the advice and counsel of his friends and colleagues. Nouwen was not a spiritual "lone ranger." Nouwen recognized that one of the purposes of community was for the benefit of guidance and confirming the leadership of God. Nouwen was also an avid reader who gleaned spiritual insights from the writings and experiences of others.

Though spiritual guidance was not one of the more prominent themes in Nouwen's work, his example and his words provide guidance in the contemporary American Christian community for two reasons. First, Americans tend to be individualistic and do not easily recognize the importance and necessity of depending on others for help and guidance. Americans tend to think they must ultimately do things on their own. Such a mentality leads to unnecessary isolation and potential lack of balance in interpreting and understanding how the Christian life is to be lived.

Second, many Protestant traditions are not accustomed to the practice of spiritual direction, and Nouwen's instruction is a healthy reminder that individual counsel or small group accountability can be very helpful for one's spiritual journey as a Christian. Some traditions practice the idea but may use another term such as discipleship, which involves more mature believers assisting the younger believers in their spiritual growth. Quakers, or the Society of Friends, emphasize the importance and wisdom of "weighty Friends" who have a gift for spiritual discernment and should be depended upon for counsel.[126] Whatever it may be called, individual believers often need the wisdom and insight that can be gleaned from others who are further along on the journey, whether in person or through their writings. Nouwen reminded American believers of this truth that spiritual direction can help a believer understand how to know God and participate in an intimate relationship with him.

Vocation

Discussing Nouwen's thought regarding relationship with God would not be complete without exploring the theme of vocation. Vocation was, for Nouwen, that unique mission which each Christian has been called to accomplish.

[126] See Thomas Kelly's essay on "The Blessed Community" in *Testament of Devotion*, 58.

We seldom realize fully that we are sent to fulfill God-given tasks. We act
as if we have to choose how, where, and with whom to live. We act as if
we were simply dropped down in creation and have to decide how to
entertain ourselves until we die. But we were sent into the world by God,
just as Jesus was. Once we start living our lives with that conviction, we
will soon know what we were sent to do.[127]

The unique call of God is important to emphasize because Nouwen did
not believe the individual Christian is called to save the world, solve all
problems, and help all people. Each is called, however, to a unique task
within his or her context. Christians must stay close to God and listen
attentively by means of the spiritual disciplines in order to understand
that call and gain the strength to live it out with confidence.[128] Nouwen
believed that understanding one's vocation could bring clarity of focus
and the freedom to say no to those opportunities that were not in keeping with God's calling regardless of what others might expect or desire.

Robert Durback writes in the introduction to his Nouwen reader,
Seeds of Hope, that "Nouwen's writings are basically the record of his
search to follow his own vocation, that is, the voice he listens to in the
silence of his own heart, the voice of God calling."[129] Durback is accurate
in that Nouwen did not speak to vocation in a direct way as much as he
continually mentioned his own desire to follow his vocation obediently
and as he struggled with what that meant. Thus Nouwen said more
about vocation through his autobiographical writing than anywhere else.
Nouwen believed a true vocation was something one *had* to do, in that
he could not imagine *not* fulfilling his vocation to "be a witness of God's
love."[130] Durback concluded, "By sharing in his search, readers were also
invited to listen for their own call."[131] A person's relationship with God
is enhanced by such obedience.

Obstacles to a Relationship with God

Nouwen did not directly address the obstacles to a relationship with
God by writing a book or chapter on them. Several barriers can be dis-
cerned, however, by exploring what he had to say about the spiritual
disciplines and the character of God.

---

[127] Nouwen, *Bread for the Journey*, April 12.
[128] Nouwen, *Bread for the Journey*, March 10.
[129] Durback, *Seeds of Hope*, xxx.
[130] Nouwen, *Genesee Diary*, 13, 110–11.
[131] Durback, *Seeds of Hope*, xxx.

One such obstacle is the modern plague of busyness. Solitude and silence, the environs of prayer, do not come easily in a world that is noisy and bustling. Even when Christians believe God desires a relationship with them and they know that all the spiritual disciplines are the means to creating space for God, they are often overcome by a life that is too busy for God. Nouwen struggled in this battle with time. He knew his life was not focused enough on the one thing that mattered most, his intimacy with the Father, and yet he filled his life with many activities and commitments, and felt the demands of many obligations. Nouwen mentioned this dilemma throughout his journals and referred to the struggle when writing about the priority of seeking first the Kingdom through prayer and other disciplines. He made the problem most plain, however, in his work about Thomas Merton, *Contemplative Critic*:

> We modern Westerners are so busy with ourselves, so preoccupied with the question of whether we do justice to our own selves, that the experience of the "transcendent" becomes practically impossible. . . . In this way of thinking there is scarcely room for Him who speaks whenever we are silent and who comes in whenever we have emptied ourselves. Instead of making ourselves susceptible to the experience of the transcendent God, we, busy with many things, begin to seek after the small flighty sensations brought about by artificial stimulation of the senses.[132]

Another obstacle to a relationship with God is fear. Nouwen acknowledged that many people live in a constant mode of fear to the point that, whether they are aware of it or not, they make their decisions based on fear and accept this as what has to be. The voice they most need to hear is God's voice, which says, "Do not be afraid."[133] Yet many people are afraid of God, and Nouwen saw this as the greatest block in the spiritual life.

> As long as we are afraid of God, we cannot love God. Love means intimacy, closeness, mutual vulnerablility, and a deep sense of safety. But all of those are impossible as long as there is fear. Fear creates suspicion, distance, defensiveness, and insecurity.[134]

The solution to this obstacle, in Nouwen's mind, was somehow to dare to believe that God's love is perfect and perfect love casts out fear. This can only happen as one is willing to spend time listening to God's voice through the Scripture and in prayer, even when fears are noisy and dis-

---

[132] Nouwen, *Contemplative Critic*, 84.
[133] Nouwen, *Lifesigns*, 15, 21.
[134] Nouwen, *Bread for the Journey*, February 29.

tracting. Nouwen called this "moving from the house of fear to the house of love."[135]

An obstacle that is related to fear of God is the idea of doubting God's love. Nouwen struggled with this obstacle as well. Nouwen believed self-acceptance was integrally related to faith in God's acceptance. As people struggle with their own failures and difficulties, low self-esteem causes a spiraling downward that is debilitating.

> My only real temptation is to doubt in your love, to think myself as be-
> yond the reach of your love, to remove myself from the healing radiance
> of your love. To do these things is to move into the darkness of despair.[136]

Nouwen believed, however, that if one allowed the full knowledge of the love of God to pervade the whole being and sink deeply in the heart, then disappointments, rejections, and criticisms do not have the same impact as before, because a believer's value is not in what he or she does or what others think about him or her. This idea is explored in much more detail in chapter 5, which discusses the relationship to self.

Nouwen fulfilled his role as a spiritual guide effectively because he warned his readers about what can prevent their progress on the spiritual journey. He helped many modern spiritual seekers to get past the obstacles that prevented them from experiencing the abundant kind of life that is characteristic of authentic Christianity.

The Fruit of Knowing and Loving God

Nouwen also gave attention to several themes related to what life in relationship to God can bring into the daily experience of life in its difficulties as well as its victories. The themes that seem to rise to the surface most are joy, hope, and gratitude.

Nouwen wrote his fullest expression on joy in his work *Lifesigns*. He dedicated a third of the book to the idea of ecstasy. Yet the theme of joy is sprinkled throughout his work. Nouwen believed that people who come to know God are joyful people. He says they "do not deny the darkness, but they choose not to live in it."[137] Joy and laughter come from a heart that strives to live in the presence of God and learns

---

[135] Nouwen, *Lifesigns*, 39.
[136] Nouwen, *Cry for Mercy*, 80.
[137] Nouwen, *Return of the Prodigal Son*, 117.

not to worry about or fear tomorrow.[138] Such an attitude is expressed through celebration and thanksgiving. Joy embraces all of life and does not shy away from the pain of life, yet it claims trust and hope in God's promises and delights in his presence even in the valley of the shadow.

Another benefit of a life that is in relationship with God is hope. Nouwen defined hope as "not a question of having a wish come true but of expressing an unlimited faith in the giver of all good things."[139] He distinguished hope from optimism in that the optimist "speaks about concrete changes in the future. The person of hope lives in the moment with the knowledge and trust that all of life is in good hands."[140] Hope, then, results in freedom. Hope frees us from the "need to predict the future and allows us to live in the present moment with the deep trust that God will never leave us alone."[141] Hope also provides the freedom to look realistically at life without being overcome with dejection, a freedom to live creatively in the present circumstances.[142]

Closely connected with joy and hope is the fruit of gratitude. Nouwen believed that a life intimately connected to "the Vine" results in the ability to acknowledge that "all that is, is a divine gift born out of love and freely given to us."[143] At times, Nouwen also wrote of gratitude as a discipline, an overt effort to be grateful instead of resentful.[144] The Eucharist itself is the symbol of thanksgiving for all that God has given in Jesus Christ. Yet gratitude, for Nouwen, was not just a ritual observed or a word spoken. Gratitude was a quality of the heart that existed in spite of the circumstances of life.[145]

Was Nouwen's thought about the life lived in relationship with God too idealistic? Nouwen's own relationship with God was not perfect, and therefore joy, hope, and gratitude were not always perfectly evident either. Nouwen's life, however, and the lives of many saints throughout church history bear witness to the truth, as does Scripture, that as one grows in the grace and knowlege of God, such fruit does become more and more evident.

---

[138] Nouwen, *Here and Now*, 31.

[139] Nouwen, *With Open Hands*, 82.

[140] Nouwen, *Bread for the Journey*, January 16.

[141] Nouwen, *Here and Now*, 33.

[142] Nouwen, *With Open Hands*, 84, and *Out of Solitude*, 59.

[143] Nouwen, *Lifesigns*, 70.

[144] Nouwen, *Return of the Prodigal Son*, 85.

[145] Nouwen, *Cry for Mercy*, 83.

Conclusion

A relationship with God, in Nouwen's thought, was dependent on understanding who God is, trusting God's love first extended in Jesus, and actively creating space in which God can speak to believers and transform their hearts through prayer and many other spiritual disciplines. Obstacles to such a relationship are fear, doubting his love, or just being too busy to nurture it. For those who will reach out to God and allow God to find them, however, a life of joy, hope, and gratitude is possible no matter what the circumstances of life bring.

Nouwen's emphasis on a personal relationship with God underscored the reality that it was not one's standing in regard to the institution of the church, as was the basis for many people's spirituality in the 1950s, but one's personal relationship with God alone that was the foundation for an authentic Christian spirituality. Nouwen's emphasis on the individual's relationship with God and the importance of the practice of the spiritual disciplines is significant in light of the fact that many Americans after the 1960s stopped looking to the institutional church as the source and medium through which to know about God and to learn how to nurture a relationship with him. Many Americans needed spiritual guidance on what it meant to nurture the primary relationship of the spiritual life within the whole context of life, not just on Sundays.

As Jesus instructed, to love the Lord with all the heart, soul, and mind must have first priority. The other spiritual relationships, then, can flourish in the best possible sense. When one's relationship to God is growing and transforming one's heart and mind, then one's relationship to self or self-identity is based on the value God places on one's life. Consequently, when one's self-identity is healthy, then and only then is one capable of loving others as God intended. It is to Nouwen's thought concerning self-identity that we turn in the next chapter.

CHAPTER FOUR

◈

Who Am I?

The Relationship with Self

Introduction

In an article entitled "The Crisis of Postmodernity," Philip Sheldrake notes: "Whereas the question at the forefront of most of the great spiritual classics is, 'What or who is God?,' the characteristic question of the contemporary spiritual quest is the more subjective, 'Who am I?' "[1] This was certainly true of American spirituality by the 1960s and that seeker-oriented spirituality that uses the language of psychology still characterizes many Americans today. Nouwen answered this foundational question of the contemporary spiritual quest with the word *beloved*. Human beings are the beloved sons and daughters of God. They have only to receive that love and live in that identity. Many people in the world today try to define their value with such things as possessions, power, or prestige. But through his own spiritual journey and a struggle with his own self-identity, Nouwen discovered that a person's relationship with self, that is, his or her self-image, had to be based on the love of God and the value that such love renders.

In the cultural milieu of America, especially, people tend to define themselves and others by what they do, what they have, or what others think of them. Is it any wonder, then, that to chase the American dream means to climb the ladder of fortune and fame? Nouwen did not believe a person's true self was based on such criteria. This chapter will explore Nouwen's thought on the relationship to self by contrasting the false self with the true self.

---

[1] Philip Sheldrake, "The Crisis of Postmodernity," *Christian Spirituality Bulletin* 4 (Summer 1996): 6.

The False Self

Nouwen believed that the greatest trap in the spiritual life was not success, popularity, or wealth, but self-rejection, which might express itself with arrogance or humiliation. Nouwen believed that arrogance indicated that someone was not comfortable with who he or she naturally was and so had to create a facade that made up for what might be lacking, while the other extreme made no attempt to hide the self-rejection at all. Either trait, according to Nouwen, was evidence that one did not know the truth of who one really was in relationship to God. Nouwen wrote, "Whether I am inflated or deflated, I lose touch with my truth and distort my vision of reality."[2]

Nouwen believed that self-rejection was the result of listening to the "wrong voices," which said, "Prove that you are worth something; do something relevant, spectacular or powerful, and then you will earn the love you so desire."[3] Listening to these voices causes people to believe that their self-esteem relies on the successful demonstration of such accomplishments, but Nouwen called these the "compulsions of the false self."[4] The solution to such a condition is to listen to the voice of God instead:

> To grow beyond self-rejection we must have the courage to listen to the voice calling us God's beloved sons and daughters, and the determination always to live our lives according to this truth.[5]

Nouwen used the illustrations of Jesus' baptism and wilderness experience to reveal the ultimate source of the "wrong voices" or the "voices of the world."[6] Although Nouwen tended to use these phrases somewhat interchangeably, both of them ultimately referred to the deception of the Evil One who also tried to tempt Jesus to do something relevant (turn stones into bread), something spectacular (jump off the pinnacle of the temple), and something powerful (inheriting all the kingdoms of the earth in return for worshipping Satan himself). In each instance Satan attempted to make Jesus doubt his true self as the Son of God or at least tempted him with the need to prove who he was. In at least two in-

[2] Nouwen, *Life of the Beloved*, 27–28.
[3] Ibid., 29.
[4] Nouwen, *Way of the Heart*, 13.
[5] Nouwen, *Bread for the Journey*, January 10.
[6] *Life of the Beloved*, 25–26; *In the Name of Jesus* in its entirety is based on Jesus' temptations in the wilderness.

stances, Satan even began his suggestion with "If you are the Son of God, then . . ." Jesus knew the truth about who he was and did not give in to Satan's suggestions. His baptism had revealed his identity with clarity— the beloved Son of God (Luke 3:21–22). Nouwen believed that every child of God was tempted in the same ways. In order not to be deceived, each person had to realize that he or she, too, was the beloved child of God. There was no need to listen to the lie that said one needed to prove oneself.

It is important to note here that Nouwen did not clearly define in his writing what was required to be a child of God. One gets the general sense from reading all of his work that he believed that all human beings were children of God. His friend, Robert Jonas, seemed to confirm this when he described Nouwen's open attitude toward the celebration of the Eucharist:

> Henri saw every person as a child of God, whether baptized or not. But he also counseled non-Christians that the full meaning and value of the Eucharist would be revealed only if they chose to be baptized. If that baptism was in the Roman Catholic Church, so much the better.[7]

Nouwen did not speak about a conversion experience as being the first step toward becoming a child of God. Nor did he designate that the children of God were only those who had been baptized into the Roman Catholic church. The fact that Nouwen would not emphasize a conversion experience is understandable within the context of his tradition as a Roman Catholic. Yet it is interesting to note that Nouwen did not even clearly imply a Roman Catholic theology of salvation. Perhaps he was assuming its implication as he wrote or perhaps he did not want to exclude readers from other Christian traditions by being too specific with his theology. His main thrust, in the end, seemed to be that God was a loving father who longed to be in relationship with his children and to empower them to become all that he intended them to be. Nouwen did attest to the fact that this relationship, however, was available only because God made it possible through the incarnation and sacrifice of Jesus Christ.[8]

---

[7] Jonas, *Henri Nouwen*, lxvii.

[8] Assuming that Nouwen did not deviate in a significant way from the theology of his own tradition, certain basic beliefs about salvation can be noted. Roman Catholic theology assumes that Christ died for all and made atonement through His blood so that His merit might be applied to human beings, who were born in original sin and who commit sins throughout their lives. All that is required of human beings is to love God and love others, and live in obedience to His Word. Grace to live as a child of God is communicated through the sacra-

Nouwen reiterated in many different ways that self-identity should not be based on what one accomplishes or on what others think. These two ideas are difficult to separate in Nouwen's work, because what people think about others is often related to what they do and whether they are "successful" or not. This false sense of self, in Nouwen's mind, could only lead to imprisonment by the fear that someone will either find out or decide that we are not good enough.

> The more we allow our accomplishments—the results of our actions—to become the criteria of our self-esteem, the more we are going to walk on our mental and spiritual toes, never sure if we will be able to live up to the expectations which we created by our last successes.[9]

Nouwen taught that this fear then leads to a tendency to withdraw from true community as we remain guarded in relationships with others. Instead of relating to one another with compassion, we are fixed on competing with one another, living as if life were "one large scoreboard" where we have to prove ourselves "winners."[10]

> When we have sold our identity to the judges of this world, we are bound to become restless, because of a growing need for affirmation and praise. Indeed we are tempted to become low-hearted because of a constant self-rejection. And we are in serious danger of becoming isolated, since friendship and love are impossible without a mutual vulnerability.[11]

Nouwen believed that such an unhealthy connection between self-esteem and what others think causes the Christian to be too attached to the world. Busyness becomes a status symbol that has to be maintained.[12] The chase of wealth, popularity and power becomes the merry-go-round that never stops.

> As long as you live in the world, yielding to its enormous pressures to prove to yourself and to others that you are somebody and knowing from

---

ments. A person lives in response to God's love through Jesus Christ in the power of the Holy Spirit as best he can and depends on God's grace for what is lacking. God's grace in Jesus Christ and the free will of the human being both participate in the work of salvation. See *Handbook of Catholic Theology*, s.v. "Salvation," 639–42.

[9] Nouwen, *Out of Solitude*, 19.

[10] Nouwen, MacNeill, and Morrison, *Compassion*, 19.

[11] Nouwen, *Out of Solitude*, 20.

[12] Nouwen, *Making All Things New*, 24.

the beginning that you will lose in the end, your life can be scarcely more than a long struggle for survival.[13]

Nouwen's overall portrayal of humanity could be interpreted as "soft on sin" in that he did not dwell on the subject of sin in his earlier work. He tended to approach humanity's spiritual dilemma more from the perspective that people are deceived by the voices of the world and do not understand how much God loves them. It is important to note, however, that Nouwen, especially in his later work *Return of the Prodigal Son*, described the false self as one who chose to rebel against God. It was only as the rebel decided to repent and return home that he claimed his true identity once again. As Nouwen identified himself with the prodigal son, he wrote:

> It's almost as if I want to prove to myself and to my world that I do not need God's love, that I can make a life on my own, that I want to be fully independent. Beneath it all is the great rebellion, the radical "No" to the Father's love, the unspoken curse: "I wish you were dead." The prodigal son's "No" reflects Adam's original rebellion: his rejection of the God in whose love we are created and by whose love we are sustained. It is the rebellion that places me outside the garden, out of reach of the tree of life. It is the rebellion that makes me dissipate myself in a "distant country."[14]

Nouwen went on in the later pages of this work to explain that the prodigal son had to repent, or turn around, before he could return home. He also went on to say that Jesus paid the price on the cross so that God's children might be able to return home and be received once again as his beloved sons and daughters, thereby able to claim their true identity.[15]

In summary, a person with a false sense of self, in Nouwen's mind, is self-rejecting. He or she lives in constant fear of not successfully proving him- or herself worthy of love or esteem. Such a person is therefore competitive with others instead of compassionate, and attached to the world, with its temporal values and compulsions to be relevant, spectacular, and powerful. The false self can also be a rebel, refusing to acknowledge his or her need for God, believing that one can live independently of him.

Nouwen struggled throughout his lifetime, vacillating between his false self and his true self. He admitted that, especially during his aca-

---

[13] Nouwen, *Life of the Beloved*, 105.

[14] Nouwen, *Return of the Prodigal Son*, 43.

[15] Ibid., 55.

demic years, he was constantly tempted to live as if accomplishment and prestige were the bases of his value as a person. He hated the pressure, the fear, and the competition that this produced. His prayer, written at the Abbey of the Genesee in 1978, summarized his struggle:

> Help me, O Lord, to let my old self die, to let die the thousand big and small ways in which I am still building up my false self and trying to cling to my false desires. Let me be reborn in you and see through you the world in the right way, so that all my actions, words, and thought can become a hymn of praise to you.[16]

Nouwen never claimed to have arrived at perfection. He did believe, however, that his own struggle with the false self was an accurate reflection of what many Americans were experiencing. Nouwen did have his finger on the pulse of American society in regard to the reasons why people tend to live out of a false sense of self. Guides for Christian spirituality throughout church history affirm the truth that the value of the human life is founded on the love of God expressed most clearly through Jesus Christ and that rejection of that love leads eventually to destruction. Nouwen's unique contribution seemed to be his capability, as a psychologist, to describe why people get caught in the web of worldly pursuits that forces them into a pattern of false selfhood. At the same time, as a pastoral theologian, he went on to demonstrate and reinforce his ideas with the truth of God's Word, which can set people free from their false compulsions and help them understand their self-identity based on the love of God. Most important, his transparency about his own struggles with the false self gave him credibility as one who had been on the journey and was thus a reliable guide to understanding how to live, even if with some inconsistency, out of the true self.

The True Self

Nouwen believed it was extremely important to come to know and understand our true selves. How was this done? Nouwen said we know ourselves for who we really are when we understand that we are sacred beings embraced by a loving God. To come to know and understand ourselves begins with coming to some understanding of God's perspective on who we are even though we may not fully be able to grasp it:

---

[16] Nouwen, *Cry for Mercy*, 17.

> To acknowledge the truth of ourselves is to claim the sacredness of our
> being, without fully understanding it. Our deepest being escapes our own
> mental or emotional grasp. But when we trust that our souls are embraced
> by a loving God, we can befriend ourselves and reach out to others in
> loving relationships.[17]

Nouwen's description of the struggle to forsake the compulsions of the
false self could easily be viewed as what theologians would call sanctification. *Sanctification* is the term used here and not *justification* because
Nouwen realized that the struggle to live with a true sense of self is on-
going for the Christian. Evidence of success is when the true self stops
trying to please others and trusts that God is enough. The true self hears
God saying, "You are accepted."[18]

Evangelicals could easily apply this kind of language to what happens
when a person is converted. The convert trusts that God loved him or
her enough to make a way for the possibility of being in relationship with
him through Jesus Christ. Yet this language is also illustrative of sanctification as one continues to grow in one's understanding and application
of God's love and what it means to be a child of God.

Self-acceptance, for Nouwen, was the result of accepting God's love,
expressed most of all through his Son. In his view, God accepts us just as
we are and longs to empower us by his Spirit to live as we were intended
to live. When we are listening to the voices of the world, we cannot
truly accept ourselves, but when we are willing to listen to the voice of
God saying through Jesus that we are fully accepted just as we are, then
we are free to grow into our truest selves.

Two themes are especially evident in Nouwen's descriptions of what
it means to let go of the false self and embrace the true self. The first
theme is the idea of making the journey "from loneliness to solitude,"
which he evidenced more in his earlier writings. The second theme is
the idea of "being the beloved," which Nouwen developed more fully
in his later writing, after he left his academic career and found a home at
Daybreak as a pastor.

From Loneliness to Solitude

Both loneliness and solitude are prominent themes in Nouwen's writing.
In earlier works, he developed one or the other idea, but not both to-

---

[17] Nouwen, *Bread for the Journey*, March 21.
[18] Nouwen, *Inner Voice of Love*, 5.

gether. In *With Open Hands*, Nouwen viewed loneliness as the opportunity to be mindful of our emptiness, and realize that only God can fill it. He said, "The Christian way of life does not take away our loneliness; it protects and cherishes it as a precious gift . . . as an invitation to transcend our limitations and look beyond the boundaries of our existence."[19] Thus Nouwen pointed out that loneliness could be destructive or filled with promise, depending on how one responded to it.

In *Out of Solitude*, Nouwen introduced the idea that solitude, being alone with God, can teach us who we really are. It forces us to realize that our worth is not based on having or doing. Self-worth is based on being:

> It is in solitude that we discover that being is more important than having, and that we are worth more than the result of our efforts. . . . In solitude we become aware that our worth is not the same as our usefulness.[20]

Nouwen contrasted loneliness and solitude most fully in *Reaching Out*. In this work, he brought the two ideas of loneliness and solitude together for contrast. Loneliness, in this context, was the situation in which so many people find themselves. The painfulness of loneliness reminds people of their vulnerability and weakness, and makes them long for togetherness as the balm with which to end their pain. Nouwen did not believe togetherness alone healed loneliness. Only in the furnace of solitude with God could a person come to grips with his or her true self by facing the false self. Our true value, apart from others, has to be realized before any relationship with others can be meaningful.[21] It was in a later work, *Clowning in Rome*, that Nouwen more fully and clearly expressed that the greatest gift of solitude was "a new identity":

> Solitude is a place of conversion. There we are converted from people who want to show each other what we have and what we can do into people who raise our open and empty hands to God in the recognition that all we are is a free gift from God.[22]

In *The Way of the Heart*, Nouwen clarified this idea even more by calling solitude the "furnace of transformation." Using the illustration of Jesus' time of solitude in the wilderness, Nouwen explained that Jesus faced the temptations to give in to the three compulsions of the world

---

[19] Nouwen, *With Open Hands*, 84.
[20] Nouwen, *Out of Solitude*, 22.
[21] Nouwen, *Reaching Out*, 25–33.
[22] Nouwen, *Clowning in Rome*, 30.

and yet chose to affirm God as the source of his identity ("You must worship the Lord your God and serve him alone"). Solitude gives us the opportunity to respond to God's first love and find our identity in him:

> Solitude is the place of the great struggle and the great encounter—the struggle against the compulsions of the false self, and the encounter with the loving God who offers himself as the substance of the new self.[23]

In *Letters to Marc About Jesus*, one can observe the slight shift in Nouwen's thought toward the idea of solitude as being the place where we hear God say we are loved and accepted. This passage is a foreshadowing of the idea of self-identity as being intimately connected with God's love and acceptance, a stepping-stone to the idea of "being the beloved":

> The mystery of the spiritual life is that Jesus desires to meet us in the seclusion of our own heart, to make his love known to us there, to free us from our fears, and to make our own deepest self known to us. . . . Self-love and self-knowledge are the fruit of knowing and loving God.[24]

These early examples of Nouwen's attempt to talk about the true self are somewhat disjointed, but at least two ideas regarding the true self are clear. The first is that Nouwen believed that when a person possessed a healthy self-esteem, being alone did not have to be threatening. The true self is not addicted to the presence of others. In fact, solitude is welcomed, because it yields the opportunity for communion with God, whose love is the source of one's sense of worth. This leads to the second idea. Solitude is not only bearable to the true self, but necessary, for it is in solitude that one is able to hear the voice of God and to come to a deeper understanding of oneself and God.

Nouwen's emphasis in these passages rests more heavily on the fact that solitude or loneliness can provide the environment for understanding who we truly are as sons and daughters of God if we will allow it to do so. His later works, however, focus not on the environment but on the relationship itself—being the beloved sons and daughters of God—as the key to true identity.

Being the Beloved

The theme of "being the beloved" took shape for Nouwen in the last fifteen years of his life. The decade of the 1980s became a decade of quest

---

[23] Nouwen, *Way of the Heart*, 13–14.
[24] Nouwen, *Letters to Marc About Jesus*, 74–75.

for Nouwen. He knew that he did not want to remain in the academic setting, and yet he did not know where to go from there. As mentioned in chapter 3, Nouwen spent some extended time in Latin America and France before deciding that God was calling him to live among the mentally and physically disabled at the L'Arche community of Daybreak in Toronto. Even after finding a home at Daybreak, Nouwen still had to settle in and face some inner battles that had been stirring inside him for many years. All the words he wrote concerning the journey from loneliness to solitude were put to the test. His writing during this time began to reflect a new way of expressing what it meant to discover and live in relation to our true selves.

In these later years, Nouwen focused more intently on the idea of what it meant to trust and receive the love of God. He wrote in his journal *Road to Daybreak*, "I realize more than ever before that a new knowledge of God's unconditional love is needed."[25] Nouwen struggled in a new way throughout the 1980s to understand who he was in God and how to integrate more fully the unconditional love of God into his own life.

Three books are the major representatives of Nouwen's thought on this theme, although the rest of his work written during the last ten years of his life echoes this concept in a variety of ways. Nouwen wrote *The Return of the Prodigal Son* with the purpose of reflecting on how belonging to God and accepting our true selves is, in essence, a homecoming. His meditation on Rembrandt's depiction of the return of the prodigal son became a way to illustrate how receiving the love of God and dwelling in his love was the true way home. Only God can satisfy the deepest desire for belonging. His experience at Daybreak helped him to grasp the full reality of what it meant to be the beloved of God.

> The move from Harvard to L'Arche proved to be but one little step from bystander to participant, from judge to repentant sinner, from teacher about love to being loved as the beloved. . . . I have been led to an inner place where I had not been before. It is the place within me where God has chosen to dwell. It is the place where I am held safe in the embrace of an all-loving Father who calls me by name and says, "You are my beloved son, on you my favor rests."[26]

As usual, Nouwen decided to write a book which shared with others his own homecoming journey in the hope that others might be shown the way. He used both sons in the parable to illustrate how people can

---

[25] Nouwen, *Road to Daybreak*, 59.
[26] Nouwen, *Return of the Prodigal Son*, 14, 16.

often leave home like the prodigal or refuse the love of the father while staying at home like the elder brother. Both sons lost touch with their true identities as sons.

Nouwen taught that we leave home like the prodigal every time we refuse to listen to the voice of the One who calls us "beloved" and listen instead to the voices of the world.[27] The farther we run from the place where God dwells, the more difficult it is to hear his voice and the more entangled we become in the power games of the world. Yet just as the son came to his senses and rediscovered his deepest self as the beloved son of his father, so we, too, can reclaim our true self by returning to the love of God and staying there.[28]

The false self is just as evident in the character of the elder son, who was resentful and complaining toward his father. When he would not participate in the celebration of his younger brother's return, his father said, "All I have is yours." To live a life of resentment and jealousy and anger is to act out of our false selves, never receiving the love of the Father, which had been available all along.

Life of the Beloved is the second book through which Nouwen expounded upon the theme of "being the beloved." This work was originally written with the hope of explaining Christian spirituality to a friend who had no faith in God. Nouwen chose to use the story of Jesus' baptism as the backdrop for explaining what it meant to be God's beloved children. As Jesus was baptized, a voice came from heaven saying, "You are my beloved son; with you I am well pleased" (Luke 3:22). For Nouwen, the words "you are my beloved" revealed the most intimate truth about all human beings, since Christians are coheirs, brothers and sisters of Christ, and the children of God.[29] Once we accept the truth of our belovedness, then we are faced with the challenge to "become who we are," which Nouwen saw as the quest of the spiritual journey.[30]

Nouwen then turned to an additional image to explain what it meant to become the beloved. He used the image of the bread in the Eucharist, which, to Nouwen, represented not only Christ's physical body in his act of redemption, but also the lives within his Body, the Church. He used four words from Luke 22:19—*taken, blessed, broken,* and *given*—to demonstrate what "being the beloved" meant.

Taken was translated by Nouwen to mean "chosen," in that the children of God are his chosen ones. "When you lose touch with your cho-

[27] Ibid., 40.
[28] Ibid., 47–48.
[29] Nouwen, *Life of the Beloved*, 26.
[30] Ibid., 37.

senness," Nouwen warned, "you expose yourself to the temptation of self-rejection."[31] The great spiritual battle is to reclaim our chosenness in the midst of a world that persists in pulling us into "the darkness of self-doubt, low self-esteem, self-rejection and depression."[32] Nouwen then spoke of ways to reclaim our chosenness through unmasking the world for what it is, continuing to look for places and people where the truth about our belovedness is spoken, and celebrating our chosenness consistently with gratitude.[33]

Blessed is a concept that is difficult to separate from the idea of being chosen in Nouwen's writing. Nouwen said that it was not enough to be chosen but that one had to be reminded of one's chosenness by an on-going blessing, reminding us of God's love. Then we can "walk through life," Nouwen said, "with a stable sense of well-being and true belonging."[34] Nouwen taught that Christians are reminded of their blessedness through listening to God's voice in prayer and the cultivation of the awareness of God's presence in our daily lives.[35]

Broken bread was the image used by Nouwen to say that the beloved child of God must also claim his or her unique brokenness just as much as chosenness and blessedness.[36] This is a rather unusual approach to addressing the reality of pain and suffering in the Christian life in that American society tries to avoid or escape pain, but Nouwen believed brokenness was a reality for every human being, something that must be faced with truthfulness, not falsehood. Nouwen encouraged his readers to embrace their brokenness and to put it "under the blessing."[37]

> When we keep listening attentively to the voice calling us Beloved, it becomes possible to live our brokenness, not as a confirmation of our fear that we are worthless, but as an opportunity to purify and deepen the blessing that rests upon us.[38]

Nouwen said a great deal about pain and brokenness in his journal *The Inner Voice of Love*. The journal entries were written to himself as lessons that he was learning in the midst of his own deep pain and woundedness

[31] Ibid., 47.
[32] Ibid., 48.
[33] Ibid., 49–52.
[34] Ibid., 59–60.
[35] Ibid., 62–66.
[36] Ibid., 71–72.
[37] Ibid., 75–78.
[38] Ibid., 79.

while recovering from his emotional breakdown. He learned in the midst of his own brokenness that pain had to be embraced in order to heal.[39] He believed that a person's unique suffering was his or her own way of salvation, a way of revealing the truth.[40] One's true identity can receive joy as well as pain and be strengthened by both.

> Your true identity is as a child of God. This is the identity you have to accept. Once you have claimed it and settled in it, you can live in a world that gives you much joy as well as pain. You can receive the praise as well as the blame that comes to you as an opportunity for strengthening your basic identity, because the identity that makes you free is anchored beyond all human praise and blame.[41]

Given is the last movement of the life of the beloved in that Nouwen believed that the children of God were meant to love and serve others. "Our humanity comes to its fullest bloom in giving."[42] Nouwen's unique point in relation to the idea of being given is that he concentrated not so much on doing good deeds to meet the needs of others, as on the idea that we can give to others by the many ways we express our own unique presence, even through our brokenness. Nouwen also believed that our own death could be a gift. This theme is explored more fully in chapter 6. The main thrust, however, is that Jesus' disciples were able to appreciate what his life among them had meant only after he had gone to be with the Father. So Nouwen believed that if we are intentional about the way we live, even our death can be a gift that inspires people to faith and hope.[43]

Adam: God's Beloved contains the lessons Nouwen learned about "being the beloved" from Adam Arnett, the young man he took care of his first year at Daybreak. As can be detected from the title, Adam's life became the living picture that Nouwen used to illustrate what it meant to be the beloved child of God. For many years Nouwen had stressed that a person's value is not in what they do or possess but in their very existence as a precious child of God. Nouwen realized this discovery afresh as he cared for Adam, who could not speak, walk, or do anything for himself because of a severe mental disability. As he told Adam's story, Nouwen expressed the essential message of the Gospel with clarity

[39] Nouwen, *Inner Voice of Love*, 3.
[40] Ibid., 88.
[41] Ibid., 70.
[42] Nouwen, *Life of the Beloved*, 84–85.
[43] Ibid., 90–95.

through the concrete history of one life, perhaps insignificant to the world, but personal and meaningful for Nouwen and others who knew Adam well.

One has to read the whole book to capture the essence of the illustration, but as Nouwen explains his reason for writing the book, a glimpse is seen as to why Adam is the symbol of all of us as the beloved children of God.

> Most people saw Adam as a disabled person who had little to give and who was a burden to his family, his community, and to society at large. And as long as he was seen that way, his truth was hidden. What was not received was not given.

> But Adam's parents loved him simply because he was Adam. Yes, they recognized and loved him for himself. Without awareness they also welcomed him as one sent to us by God in utter vulnerability to be an instrument of God's blessing. That vision of him changes everything quite radically because then Adam emerges as someone, as special, as a wonderful, gifted, child of promise. . . . His wonderful presence and his incredible worth would enlighten us to comprehend that we, like him, are also precious, graced, and beloved children of God. . . . In relationship with him we would discover a deeper, truer identity.[44]

In the later years of his life, Nouwen came much closer to expressing the heart of the gospel and how it is experienced on a daily basis through his emphasis on being the beloved. To be a Christian means to be a follower of Christ. Jesus understood that his identity and his mission were based on his unconditional love relationship with God the Father. The Christian's identity and mission are also based on the unconditional love relationship with God through Jesus Christ. The whole of Scripture points to the fact that human beings are God's creations and totally dependent on him for the full abundance of life that he created them to experience. Nouwen chose not to communicate the Gospel from the standpoint of where a person was liable to spend eternity, as some more conservative evangelicals would tend to do, but from the standpoint of who they were created to love and be loved by as the ultimate fulfillment of meaning and purpose for this life and beyond.

Nouwen left himself open to the criticism of those who require more theological definition on how and why this relationship with God is possible. A person who is already grounded in his or her own tradition of Christian theology concerning salvation can use such a background as a grid upon which to place Nouwen's ideas and will most likely still find

---

[44] Nouwen, *Adam: God's Beloved*, 34.

him insightful, inspiring, and practical. Readers who do not have some kind of foundation in Christian theology, however, might find themselves swimming in some undefined waters, which may or may not trouble them.

Conclusion

To say "God loves you" is not original with Nouwen. Jesus announced it through his incarnation and his disciples have communicated the message ever since. Nor is the message of "detachment from the world" unique. Spiritual guides throughout the history of Christianity have continued to caution believers that buying into the system of the world will lead them astray.

What is unique to Nouwen is the manner in which he connected the two concepts with the use of psychology. Nouwen was an effective spiritual guide because he knew the language of later-twentieth-century Americans who were turning inward through the influence of psychology and he used it to help them connect their questions about meaning and purpose with the answers of the Christian faith. He used his own personal struggle with self-esteem to teach the lesson that the world's view of what makes human beings valuable and God's view are very different. Many Americans longed for material possessions, prestige, and success. Nouwen told them that such things would never give them what they truly needed. He argued that only accepting the love of God the Father, their Creator, results in the ability to live with freedom and true self-acceptance. But to say such a thing and to truly trust it and believe it and live as if it were true is another matter.

Nouwen struggled to live what he believed in regard to his true identity as a beloved son of God. Nouwen also saw many Americans chasing the American dream only to find that their narcissistic, pragmatic, restless selves were being deceived by a lie. Nouwen saw the lie at work in himself and wrote about his spiritual struggle to receive the love of the Father so that others might be encouraged to do the same.

Beumer posed the question whether Nouwen chose to emphasize the idea of being the beloved because he was insecure about his earthly father's love and approval. Certainly Nouwen was not immune to his own psychological baggage, but he did not base his thought on experience alone. It is logical to think that being the beloved was an important theme for Nouwen because he longed to be beloved to someone, but such psychoanalysis, as accurate as it may or may not be, does not negate the truth of the concept that God created human beings to live in rela-

tionship with him who is the perfect and loving Father. Surely the teachings of Jesus support the truth of this concept.

To the very end of his life Nouwen fought against the temptation to
make accomplishments or relationships with others the basis for his self-
worth. One might question if he ever learned to practice what he
preached. He inevitably longed for the affection and attention of others.
He became so attached to one friendship that when it was interrupted,
he temporarily lost his bearings, not sure that he wanted to live. Yet the
spiritual journey for Nouwen was not about perfection, but about struggling to live in a deep and meaningful relationship with God that would
bear fruit in the lives of others.

Nouwen knew that whenever he was faithful to trust in God's deep
and abiding love, his ability to love others deepened as well. His emphasis on being the beloved was not a sentimentality devoid of ethic. He
wrote on one occasion, "Self-understanding can never be its own goal.
We are for others."[45] Trusting in his own belovedness gave him the ability, he believed, to see the belovedness of others and therefore love them
in the way that God intended. Nouwen's spirituality in regard to one's
relationship with others is the focus of the next chapter.

---

[45] Nouwen, *Aging*, 117.

CHAPTER FIVE

❖

What Is My Purpose?
The Relationship with Others

Introduction

Jesus taught his disciples in Matthew 22 that the greatest command-ment was to love God with everything that they were—heart, soul, mind, and strength. His second commandment was to love their neigh-bor as themselves. Nouwen believed the ability to love one's neighbor was intricately tied to loving God. He wrote, "An unconditional, total love of God makes a very articulate, alert, attentive love for the neighbor possible."[1] Love for one's neighbor completes the circle of spiritual rela-tionships. "Laying our hearts totally open to God leads to a love of our-selves that enables us to give whole-hearted love to our fellow human beings."[2] Loving others enables people to see God or find God in a new way, and so the circle continues.

For Nouwen, the purpose of the Christian life was to "make God's love visible to the world."[3] Therefore, loving others, in Nouwen's mind, was not based on a feeling. For Nouwen, to love meant to "think, speak, and act according to the spiritual knowledge that we are infinitely loved by God and called to make that love visible in this world."[4] Such a calling immediately brings to mind issues of social justice and the challenge to transform a culture rife with social ills. Nouwen gave attention to these issues. But Nouwen also believed such a calling involved the more fun-

[1] Nouwen, *Genesee Diary*, 84–85.

[2] Nouwen, *Letters to Marc About Jesus*, 75. This interrelationship is present in several of Nouwen's books. For example, see also *Intimacy*, 149; *With Open Hands*, 114; *Lifesigns*, 43; *Reaching Out*, 65; *Life of the Beloved*, 84; and *Return of the Prodigal Son*, 121.

[3] Nouwen, *Here and Now*, 127–28, and *Bread for the Journey*, June 16.

[4] Nouwen, *Bread for the Journey*, June 16.

damental challenge of learning to live in intimacy and community with one another within the Christian community.

Nouwen saw the Christian life as much more than doing the right things. He said, "The real question is not 'What can we offer each other?' but 'Who can we be for each other?' "[5] Nouwen saw personal character and lifestyle in relationship to others as the outward manifestations of an inner reality—the transforming power of God's Spirit. This chapter will explore the various facets of Nouwen's thought on what it means to love others, including such themes as intimacy, friendship, community, death as a gift, compassion, social activism, and ministry.

Intimacy

Nouwen believed that all human beings were meant to love others and be loved by them. "We belong together in the embrace of God's perfect love," he wrote.[6] Nouwen defined intimacy as "the mutuality of the confession of our total self to each other,"[7] and he believed that intimacy was a gift from God.

Nouwen contrasted two kinds of intimacy in his writing, one that was based on fear and one that was based on love. In his first book, *Intimacy*, Nouwen spoke of the two forms as "taking" and "forgiving." Intimacy based on taking is when people manipulate relationships by the use of power motivated by fear. Such persons have to dominate in order to get what they need and not show any weakness or vulnerability for fear that it will be held against them. On the other hand, intimacy based on forgiving is a relationship that is motivated by love and demonstrated by the willingness to reveal one's self with truth, tenderness, and vulnerability. Even sexual intimacy, Nouwen wrote, can be a "taking" kind of experience or a "mutual self-surrender."[8] In *Lifesigns*, Nouwen also used the same contrast of love and fear in explaining intimacy, affirming that fear prevents true intimacy from occurring:

> Fear makes us move away from each other to a "safe" distance, or move toward each other to a "safe" closeness, but fear does not create the space where true intimacy can exist. Fear does not create a home. . . . Fear conjures either too much distance or too much closeness.[9]

[5] Nouwen, *Life of the Beloved*, 90.
[6] Nouwen, *Lifesigns*, 46.
[7] Nouwen, *Intimacy*, 29.
[8] Ibid., 23–37.
[9] Nouwen, *Lifesigns*, 30.

In *Reaching Out*, Nouwen contrasted these two types of intimacy by using the words hostility and hospitality. Intimacy based on fear eventually leads to hostility, even violence. Intimacy based on love and mutual forgiveness, however, creates a hospitality in which "guest and host can reveal their most precious gifts and bring new life to each other."[10] Hospitality is the creation of space where the stranger can become a friend. Nouwen admitted that creating space is far from easy in modern society, but hospitality is an important attitude because it offers people an environment in which to be encouraged and to disarm themselves.[11] In *Compassion*, Nouwen and his coauthors used a similar approach to describe compassion:

> When, through discipline, we have overcome the power of our impatient impulses to flee or to fight, to become fearful or angry, we discover a limitless space in which we can welcome all the people of the world.[12]

Nouwen cautioned his readers against clinging to others too tightly. Here the idea of space is used in another sense. Nouwen believed that when people fear loneliness they tend to "cling to others instead of creating space for them."[13] He believed no human being can meet all of a person's deepest needs. Nouwen wrote:

> No human being can understand us fully, no human being can give us unconditional love, no human being can offer constant affection, no human being can enter into the core of our being and heal our deepest brokenness. When we forget that and expect from others more than they can give, we will quickly become disillusioned.[14]

Nouwen wrote that instead of clinging tightly to someone, intimacy is like a cupped hand that holds a bird, neither totally open nor totally closed. "It is the space where growth can take place."[15] In *Bread for the Journey*, Nouwen used the image of a dance:

> For love to be possible we need the courage to create space between us and to trust that this space allows us to dance together. . . . Sometimes we are very close, touching each other or holding each other; sometimes we

[10] Nouwen, *Reaching Out*, 67.

[11] Ibid., 76.

[12] Nouwen, MacNeill, and Morrison, *Compassion*, 109.

[13] Nouwen, *Reaching Out*, 101.

[14] Nouwen, *Clowning in Rome*, 41.

[15] Nouwen, *Lifesigns*, 34.

move away from each other and let the space between us become the area where we can freely move.[16]

These insights concerning intimacy reflect Nouwen's psychological counsel more than a theological premise. Nouwen knew that no human being could meet a person's every need. Ultimately, he believed only God could fulfill totally the desires of the human heart to be loved unconditionally. Nouwen's own personal application of this belief was one of his greatest spiritual struggles until the day he died, and yet even his greatest trial, which he wrote about in *The Inner Voice of Love*, bears out his convictions in the end. He withdrew from that relationship until he could get help, regain his emotional stability, and create the emotional space that was needed for a more healthy relationship. Once this was accomplished, the friendship was restored, and Nouwen's instruction on intimacy became enfleshed as a lesson for himself and those who benefited from his willingness to share the experience through his writing.

Nouwen's role model, Jesus, also demonstrated that a relationship with others must be tempered by a deeper love for God. Jesus encouraged his disciples to love others based on his own love for them. Jesus obviously had close, intimate friendships with several of his followers, including Peter, James, John, Mary, Martha, and Lazarus. He loved them, cared for them, instructed them, encouraged them, and served them. Yet Jesus' relationship with his Father was such that he had no need to try to force those relationships to be any more than they could be. Thus Nouwen's words are a reflection of the attempt to follow the example of Jesus.

Nouwen's commitment to celibacy played a role in his views of intimacy. Nouwen's vow of celibacy prohibited any exclusive relationship. It was this commitment that created great loneliness for him at times and a great sense of loss because he could not have the most intimate of human relationships with another person. One cannot help but wonder what Nouwen would have been like if he had not been forced to take such a vow in order to be a priest, as the Roman Catholic tradition requires. Perhaps Nouwen would not have suffered so much with his neediness for affection. Was this his whole problem? Did his religious tradition prevent him from having a healthy psyche in regard to intimacy? Should one take his instruction on intimacy with a grain of salt since he obviously was not free to form a marriage relationsip? Of course, Nouwen would have answered this question in the negative. Nouwen perceived celibacy as a gift that opens up a huge space for God to fill with his unconditional love. Nouwen was human, and he struggled with his

---

[16] Nouwen, *Bread for the Journey*, February 19, 22.

commitment but he also believed the ultimate lessons about intimacy could be learned by one who longed to "discover the Author of love."[17]

In an American culture that places so much importance on intimacy, especially physical intimacy, Nouwen attempted to be an example of the importance of loving God most of all and allowing all other relationships to flow from that first love. Nouwen's struggle was indeed the struggle of many Americans who long for true intimacy with another human being or who desperately depend on the relationships they have, to the point of inadvertently destroying them. One does not have to be an expert to discern that many Americans do not understand how to relate to one another in a healthy and fulfilling manner. Nouwen believed that a relationship with God must be the source from which people can grow in their capability to love others in a balanced and healthy way.

Can the nonbeliever be intimate in a balanced and healthy way? Nouwen would not condemn or judge others to the point of sounding exclusive. Nouwen did seem to be convinced, however, that God created human beings to relate to each other in the highest possible sense based on a loving relationship with God himself. To believe that God is who he says he is implies that he knows what is best for his creation, and to ignore this reality diminishes the human potential for fulfilling relationships with others.

Friendship

Nouwen did not write about friendship until his later years, after moving to Daybreak. In the earlier years, he wrote about the need for community, but friendship was not a prominent theme. Nouwen had many friends all over the world, but Daybreak gave him the opportunity to learn new lessons about loving and being loved through close friendships.

In *Life of the Beloved*, as might be expected, Nouwen described friendship as "the calling forth of each other's chosenness and a mutual affirmation of being precious in God's eyes."[18] Nouwen believed God provided friends as gifts, channels of his love to those who "make God their sole concern."[19] *Here and Now* continued this line of thinking as

[17] The author is indebted to Sue Mosteller for this phrase as we corresponded about her perceptions concerning Nouwen's thoughts about intimacy from the vantage point of a close friend and colleague.

[18] Nouwen, *Life of the Beloved*, 54.

[19] Nouwen, *Can You Drink the Cup?*, 98.

Nouwen pointed out that because God loves his children, he will provide men and women who are eager to show them God's love. Yet Nouwen went on to say that one should not wait passively for such
relationships but, instead, must have the courage and confidence to initiate a relationship with those who seem to demonstrate God's love. Such
risk can result in rejection, but Nouwen believed people have to intentionally create the milieu where they can "grow stronger and deeper in
love."[20] Nouwen also cautioned that friends are limited and can never
love as God does.

> Friends cannot replace God. They have limitations and weaknesses like
> we have. Their love is never faultless, never complete. But in their limi-
> tations they can be signposts on our journey toward the unlimited and
> unconditional love of God.[21]

His thought about friendship is sprinkled throughout his later books,
but *Bread for the Journey* includes the majority of his ideas on this point.
This is noteworthy because this daily devotional book summarizes, for
the most part, thoughts and concepts that he had already written about
in other works. On this topic, however, the book offers some original
material. In *Bread for the Journey* Nouwen expressed how each friend is
unique. Some may offer affection. Others may challenge our mind or
inspire our souls, but each has a unique gift to give. "Thus, friendships
create a beautiful tapestry of love."[22]

Nouwen believed close friends should share one's deep pain as well
the joys. Such a unity of souls brings life and light and inner healing.[23]
Nouwen went on to observe that friends can see the twilight zone in our
heart that we cannot see. He explained that even though we know much
about ourselves, there are parts of ourselves that remain in the shadow of
our consciousness. We will never fully know the significance of our presence in the lives of others. This is good, Nouwen said, because it keeps
us humble and requires us to trust those who love us.[24]

Nouwen believed it was important to tell people that they are loved.
Words are important and need to be expressed and heard. Nouwen also
believed touch was important. He said, "When a friend touches us with
free, nonpossessive love, it is God's incarnate love that touches us and

---

[20] Nouwen, *Here and Now*, 131–32.

[21] Nouwen, *Bread for the Journey*, May 1.

[22] Ibid., May 2.

[23] Ibid., January 7 and February 24.

[24] Ibid., March 24.

God's power that heals us."[25] Yet, most important, Nouwen believed a friend was one with whom to share silence. Friends do not have to say or do anything. "With a friend we can be still and know that God is there with both of us."[26]

None of these thoughts about friendship are particularly unique. Yet Nouwen's words about friendship are solidly grounded in the concept that relationships are a gift from God. Nouwen believed friends are never to take the place of God, but instead should lead people closer to God as the source of all love. Nouwen's thought here is much more than some self-help advice on friendship, even though he might sound more like a psychologist than a theologian at times. It seems that, to Nouwen, God is intimately involved in all of life and in all relationships. Such thinking is in keeping with a holistic Christianity that has its center in God.

Nouwen did not propose a life of faith focused on God alone in that one should become a hermit and eliminate all other relationships. Nouwen himself was not a hermit or a monastic. He was very much involved in the lives of others and wrote for an American audience whose culture is very much plagued by the irony that one cannot live without relationships and yet few of them can be trusted. Nouwen seemed to welcome all of life's typical human relationships as expressions of the God of love and gifts from his hand. All of these relationships were to be nurtured and cherished and enjoyed, but ultimately served the purpose of knowing and experiencing more of God himself.

Community

While Nouwen's thought on intimacy and friendship speaks to a smaller circle of loved ones, Nouwen stressed the importance of being a part of the larger Christian community. Community, like prayer, is one of the larger themes in Nouwen's writing. Just as communion with God was of ultimate importance in Nouwen's mind, so community with other Christians was also an imperative for the Christian life for Nouwen. Jesus told his disciples that the world would recognize them by the way they loved each other. Nouwen gave as much or more attention to teaching about how the people of God were to love each other as to how to love those who do not know God.

[25] Ibid., March 25.
[26] Ibid., March 23.

The Church

It is probably safe to assume that when Nouwen used the word *community*, he was referring to the Christian church, although he used the word *community* much more often than the word *church*. Interestingly, whenever Nouwen specifically wrote about the institution of the church, his comments were not usually positive. In the 1960s and 1970s, Nouwen saw the church as more of an obstacle than a channel to God. This is in keeping with common attitudes during those years as many sincere believers challenged the relevance of the church. Yet Nouwen could see that many people longed for a community through which sincerely to experience God. As he saw them leaving the church to experiment with other avenues of spiritual expression, he knew the time was ripe for the church to take advantage of such hunger, and he called on the church to stop arguing over internal matters and respond.[27] While many young people were turning to the newly popular spiritualities of the East, Nouwen longed for churches to stop being distracted and "read the signs well" of a new opportunity to make God known:

> The churches, in many ways entangled in their own structural problems, often seem hardly ready to respond to this growing need to live a spiritual life. The tragedy is that many find the church more in the way to God than the way to God, and are looking for religious experiences far away from the ecclesiastical institutions. But if we read the signs well, we are on the threshold of a new area of spiritual life, the nature and ramifications of which we can hardly foresee. Hopefully, we will not be distracted by the trivia of churchy family quarrels and overlook the great questions which really matter. Hopefully, we will be sensitive enough to feel the gentle breeze by which God makes His presence known.[28]

Nouwen wrote a great deal about Christian community without mentioning the institution of the church in any noticeable way until the last year of his life. In his daily devotional book, *Bread for the Journey*, Nouwen devoted the last two weeks of October to his thought on the church. In this work, written more than twenty-five years later than the quote above, Nouwen still admitted the many imperfections of the institutional church and its hierarchy. Yet Nouwen said repeatedly that one cannot love God and not love the church. This is because, although the church is a very human organization, it is also the "garden of God's

---

[27] Nouwen, *Intimacy*, 66–67; Nouwen, *Creative Ministry*, 117.
[28] Nouwen, *Intimacy*, 150.

grace."[29] For there are many people within it who make the living Christ visible. Therefore, the "Church as an often fallible organization needs our forgiveness, while the Church as the living Christ among us continues to offer us forgiveness."[30] Nouwen believed it was important to love the church and to continue to be a part of it. He wrote:

> Loving the Church is our sacred duty. Without a true love for the Church, we cannot live in it in joy and peace. And without a true love for the Church, we cannot call people to it.[31]

The church continues to be God's people, "called together to make his presence visible in today's world."[32] It is against this backdrop of Nouwen's love and commitment to the church, as well as his honest assessment of its human weaknesses, that the rest of his thought on Christian community must be seen.

Community Defined

A place of refuge. Nouwen saw the Christian community as a place of refuge and belonging, a safe harbor in the midst of a competitive, demanding world.[33] In this safe harbor people form a fellowship that reminds them that they need not be afraid. They are accepted.[34] Like a harbor that provides calm water and needed support, so the community assures, comforts, and holds people close to the heart of God and demonstrates his faithful love.[35]

This definition must have struck to the heart of many Americans who read Nouwen's work. In a culture that is fragmented and often malignant with hate and cruelty, Nouwen's description of the Christian community as a refuge would have been very appealing. If Nouwen had stopped here, however, his definition would have been only a half-truth. The Christian community was definitely charged by Jesus to love and care for one another, but this was only part of the purpose of the church. The church not only helps to meet the needs of self, but each must also point the other to God.

---

[29] Nouwen, *Bread for the Journey*, October 22.

[30] Ibid., October 27.

[31] Ibid., October 24.

[32] Ibid., October 21.

[33] Nouwen, *Reaching Out*, 65.

[34] Nouwen, *Out of Solitude*, 24.

[35] Nouwen, *Inner Voice of Love*, 7, 76.

A window through which we see God in each other. Nouwen did not believe that a vital relationship with Christ was possible apart from a vital relationship with a caring Christian community.[36] Our common focus on knowing God in solitude then creates the possibility of protecting, encouraging, and guiding one another in our common endeavor.[37] "Together," Nouwen wrote, "we can reveal something of God that none of us is able to reveal on our own."[38] And during times of doubt or unbelief, the community can "carry us" and help us to "recognize the Lord again."[39]

Nouwen's instruction is valid because it is in keeping with authentic Christian spirituality as exhibited in the activity of the early church. The book of the Acts readily demonstrates that the early Christians met regularly to instruct and encourage one another. God through Jesus had been revealed to each of them in a variety of ways. Such diversity of experience enhanced their understanding of how God was working in their midst. They sometimes disagreed. The issue of Gentiles becoming members of the church (Acts 15) is one example. Yet such circumstances forced them to depend on each other and to seek the will of God together if they were going to fulfill the mission of the church as God intended.

A channel for the expression of our unique gifts. Nouwen viewed community as a place where space is created to serve one another and the world.[40] Because believers are assured of their own belovedness, they can recognize the belovedness of others, with no compulsion to compete with them. Instead, they are free to affirm each other's giftedness and allow those gifts to be expressed for the benefit of all.[41]

> When we have discovered that our sense of self does not depend on our differences and that our self-esteem is based on a love much deeper than the praise that can be acquired by unusual performances, we can see our unique talents as gifts for others. Then, too, we will notice that the sharing of our gifts does not diminish our own value as persons but enhances it. . . . Thus, our dominant feeling toward each other can shift from jealousy to gratitude. With increasing clarity, we can see the beauty in each

[36] Nouwen, MacNeill, and Morrison, *Compassion*, 61.
[37] Nouwen, *Reaching Out*, 46.
[38] Nouwen, *Here and Now*, 86; see also *Genesee Diary*, 29, and *Making All Things New*, 81.
[39] Nouwen, *Genesee Diary*, 56.
[40] Nouwen, *Reaching Out*, 97.
[41] Nouwen, MacNeill, and Morrison, *Compassion*, 78.

other and call it forth so that it may become a part of our total life together.[42]

Nouwen seems to create a helpful connection in reminding his readers
that human value is not in the functions performed but in the fact that
everyone is loved by God and can therefore let go of competition with
one another and rejoice in each other's unique gifts.

Churches in America today struggle to find a way to incorporate the
gifts of everyone. This is partly because some do not see the need to
contribute their gifts and partly because certain gifts are valued more
highly than others in a culture that lauds popularity and public perfor-
mance. Nouwen's definition is a useful reminder to the American church
that every person is uniquely gifted and should be valued simply because
he or she is also God's beloved.

A mosaic that reveals the face of God in the world. Nouwen saw the Christian community as a mosaic where each person is a stone. One stone by
itself cannot provide the entire picture, but when seen all together the
picture is clear.[43] As a people "fashioned by God," the Christian community is bound together by the same Spirit that calls them to make
God's compassion visible in the concreteness of everyday living in the
world.[44] Thus the purpose of the community is not just for the well-
being of its members, but primarily for the purpose of relying on one
another to hear the voice of God and moving forward together in obedience to him.[45]

This aspect of Nouwen's definition of the church is very important
because it prevents the church from being portrayed in his thought as a
self-help group or a therapy group that is totally focused on providing for
the needs of its own members. Nouwen's view of the Christian community challenges the American church to leave the walls of its buildings
and be obedient to the mission of extending the Kingdom of God.
Everything in Nouwen's thought points back to God and his purposes.

Characteristics of the Christian Community

Nouwen pointed to a variety of ways in which the community can fulfill
its purposes: he used the images of a refuge, a window, a channel, and a

[42] Ibid., 79.

[43] Nouwen, *Bread for the Journey*, May 3.

[44] Nouwen, *Reaching Out*, 154–55.

[45] Nouwen, *Behold the Beauty of the Lord*, 67; *Compassion*, 60, 76; *Making All Things New*,
87–88.

mosaic. The themes that are most evident in his description of how this fulfillment takes place are prayer, worship, celebration, forgiveness, and presence and absence.

Prayer. Nouwen emphasized the importance of prayer in the community above all other practices. First of all, it is individual prayer that compels believers to see their responsibility to the community, to realize that nothing human is alien to them.[46] Yet individual prayer and communal prayer are inseparable for Nouwen. He believed prayer should be the community's primary concern:

> Communal and individual prayer belong together as two folded hands. Without community, individual prayer easily degenerates into egocentric and eccentric behavior, but without individual prayer, the prayer of the community quickly becomes a meaningless routine.[47]

Communal prayer, according to Nouwen, serves at least two purposes. One is the discipline of intercessory prayer, praying for the specific needs of community members and others. Intercessory prayer enables the community to "enter into the center of the world and pray to God from there."[48] It helps the community stand in solidarity with those who have needs so that they might be touched by the healing presence of God by receiving new light, new hope, new courage."[49] Communal prayer also helps to erase the barriers that prevent solidarity. Communal prayer acknowledges that "we belong to each other as children of the same God."[50] Nouwen acknowledged that this kind of intercessory prayer also requires Christians to pray for their enemies, who are no more and no less worthy of being loved.[51]

The second purpose of communal prayer is to enable the community to discern its vocation, listening carefully to the same Spirit that speaks in each heart. Nouwen pointed out the troubling fact that many Christian communities keep one another too busy and too distracted to listen carefully to the voice of God. Communal prayer provides the opportunity for the discovery together of a common vocation.[52]

---

[46] Nouwen, *Contemplative Critic*, 50; *Out of Solitude*, 31; *Reaching Out*, 42; *Way of the Heart*, 20; and Nouwen, MacNeill, and Morrison, *Compassion*, 109.

[47] Nouwen, *Reaching Out*, 158.

[48] Nouwen, *Genesee Diary*, 144–45; *Clowning in Rome*, 32.

[49] Nouwen, MacNeill, and Morrison, *Compassion*, 110.

[50] Nouwen, *Here and Now*, 22.

[51] Nouwen, *Letters to Marc About Jesus*, 62.

[52] Nouwen, *Clowning in Rome*, 20–24; *Reaching Out*, 73.

Especially important in Nouwen's thought is the emphasis on listening together. Few American churches experience the fullness of participating with God in his Kingdom plan because they are full of individuals who fail to see the importance of listening in their own prayer lives. Some expect their professional ministers to listen for them. Nouwen challenged American Christians to be faithful to praying individually and corporately in order to understand what God is calling them to do.

Worship. Nouwen believed the celebration of the Eucharist as an act of worship was important for the fellowship of the community as well as for the individual's fellowship with God. For where the Eucharist is, there Jesus is present, and there the church is a body sharing together in eternal life.

> The self-surrendering love which we encounter in the Eucharist is the source of true Christian community. . . . I feel more and more certain that the way of Jesus can't be found outside the community of those who believe in Jesus and make their belief visible by coming together around the eucharistic table.[53]

Nouwen saw the Eucharist as a true picture not only of what Christ had done for the church but of what each believer and the Christian community as a whole is supposed to be—a living sacrifice. Those of his readers who participate in a tradition where the Eucharist is central in worship can easily relate to his words. Those traditions that do not as often observe the practice of remembering Jesus' last supper with his disciples might have a more difficult time relating to Nouwen on this point. Yet his encouragement to worship together as a community is not lost on anyone. Worship in song, reading and listening to the Word, baptism, and communion all create an atmosphere in which the community can focus on God, his love and his purposes. The Christian life cannot be lived apart from the worship of the community. Yet many Americans who have continued to reject organized religion since the 1960s fail to see the purpose of corporate worship and the life-giving sustenance that can be found in it. Nouwen challenged American Christians that worship of God on one's own is not enough. Communal worship keeps Christians from straying as easily from the path and provides help, encouragement, instruction, and a re-centering upon a narrow way.

Celebration. Nouwen believed not only that joy was a characteristic of the individual life in relationship to God, but that it must also be a char-

---

[53] Nouwen, *Letters to Marc About Jesus,* 48–49, 82.

acteristic of the Christian community. Celebration is, first of all, the "full affirmation of our present condition." Nouwen believed many had lost the capability of living in the present moment. Thus celebration is the "recognition that something is there and needs to be made visible so that all can say 'yes' to it."[54]

Celebration, secondly, is remembering both the positive and negative of the past and acknowledging that history has helped to shape who people are today and who they are becoming. The past having been accepted, the future can be celebrated as well.[55] Celebration is also something to be shared with honesty, affirming that "underneath all the ups and downs of life there flows a solid current of joy."[56] Joyful living in community requires breaking through the walls of isolation and becoming a people of God, realizing that all are fragile and mortal but also friends, companions, and fellow travelers on the way of eternal life.[57]

Nouwen was even so specific as to say that meals and birthdays are important ways to celebrate. Meals offer the opportunity to know one another more intimately.[58] Birthdays especially provide the chance to rejoice in one life and celebrate one's existence.[59] They serve as reminders that *being* is the most important thing:

> We should never forget our birthdays or the birthdays of those who are close to us. Birthdays keep us childlike. They remind us that what is important is not what we do or accomplish, not what we have or who we know, but that we *are*, here and now.[60]

Nouwen's words about celebration are certainly relevant to the modern Christian community. For those who tend to be too sober, too conservative with resources, or too task driven, the reminder to celebrate is a useful one. Scripture reminds us as well that the "joy of the Lord is our strength" (Neh. 8:10). Joy is one of the fruits of the Spirit (Gal. 5:22), and Paul admonishes believers to "rejoice in the Lord always" (Phil. 4:4).

Hannah Whitall Smith wrote a book in the 1870s called *The Christian's Secret of a Happy Life*. In it she writes that celebration, or joy, is the natural result of living in obedience to God. True Christianity brings joy when

[54] Nouwen, *Creative Ministry*, 96.
[55] Ibid., 97, 99.
[56] Nouwen, *Lifesigns*, 102.
[57] Nouwen, *Bread for the Journey*, January 31.
[58] Ibid., February 15, 16.
[59] Nouwen, *Here and Now*, 19.
[60] Nouwen, *Bread for the Journey*, February 13.

there is celebratory conformity to God's way.[61] The contemporary author on spirituality Richard Foster also includes a chapter on celebration in his work *Celebration of Discipline*. Foster writes, "The carefree spirit of joyous festivity is absent in contemporary society. Apathy, even melancholy, dominates the times."[62] Foster lists several benefits of celebration in the community that are in keeping with Nouwen's thought, but he perhaps states them more succinctly. Foster writes that celebration saves people from taking themselves too seriously and is an antidote for sadness of heart; celebration also can provide perspective and freedom from a judgmental spirit as believers strive to love and serve one another.[63]

Forgiveness. Nouwen called forgiveness the "cement of the community."[64] Such forgiveness requires first that Christians stop judging others as if they themselves are perfect. "To the degree that we embrace the truth that our identity is not rooted in our success, power, or popularity, but in God's infinite love, to that degree we can let go of our need to judge."[65] In an article for *Leadership* magazine, Nouwen summarized the importance of forgiveness for the community. Nouwen said, "Forgiveness is allowing other people not to be God."[66] No one will love perfectly. No one can meet every need except God himself. Forgiveness is a must so that Christians can be free to love each other without resentment or bitterness. Forgiveness requires letting go of hurts and disappointments and realizing that only God is capable of loving fully. It is futile to expect others to fulfill his role.[67]

Forgiveness is a prominent theme in psychological counseling, but Nouwen shifts the motivation for forgiveness. As Nouwen pointed out, forgiveness is not just for the purpose of one's own peace of mind. Forgiveness is based on the fact that God loved his children enough to offer them forgiveness and so they must also forgive one another.

Presence and absence. Nouwen called consolation the "gift of presence." Presence was important for Nouwen in that people have the capability

---

[61] Hannah Whitall Smith, *The Christian's Secret of a Happy Life* (Uhrichsville, Ohio: Barbour Publishing, 1998), 199–206.

[62] Foster, *Celebration of Discipline*, 191.

[63] Ibid., 196–97.

[64] Nouwen, *Bread for the Journey*, January 24.

[65] Nouwen, *Here and Now*, 62.

[66] Nouwen, "Moving from Solitude to Community to Ministry," 85.

[67] Ibid.

to offer something very precious to one another simply by being present with one another. One does not have to say anything or do anything or accomplish anything. Community is communing, being with one another. At times there is not even a need for conversation. People can simply love with their presence.[68]

Nouwen's idea about presence is not unique in that many people would acknowledge the value of just being together. But Nouwen goes a step further in proposing that absence can also be a gift, even death can be a gift. Nouwen believed that being present is not always the best gift to give someone. He said sometimes the best thing to do for someone is to leave and allow the Spirit of God to work and become present in an entirely new way. If people are dependent on our presence, he would say, then they will never grow past a certain point in their ability to depend on God above all. Jesus did this for his disciples. He left so the Holy Spirit could come.[69]

Death as a Gift

Over many years Nouwen developed the unique idea of death being a gift. He first mentioned this idea in *Creative Ministry* while describing how a hospital chaplain's task is to help make death an "ultimate human gift."[70] Yet Nouwen's own personal encounter with the death of his mother, and a brush with death himself, made him articulate this idea more fully. He wrote in *Aging,* "death can be made into our final gift" if we have lived carefully and gracefully.[71]

When his mother died, Nouwen had the opportunity to experience his mother's death as a gift to him. She taught him with her life, and she also taught him in her death. He came to realize that her life had truly borne fruit, fruit that was not realized until her death.[72] What Nouwen seemed to mean by this unusual perspective on death was that he came to appreciate fully who his mother was in life through her death because he came to realize more fully how she had lived a life that focused on those things that had eternal value. When one chooses to love others and sow acts of kindness and goodness, thereby demonstrating the love of God, then even one's own death becomes a gift though which people

[68] Nouwen, *Reaching Out,* 45–46.

[69] Nouwen, *Living Reminder,* 44; Nouwen, *Reaching Out,* 46–47.

[70] Nouwen, *Creative Ministry,* 47.

[71] Nouwen *Aging,* 14.

[72] Nouwen, *In Memoriam,* 80.

can, though grieving the loss, remember the fruit and gain strength and courage to make life count in the fullest way possible.

> If, however, mother's life was indeed a life lived for us, we must be willing to accept her death as a death for us, a death that is not meant to paralyze us, make us totally dependent, or provide an excuse for all sorts of complaints, but a death that should makes us stronger, freer, and more mature.[73]

Nouwen wrote more about death as a gift after having the experience of thinking that his own death was imminent. Nouwen discovered that his own death could be a gift only if he was willing to love others in his life to the point that he could set them free with gratitude and forgiveness rather than binding them with guilt.[74] He wrote, "I knew that my dying could be good or bad for others, depending on the choice I made in the face of it."[75] Later on, in *Life of the Beloved*, Nouwen summarized his thought about the gift given through death:

> The death of the Beloved bears fruit in many lives. You and I have to trust that our short little lives can bear fruit far beyond the boundaries of our chronologies. But we have to choose this and trust deeply that we have a spirit to send that will bring joy, peace and life to those who will remember us.[76]

Up to this point in Nouwen's work, the question still remained as to how to do this. How does one "die well?" This question became the focus of another book, *Our Greatest Gift*. This writing project forced Nouwen to face the question of how to prepare for his own death and how to lead others to do the same. Nouwen admitted that he had always been afraid of death. The brush with death in 1990 taught him that he did not have to fear it, but that he could welcome it as the ultimate expression of going home. Yet because he did not die, he was left with the question of how to prepare more fully for that inevitable moment.

Our Greatest Gift consolidates some of Nouwen's most prominent themes on the spiritual life, specifically relating them to the context of death. First, Nouwen explained that death can only be a gift when people realize they are the beloved of God and can welcome death instead of fearing it.[77]

---

[73] Nouwen, *Letter of Consolation*, 57.
[74] Nouwen, *Beyond the Mirror*, 52.
[75] Ibid., 42.
[76] Nouwen, *Life of the Beloved*, 96.
[77] Nouwen, *Our Greatest Gift*, 25.

Secondly, Nouwen taught that the intense awareness of mortality is an experience encountered by all human beings. Thus, facing death with hope, believers can believe that death does not separate them from people. Instead, death creates solidarity as people become mindful of their powerlessness and fragility. No one is alone in the journey. Nouwen believed that humans are eternal beings and the bonds between them are stronger than death. Death can be a celebration in the midst of temporary sorrow. In the meantime, Christians can have hope and can live generously toward one another.[78]

Finally, Christians have the opportunity to die well when they realize that their lives can be of more benefit to the generations that follow if they live fruitful lives so that, in their absence after death, that fruit becomes fully manifested:

> How can I live so that I can continue to be fruitful when I am no longer here among my family and friends? That question shifts our attention from doing to being. Our doing brings success, but our being bears fruit. The great paradox of our lives is that we are often concerned about what we do or still can do, but we are most likely to be remembered for who we were.[79]

There is value in considering what it means to "die well." Yet in his attempt to distinguish fruitfulness from productiveness, Nouwen seems to identify *being* as all good and *doing* as somehow bad. There are times when the two cannot be neatly separated. It is true that character is very important in the Christian faith. Achievement or success, based on the world's definition, is certainly not necessary in order to be of value to God and his Kingdom. Yet sometimes a person's legacy surely includes not only who he or she is, but also what he or she has done for the sake of Christ and others. Nouwen does advocate the importance of doing or taking action. So what is the difference? His distinction between what is fruitful and what is productive is not always helpful or clear. Being and doing are both inescapable human endeavors.

On the other hand, it remains important to keep in mind the context in which Nouwen wrote and the audience to which he was speaking. Americans tend to emphasize doing over being. Perhaps Nouwen was seeking to swing the pendulum in the other direction and emphasize the importance of being to a generation that was fully immersed in the goal of climbing the ladder of success without giving enough attention to that which is eternal.

[78] Ibid., 26–28.
[79] Ibid., 41.

In his biography of Nouwen, Beumer made a useful observation about the place of death in Nouwen's work. Beumer wrote that Nouwen sought to incorporate death fully into his spirituality and that this "spiritually faithful vision of death" is extraordinarily important.[80] Death is an important part of the process of life for one who believes in an eternal relationship with God. It is as if Nouwen eventually learned to embrace not only suffering but death itself. He no longer feared death, but saw it as an important facet of being a spiritual being. Americans, however, tend to view aging and death as enemies, and they agonize over the reality that such experiences are inevitable. Nouwen challenged the American Christian to embrace the reality of death. He gave his readers the opportunity to replace their fear of death with the realization that even death has a spiritual purpose and that such a realization could change the way they lived.

Compassion

Nouwen's spirituality regarding the relationship with others had a great deal to say about compassion. Nouwen used the terms *compassion* and *care* to describe the idea of ministering to or serving those who suffer, taking the meaning of compassion from its Latin derivative, which means "to suffer with."[81] In *The Return of the Prodigal Son*, Nouwen uses the metaphor of the prodigal son's father to illustrate the idea that Christians are to become like the Father, to be "compassionate as your heavenly Father is compassionate," to offer the same compassion that he has offered them and to become transformed into his image.[82] A Christian is called to the compassionate life, to suffer with those who suffer, to offer care, and to reveal "the gentle presence of a compassionate God in the midst of our broken world."[83]

> Compassion asks us to go where it hurts, to enter into places of pain, to share in brokenness, fear, confusion, and anguish. Compassion challenges us to cry out with those in misery, to mourn with those who are lonely, to weep with those in tears. Compassion requires us to be weak with the weak, vulnerable with the vulnerable, and powerless with the powerless. Compassion means full immersion in the condition of being human.[84]

[80] Beumer, *Henri Nouwen: A Restless Seeking for God*, 110–11, 118.
[81] Nouwen, MacNeill, and Morrison, *Compassion*, 4.
[82] Nouwen, *Return of the Prodigal Son*, 123.
[83] Nouwen, MacNeill, and Morrison, *Compassion*, 32.
[84] Ibid., 4.

Nouwen and his coauthors, in *Compassion*, noted that the natural human being tends to be not compassionate but competitive. Compassion goes against the grain and is, therefore, a radical call.[85] Nouwen expounded upon this in a later work by incorporating what he had been saying about being the beloved. He wrote that the compassionate life is possible "only when we dare to live with the radical faith that we do not have to compete for love, but that love is freely given to us by the One who calls us to compassion."[86]

A survey of Nouwen's thought on compassion brings to light several requirements for the compassionate life. The first is that compassion requires dependence, dependence on God and dependence on others. If a person relies on his or her own strength to live the compassionate life, it will not take long to be overwhelmed to the point of becoming numb or angry.[87] Compassion must therefore be rooted in prayer, because compassion must be rooted in love for and trust in God.[88] Some people view the compassionate life as a morbid focus on pain and suffering. Others see it as the opportunity to be a hero. Neither is characteristic of the truly compassionate life because the compassionate life for Nouwen was focused solely on being devoted and obedient to God.[89]

Nouwen pointed out in *Out of Solitude* that compassion, or caring, is required of all who live in relationship with God. Yet, he explained, many Christians have no space left in their lives to listen or to allow others to come close to them in the busyness of their self-absorbed lives. The compassionate life will arise only out of those who practice solitude. Solitude allows for the rest, centering, and emptying needed to be involved with the suffering. Solitude also provides the quietness from which to hear his voice which calls believers to this radical lifestyle of compassion.[90]

Yet the compassionate life is not only dependent on God, but also dependent on the community. Christians must depend on the community to reveal the whole of God's compassion. They cannot do so on their own. The community also provides support, encouragement, and direction as believers live and work together to reveal God's presence in the world.[91]

[85] Ibid., 8.
[86] Nouwen, *Here and Now*, 99.
[87] Nouwen, MacNeill, and Morrison, *Compassion*, 52–55.
[88] Nouwen, *With Open Hands*, 114.
[89] Nouwen, MacNeill, and Morrison, *Compassion*, 32, 39, 42.
[90] Nouwen, *Out of Solitude*, 39–43.
[91] Nouwen, MacNeill, and Morrison, *Compassion*, 50.

The compassionate life requires not only dependence but also patience, gentleness, gratitude, and hope. A compassionate life requires the discipline of patience so that Christians are not anxious and restless, but calm and forbearing.[92] Linked to patience is the quality of gentleness. Compassionate people must be gentle and tender people. Nouwen uses a unique metaphor to describe a heart that is gentle:

> If I could have a gentle "interiority"—a heart of flesh and not of stone, a room with spots on which one might walk barefooted—then God and my fellow humans could meet each other there.[93]

Finally, Nouwen believed that the compassionate life is a grateful life and a hopeful life. The compassionate action must be one that is freely given with joy, not compulsive, somber, or fanatical. Such compassionate living is the result of being grateful to God.[94] Compassionate living is also the result of hope—hope that compassion points beyond itself to the expectation of a new heaven and a new earth. Apart from Christ establishing his Kingdom in eternity, life in this broken world will never see total transformation. One day all will be made right.[95]

Nouwen's image of compassion is compelling and insightful. To Americans living in a society that is indeed competitive, isolating, and fragmented, Nouwen utilized concepts like dependence, community, and hope to describe how the Christian faith should be expressed through compassion. Such ideas are totally in keeping with the teachings of Jesus, but they are antagonistic to what American society promotes.

Nouwen offered some instruction on how to be compassionate and care for others. *Aging* and *Our Greatest Gift*, as well as *Compassion*, speak more at length on how to care for others, but other works provide some insights as well. Nouwen is careful to point out, especially to professional ministers, that caring is not about manipulating people. Caring does not mean to control or dominate. Caring creates an environment through which people are enabled to flourish, search for new direction, and make new choices.[96] Caring is also not necessarily the same as curing. "Often we are not able to cure, but we are always able to care."[97]

If compassion is not manipulation or cure, then what is it? Nouwen gave several concrete principles on how to care. The most prominent in

[92] Ibid., 95, 101.
[93] Nouwen, *Genesee Diary*, 145.
[94] Nouwen, MacNeill, and Morrison, *Compassion*, 126.
[95] Ibid., 134.
[96] Nouwen, *Lifesigns*, 71.
[97] Nouwen, *Bread for the Journey*, February 8.

his writing goes back to the idea of being present. Nouwen believed that caring means, first of all, to be present with each other,[98] "offering one's own vulnerable self to others as a source of healing."[99] One does not need to be useful as much as to be present.[100] To be present is to listen and to identify with each other as mortal, fragile human beings who need to be heard and sustained by one another, not distracted or entertained.[101] Nouwen's most powerful expression of this idea is found in *Here and Now*:

> When I reflect on my own life, I realize that the moments of greatest comfort and consolation were moments when someone said: "I cannot take your pain away, I cannot offer you a solution for your problem, but I can promise you that I won't leave you alone and will hold on to you as long and as well as I can." There is much grief and pain in our lives, but what a blessing it is when we do not have to live our grief and pain alone.[102]

Nouwen believed that caring also involved acceptance as well as confrontation. Caring for those who suffer often means that God's people must help those who suffer to realize their belovedness and embrace it.[103] People often interpret their suffering to mean that God is rejecting them or punishing them. Care involves helping people to overcome self-rejection and accept themselves as truly loved by God. Caring also involves helping those who suffer to realize that there are many who suffer alongside them.[104] Nouwen also proposed that suffering people do not necessarily need to be shielded from the suffering of others. They need to know about others' suffering so that they may realize they are not alone. Finally, Nouwen taught that caring can mean helping others to accept that it is in their weakness that God's strength is made visible and fruitful.[105] As difficult as it may be to understand, suffering offers the opportunity to recognize and receive all that God is capable of doing for his people and in his people.

Compassion sometimes requires confrontation. To care for someone might mean confronting and challenging that person to make different

---

[98] Nouwen, *Aging*, 120; *Out of Solitude*, 36.
[99] Nouwen, *Aging*, 97.
[100] Nouwen, MacNeill, and Morrison, *Compassion*, 13–14.
[101] Nouwen, *Aging*, 103.
[102] Nouwen, *Here and Now*, 105.
[103] Nouwen, *Our Greatest Gift*, 60.
[104] Ibid., 77.
[105] Ibid., 94.

choices or to change an attitude. Such confrontation must be balanced
so as not to become oppressive or hurtful, yet tough love is sometimes
the key to healing.[106]

Throughout his discussions on the subject of compassion, Nouwen's
role and expertise in the field of pastoral care becomes obvious. Nouwen
was acknowledged by many as a strong contributor to the field,[107] and
many of his early books, especially, were dedicated to pastoral care. Yet
one cannot help but wonder what real experiences Nouwen had as a
pastor or minister to others before going to Daybreak. Nouwen was either a professor in highly prestigious universities or he was traveling as a
speaker and author. Nouwen knew the right principles, based on a biblical model, and perhaps he had some opportunities to put them to work
as one human being who was mindful of his responsibility to care for
others. It was in making the decision to go to Daybreak, however, that
Nouwen truly experienced the challenges inherent in what he was trying
to say about compassion and caring. At Daybreak, his perspectives on
caring and compassion received a jolt of reality. Nouwen no longer had
the leisure to move on once the speech was over. He had to live what he
had been preaching and this new situation brought a certain depth to his
later work.

In his dissertation on Nouwen's influence on the field of pastoral care,
Kyle Henderson makes two observations that are worth repeating. First
of all, Nouwen placed much more emphasis upon Jesus as the one who
came to suffer with and for humanity than he does on the Spirit, who
comes to empower and heal. If Jesus is left on the cross, so to speak,
Nouwen's thought produces a model that is somewhat void of true healing and restoration. This leads us to Henderson's second observation in
that Henderson believed Nouwen's spirituality to be lacking in emphasis
on the role of the Spirit in the Christian life. Nouwen used the phrase
"life in the Spirit" often, but he rarely taught practical lessons about the
role of the Holy Spirit in the life of the believer.[108]

Henderson admits that no author should be expected to cover every
subject with equal weight,[109] but it is curious that Nouwen did not speak
more to the Holy Spirit's place in the Christian life. Perhaps Nouwen
tended to give more weight to the ministry and death of Jesus because
this was a narrative that rational Americans could identify with more

[106] Nouwen, *Aging*, 136–37; *Reaching Out*, 99.

[107] Hiltner, "Henri Nouwen: Pastoral Theologian of the Year," 6.

[108] Kyle L. Henderson, "The Reformation of Pastoral Theology in the Life of Henri J. M.
Nouwen" (Ph.D. diss., Southwestern Baptist Theological Seminary, 1994), 211–12.

[109] Henderson, "Reformation of Pastoral Theology," 211.

easily, whether they were seekers or mature believers. Whatever the reasoning, Americans, like most human beings, are not eager to enter into suffering and brokenness. Nouwen's words about compassion are sorely needed in a society that tends to err on the side of making care of self the priority. As Annice Callahan observed, Nouwen "challenges us to inclusive living."[110]

Social Activism

Nouwen taught that compassionate people also must be willing to confront those sources which cause the suffering of human beings. This leads to a discussion of another major theme in Nouwen's writings concerning one's relationship with others, that of social activism. He wrote:

> This is compassion. We cannot suffer with the poor when we are unwilling to confront those persons and systems that cause poverty. We cannot set the captive free when we do not want to confront those who carry the keys. We cannot profess our solidarity with those who are oppressed when we are unwilling to confront the oppressor. Compassion without confrontation fades quickly into fruitless sentimental commiseration.[111]

Nouwen believed that conversion was necessary not only for the individual and his neighbors, but for the entire human community.[112] Such conversion calls for a "prophetic witness who dares to criticize the world."[113] Yet Nouwen never separated the revolutionary way from the mystical way because he believed that in Jesus the two come together.[114] This is the critical difference for Nouwen in his assessment of liberation theology. Nouwen definitely believed the individual Christian and the church had an important role to play in social activism, but he did not believe that this could be done in keeping with the example of Christ if such activism led one away from the primary importance of a relationship with God in prayer. Activism that was not inspired by a deep relationship with God, Nouwen believed, was in danger of becoming an activism that did not have the right motive, love. In his review of Gustavo Gutiérrez's book *We Drink from Our Own Wells*, Nouwen affirmed the need for a liberation spirituality to undergird a liberation theology.

---

[110] Callahan, *Spiritual Guides for Today*, 131–32.
[111] Nouwen, MacNeill, and Morrison, *Compassion*, 124.
[112] Nouwen, *With Open Hands*, 120.
[113] Ibid., 97.
[114] Nouwen, *Wounded Healer*, 15–19.

Those who see in liberation theology a theological rationale for a class struggle in which the poor claim their rights and try to break the power of their oppressors have ignored the center of the struggle for freedom. Jesus is the center. . . . The good news that Jesus announces is the news that love is stronger than death and that the evil of hatred, destruction, exploitation and oppression can only be overcome by the power of love that comes from God.[115]

Nouwen sometimes referred to social activism, especially on an international scale, as "global spirituality." He wrote in *Lifesigns*, "We must continually search for a Christian spirituality which is global in its dimensions and unafraid to take seriously the dark forces at work on the international level."[116] This did not involve, however, merely an anxious human effort to create a better world, but the confident expression of the truth that in Christ, death, evil, and destruction have been overcome.[117] He wrote:

The great spiritual leaders, from St. Benedict to St. Catherine of Siena to Martin Luther King, Jr., to Thomas Merton, have all grasped this truth: the power of the renewing Word of God cannot be kept within the safe boundaries of the personal or interpersonal. They call for a new Jerusalem, a new earth, a new global community.[118]

In his earlier years, Nouwen was much more involved in social activism on an international scale. His involvement in Latin America and his tour of the United States in which he called Christians to protest against U.S. foreign policy in Central America are just two examples.[119] He was especially passionate about peacemaking and protested against the supplying of weapons to nations at war and the making of nuclear weapons. Nouwen did not advocate, however, that world peace would be achieved only by activism on the political level. He reminded Christians that true peace is not of this world and comes not through human effort but rather through the indwelling presence of Christ in both the individual and the community.[120]

[115] Henri Nouwen, "A Review of *We Drink from Our Own Wells*," *America*, 15 October 1983, 207–8.

[116] Nouwen, *Lifesigns*, 107.

[117] Ibid., 48.

[118] Ibid., 112.

[119] See Nouwen's book, *¡Gracias!*, for a description of his time in South America and Yvonne Goulet's article, "Father Nouwen on Nicaragua" in *The Church World* (29 September 1983): 3, 12–13 for a description of his tour of the United States.

[120] This idea is taken from Nouwen's unpublished book on peacemaking that was probably

In his introduction to the reader of Nouwen's writings on peace called *The Road to Peace*, John Dear summarizes Nouwen's challenge to Christian peacemakers: (1) all actions must be rooted in prayer; (2) peacemakers must move beyond judgmentalism and self-righteousness to speak not from anger or fear but love; (3) peacemaking calls Christians to community and challenges individualism; (4) all peacemakers must seek intimacy with Jesus and allow that relationship to guide all actions; (5) the work of peace must be rooted in searching for God, listening to God, and obeying God.[121]

Dear believed that Nouwen's essays on peace and justice offer some of his most mature spiritual insights and that they "stand at the center of his thought."[122] I do not agree. The center of Nouwen's thought was a personal relationship with God. He obviously believed that such a relationship would express itself through social activism, but this was not the center of his thought and work. Loving God and loving others as much as self was at the center of his work. Social activism was only one expression of these relationships at work.

Beumer questioned whether Nouwen's commitment to social activism ever went beyond a "romanticized spirituality" that Nouwen admitted he had when first confronted with Gutiérrez's spirituality of liberation in South America. After all, Nouwen did not stay among the poor and oppressed in Latin America. Was his talk of social justice just that—talk? I do not believe this to be the case. Perhaps it is true that Nouwen determined he was not cut out to live among those committed to the political liberation of the poor and oppressed in Latin America. Yet Nouwen remained committed to the idea that all Christians are called to live in compassion towards others, especially towards the poor. I believe Nouwen was deeply committed to the idea that God had called him to minister among the poor. When he discovered L'Arche and the Daybreak community, he discovered his own specific place to live out that vocation. Nouwen could have remained in the academic world. He could have decided that his gifts were best expressed from the study and the classroom. There is certainly nothing inherently wrong with being a scholar, author, and teacher. He could have left the hands-on work to others. Yet Nouwen believed that obedience required that he live out his calling among the mentally disabled at Daybreak.

---

written in 1984 and has been reprinted in a reader of his work on peacemaking called *The Road to Peace*, edited by John Dear (Maryknoll, N.Y.: Orbis Books, 1998), 43.

[121] Dear, *Road to Peace*, xxx–xxxii.

[122] Ibid., xxix.

To elaborate on the Christian's responsibility to live an actively compassionate life for others, Nouwen used several other themes such as solidarity, "poverty of spirit," and "downward mobility." Nouwen believed that the basis for all social action must be the sense of solidarity. By solidarity Nouwen meant a willingness to "enter into the problems, confusions, and questions" of others.[123] Solidarity is the common sharing of the human condition. Nouwen believed such camaraderie prevented self-righteousness and made true compassion the motivation for action.[124] This is exactly what Nouwen believed Jesus did through his incarnation. He entered into solidarity with humanity. Nouwen wrote:

> This is what we mean when we say that Jesus Christ reveals God's solidarity with us. In and through Jesus Christ we know that God is our God, a God who has experienced our brokenness, who has become sin for us.[125]

Nouwen believed Jesus demonstrated the unconditional love of God, who was willing to enter into the human condition in order to bring redemption. Thus Christians find the motivation to enter into solidarity with others and to give in a sacrificial manner because Christ did the same for them. This reasoning, however, was not meant to heap the cares of the world on the shoulders of a follower of Christ. Solidarity did not mean that one had to save the world or die trying. Nouwen believed guilt and feelings of impotence could all too easily paralyze one who is overwhelmed by human suffering and yet desires to offer a healing response. Nouwen believed each Christian must simply concentrate on being faithful to whatever God has called him or her to do. Nouwen wrote about his own struggle with this issue:

> More important than ever is to be very faithful to my vocation to do well the few things that I am called to do and hold on to the joy and peace they bring me. I must resist the temptation to let the forces of darkness pull me into despair and make me one more of their many victims. I have to keep my eyes fixed on Jesus and on those who followed him and trust that I will know how to live out my mission to be a sign of hope in this world.[126]

Nouwen expressed the same idea in another way in his use of the phrase "poverty of spirit." He defined this phrase as the ability to realize that "nothing human is alien to us, that the roots of all conflicts, war,

[123] Nouwen, MacNeill, and Morrison, *Compassion*, 14.
[124] Nouwen, *Reaching Out*, 59.
[125] Nouwen, MacNeill, and Morrison, *Compassion*, 17.
[126] Nouwen, *Here and Now*, 46–47.

injustice, cruelty, hatred, jealousy, and envy are deeply anchored in our own hearts."[127] Poverty of spirit is to understand that no one is good but God alone. As the Christian surrenders to the lordship of Jesus, he or she can receive all humans as spiritual equals. If God loves all people, his followers can do no less. Nouwen saw this reality at work in the lives of Mother Teresa of Calcutta and Dorothy Day as each expressed her "compassionate solidarity with those in whom the brokenness of the human condition was most visible."[128] Of course, he believed such a life was most visibly expressed in Jesus himself.

"Downward mobility" is another phrase that Nouwen used to express the idea of solidarity. Instead of choosing the path of upward mobility, which is what the world promotes as the best way to approach life, especially in America, Nouwen described the Christian approach as downward mobility. He believed this "descending way of love" had to be sought out individually. It is not expressed in the same way for every Christian. It has nothing to do, Nouwen said, with "spiritual heroics or dramatically throwing everything overboard to follow Jesus." Instead, it is a way that finds unique expression as each person seeks God's guidance and listens to him in prayer.[129]

In his work *In the Name of Jesus*, Nouwen described downward mobility as a powerlessness and as a humility where power is constantly abandoned in favor of love. The Christian does not follow the way of the world but rather follows the way of Jesus and the cross, confident that such a path produces abundant life.[130] A certain passage in *Compassion* seems to define the idea of downward mobility most clearly:

> Jesus' whole life and mission involve accepting powerlessness and revealing in this powerlessness the limitlessness of God's love. Here we see what compassion means. It is not a bending toward the underprivileged from a privileged position; it is not a reaching out from on high to those who are less fortunate below; it is not a gesture of sympathy or pity for those who fail to make it in the upward pull. On the contrary, compassion means going directly to those people and places where suffering is most acute and building a home there.[131]

Nouwen exemplified his teaching on downward mobility when he came to live at Daybreak. Nouwen knew when he agreed to come that

---

[127] Nouwen, *With Open Hands*, 105.
[128] Nouwen, MacNeill, and Morrison, *Compassion*, 68.
[129] Nouwen, *Letters to Marc About Jesus*, 47.
[130] Nouwen, *In the Name of Jesus*, 62–64.
[131] Nouwen, MacNeill, and Morrison, *Compassion*, 27.

there would be no salary for the first three years. He also gave all of his material possessions to the community, including furniture, dishes, beds, linens, and his library. Nouwen also stipulated in his will that most of the royalties from his books be given to Daybreak.[132]

Closely related to Nouwen's theme of downward mobility was his idea of a "theology of weakness." Most of his thought on this subject is encapsulated in his booklet *The Path of Power*. Nouwen acknowledged that the lust for power has often "entrapped and corrupted" the human spirit and the Church.[133] Nouwen reminded all those involved in ministering to society that Jesus' example teaches a "theology of weakness," which Nouwen defined as a "total and unconditional dependence on God that opens us to be true channels of the divine power that heals the wounds of humanity" through the "all-transforming power of love."[134] Nouwen cautioned Christians against the temptation to control or manipulate people. To choose power over love is always bad news, not good news.[135] In his book *In the Name of Jesus*, Nouwen wrote to ministers and others involved in social activism:

> What makes the temptation of power so seemingly irresistible? Maybe it is that power offers an easy substitute for the hard task of love. It seems easier to be God than to love God, easier to control people than to love people, easier to own life than to love life. . . . The long painful history of the Church is the history of people ever and again tempted to choose power over love, control over the cross, being a leader over being led. Those who resisted this temptation to the end and thereby give us hope are true saints.[136]

Beumer makes several significant observations regarding Nouwen's thought on social involvement. First, it is important to point out that Nouwen's spirituality is neither otherworldly nor cynical. His was an earthly spirituality that said that Christians should be active in their society for the purpose of promoting love and compassion. Yet Nouwen acknowledged that the total redemption of the world would only come at the end of time, when Christ's victory would be total.[137]

---

[132] This information was confirmed in a conversation with Sue Mosteller via electronic mail on 3 April 1999.

[133] Nouwen, *Path of Power*, 8.

[134] Ibid., 33.

[135] Ibid., 16.

[136] Nouwen, *In the Name of Jesus*, 59–60.

[137] Beumer, *Henri Nouwen: A Restless Seeking for God*, 121–22.

Second, Nouwen's ethic was kenotic, within the tradition of the self-emptying and self-denying model of Jesus.[138] It is interesting to note that Nouwen's emphasis on social activism lessens after the mid-1980s. Beumer suggests that perhaps this is because social activism was not "in" as much in the last ten years of his life as it had been in the 1960s and 1970s.[139] Had Nouwen compromised on his commitment to social activism later in life just because the topic was not as central in the late 1980s and 1990s? Nouwen remained sensitive to the changing issues of the times in order to remain relevant. I do not believe, however, that Nouwen ever wandered from his commitment to the importance of offering one's self for the sake of others. Nouwen practiced such a commitment through his service and accountability to the Daybreak community, but he also moved on to other facets of spirituality which he saw a need to address in his writing.

Finally, it is important to note that Nouwen was more social and less political overall in his discussions. Nouwen had few opinions on political systems. He was quite outspoken on U.S. involvement in Nicaragua but the political systems involved were less important to him than the fact that U.S. money and weapons were being used to kill and destroy lives. More than anything, however, Nouwen constantly emphasized that peace was not possible without a spiritual anchor. Nouwen was less interested in what political systems were rising or falling than he was in whether Christians were being faithful in listening to God and obeying him in every facet of life, including their responsibility to their neighbors.[140] As Beumer observed, Nouwen observed the world scene not as an analyst but as a contemplative who emphasized the importance of seeing everything through the eyes of God.[141] The ultimate goal of social activism, for Nouwen, was to please God.[142]

The self-centered spirituality that characterizes many Americans in the 1980s and 1990s seems to point to the fact that some American Christians today are dangerously close to practicing a kind of modern gnosticism where the desire to know God and experience him results in a tendency to forget about or ignore one's obligation to love and care for others. Nouwen's thought concerning social activism is relevant and in keeping with the teachings of Scripture and the examples of many throughout the history of the Christian church, and it is a message that the American

[138] Ibid., 125.
[139] Ibid., 100.
[140] Ibid., 130–31.
[141] Ibid., 122–24.
[142] Ibid., 126–27.

church needs. American society is driven by the upward pull of success, prestige, and wealth. Nouwen's insistence upon downward mobility is not appealing from the worldly point of view and surely many of his American readers must squirm when forced to consider whether they truly will apply what he said. Nouwen admitted that he was never totally free from the upward pull himself, but his writings and his personal example offer a challenge to American Christians to live an authentic faith that recognizes that a "faith by itself, if it is not accompanied by action, is dead" (James 2:17).

Professional Ministry

"In Nouwen's thought, spirituality is not sharply divided between a clerical and a lay spirituality."[143] Nouwen believed that every Christian is called by God to be a minister; therefore, every Christian has the responsibility to listen to God and to be obedient.[144] All Christians who take this call to be ministers seriously can glean insight from what Nouwen had to say to professional ministers, and it seems fitting to conclude this chapter on Nouwen's thought concerning the relationship with others by exploring what Nouwen had to say about professional ministry.

In his earlier works, such as *Intimacy, Creative Ministry*, and *The Wounded Healer*, Nouwen concentrated on the more practical aspects of how ministers fulfill their role. Much of his advice in these works was very specific and very practical, related to preaching, teaching, pastoral care, counseling, and organizational duties. We will not explore these areas of practical instruction since much of what is written above in this chapter would apply to professional ministers as well in how to relate to others and meet their needs. Let us explore these early writings, however, to gain insight into what Nouwen believed to be the purpose, or role, of a minister.

Two metaphors express Nouwen's definition of what it means to be a minister. One metaphor is that of a bridge. Nouwen believed that the purpose of a minister was to "continuously make connections between the human story and the divine story."[145] Nouwen believed the challenge of ministry was to help people in very concrete situations of daily life see and experience their story as part of God's ongoing redemptive work in

[143] Durback, *Seeds of Hope*, xxxi.
[144] Nouwen, MacNeill, and Morrison, *Compassion*, 85; Nouwen, *Reaching Out*, 93–96.
[145] Nouwen, *Living Reminder*, 24–25.

the world.[146] In other words, the minister must communicate God's perspective through the truth of his Word and become the conduit through which God's unconditional love is expressed.[147]

Another metaphor that is applicable to Nouwen's view of a minister is that of a transparent role model. It is this model that is perhaps the most well known, as Nouwen used the phrase "wounded healer" as the title for one of his books. Referring to John 15:13, Nouwen believed that the Christian minister's purpose was to "lay down his life for his friends." Nouwen interpreted this to mean that every minister must allow his own life to become a guide and an example in the search for God. These two passages from different sources in his work illuminate the idea:

> Christian ministry is the ongoing attempt to put one's own search for God, with all the moments of pain and joy, despair and hope, at the disposal of those who want to join this search but do not know how.[148]

> The minister is called to recognize the sufferings of his time in his own heart and make that recognition the starting point of his service. . . . Thus, like Jesus, he who proclaims liberation is called not only to care for his own wounds and the wounds of others, but also to make his wounds into a major source of his healing power.[149]

Nouwen most certainly applied both of these models himself through his writing. He spoke directly to the human condition and attempted to connect God's story with the human story, helping his readers to understand their circumstances or their responsibilities in the light of God's will for his creation. Nouwen also exemplified the transparent guide who was willing to share his own journey for the sake of helping others on their own journeys.

Nouwen's later works addressed to ministers seemed to leave the more practical aspects of ministry behind as he focused on the spirituality of the minister. *Clowning in Rome, The Living Reminder, The Way of the Heart,* and *In the Name of Jesus* are the examples of this emphasis. In short, one could say that those themes of spirituality mentioned in the previous two chapters apply to ministers as well. Ministers must love God and nurture a relationship to him through the spiritual disciplines. Ministers must also learn to live out of their true selves and find their identity in the unconditional love of God. It is fitting to explore more fully, however, how Nouwen applied these truths to the life of one who is usually

[146] Ibid., 26.
[147] Nouwen, *In the Name of Jesus*, 44, 67–68.
[148] Nouwen, *Creative Ministry*, 114.
[149] Nouwen, *Wounded Healer*, xvi, 82–83.

tempted to focus solely on the work of meeting the spiritual needs of others.

First of all, ministers are not immune to the temptation of defining themselves by the world's standards. Nouwen underscored the necessity for ministers to understand who they are in light of God's perspective rather than their cultural milieu. Just as any Christian can get caught up in the compulsions of the false self, which are to be powerful, relevant, and spectacular, the minister can do the same. Nouwen wrote:

> Our society is not a community radiant with the love of Christ, but a dangerous network of domination and manipulation in which we can easily get entangled and lose our soul. The basic question is whether we ministers of Jesus Christ have not already been so deeply molded by the seductive powers of our dark world that we have become blind to our own and other people's fatal state and have lost the power and motivation to swim for our lives.[150]

Nouwen went on to express his concern that many ministers are "horrendously secular" because they are dependent upon their milieu to define who they are and what they should be about. Thus they strive for success, prestige, and the approval of others. They are compulsive and driven.[151] One minister wrote of what Nouwen taught him in this regard:

> My work on God's behalf must be rooted in God's love and grace. When it is thus rooted, my work will be neither compelled nor driven nor frantic. When it is thus rooted, I will once again find the balance, working with conviction and calm, trusting in God's purposes and ways.[152]

One does not have to look too closely into recent history to discover the numbers of prominent ministers who lost sight of their true identity as ministers and ended up exposed in shameful disgrace because they lived according to the compulsions of the false self. Such words are pertinent for American ministers today. The temptation to live according to the world's standards is just as strong for those called to be professional ministers as for anyone else. This is why Nouwen underscored the importance that ministers, of all people, must maintain an intimate relationship with God, which provides perspective and the power to be who they are called to be.

[150] Nouwen, *Way of the Heart*, 9.

[151] Ibid., 10.

[152] Arthur Boers, "Abide in Me," *The Other Side* 27 (January-February 1991): 13.

Nouwen constantly lamented the fact that ministers no longer receive enough spiritual formation in their seminary training, which he saw as one explanation for why many ministers lacked a deep and nurturing relationship with God. Many Roman Catholic seminaries had abandoned the routine of spiritual exercises because prayer was viewed as a way to avoid the burning issues of parish life. More attention was focused on practical pastoral training. Nouwen called this a "separation of professionalism and spirituality."[153] Nouwen wrote, "Education to ministry is an education not to master God but to be mastered by God."[154] "Seminary training should provide deep spiritual formation in the mind of Christ."[155] "It is sad that most ministers have more hours of training in how to talk and be with people than how to talk and be with God."[156]

> In no way am I trying to minimize or even to criticize the importance of training for the ministry. I am simply suggesting that this training will bear more fruit when it occurs in the context of a spirituality, a way of life in which we are primarily concerned, not to be with people but to be with God, not to walk in the presence of anyone who asks for our attention but to walk in the presence of God—a spirituality, in short, which helps us to distinguish service from our need to be liked, praised, or respected.[157]

Nouwen believed the separation of professionalism and spirituality, which ministers were inadvertently taught in seminary, resulted in ministers who prayed little and worked much. Nouwen suggested that such a lifestyle was to blame for many of the frustrations and disappointments in ministry.[158] Nouwen saw too many ministers treating prayer and service as if they were mutually exclusive. To them, there was no time to pray. There was too much to do, too many expectations, and too many needs. Nouwen addressed this dichotomy by reminding ministers of what their primary vocation was. It was not to meet the needs of people, but to be obedient to God, living constantly in his presence and listening to his voice. Nouwen viewed Jesus as the primary role model for ministers in this respect in that Jesus' relationship with the Father was the "center, beginning and end of his ministry."[159] He wrote:

[153] Nouwen, *Creative Ministry*, xvii.
[154] Nouwen, *Reaching Out*, 104.
[155] Nouwen, *In the Name of Jesus*, 69.
[156] Nouwen, *Living Reminder*, 69.
[157] Ibid., 30.
[158] Nouwen, *Creative Ministry*, xvii.
[159] Nouwen, *Living Reminder*, 50–51.

It seems in fact we live as if we should give as much of our heart, soul and mind as possible to our fellow human beings, while trying hard not to forget God. At least we feel that our attention should be divided evenly between God and our neighbor. But Jesus' claim is much more radical. He asks for single-minded commitment to God and God alone. God wants all of our heart, all of our mind, all of our soul. It is this unconditional and unreserved love for God that leads to the care for our neighbor, not as an activity which distracts us from God or competes with our attention to God, but an expression of our love for God who reveals himself to us as the God of all people. It is in God that we find our neighbors and discover our responsibility to them.[160]

Such words sound good, but are they practical? How much prayer is enough so that one is obeying God and not working out of one's own egotistical strength? How does a minister justify time away from the demands that cry for attention? Nouwen addressed two misconceptions about the relationship between service and prayer that help to answer these questions. First, Nouwen insisted that prayer was not for the purpose of "charging up" in order to be able to do ministry. Nouwen believed it was important to view prayer itself as ministry. Ministry is taking place when ministers are alone with God.[161] Prayer is a vital part of a minister's responsibilities. Nouwen wrote, "We ought to schedule our time with God with the same realism that we schedule our time with people."[162] Prayer is ministry.

The second misconception about ministry and prayer that Nouwen addressed is the illusion of indispensability.[163] Ministers tend to think that the demands of their service to others make it impossible for them to get away for seasons of prayer. Yet Nouwen argued that a certain unavailability for the purpose of prayer is indispensable. Prayer is essential for the life of the minister and the fruitfulness of his service. If a minister lives as if he has no time for prayer, his ministry is based on his own wisdom and his own strength. This was not to imply that ministers should not be involved in the lives of people or that society should be abandoned to its many struggles. Nouwen simply reminded ministers that they were not capable of meeting every need, of solving every problem, or saving every life that was teetering on the edge of disaster. Prayer, therefore, gives the minister the ability to discern those activities with which God desires his

[160] Ibid., 31.
[161] Ibid., 51.
[162] Ibid., 54.
[163] Ibid., 49.

or her involvement for the glory of God and those activities that are "primarily for the glory of our unconverted ego."[164] Nouwen also reminded ministers that it was only through prayer that a minister could receive a restful heart through which others will be drawn to God.

> It is this restful heart that will attract those who are groping to find their way through life. When we have found our rest in God we can do nothing other than minister. God's rest will be visible wherever we go and whoever we meet. And before we speak any words, the Spirit of God, praying in us, will make his presence known and gather people into a new body, the body of Christ himself.[165]

Nouwen reminded ministers that ministry is not about results or success or impressing those they serve. Ministry is about knowing God first and foremost and then becoming a bridge or a guide so that others might know him, too. Nouwen summarized this thought best in a speech he made about Christian leadership in the twenty-first century: "For the future of Christian leadership it is of vital importance to reclaim the mystical aspect of theology so that every word spoken, every advice given, and every strategy developed can come from a heart that knows God intimately."[166]

Nouwen's words about prayer and ministry ring true when measured against the life of Jesus. Of course, it is one thing to say such words and it is another thing to do them, because Jesus sets the highest of standards and no human can fully measure up. Nouwen struggled to make prayer a priority in his own busy, hectic ministry. He understood the pressures of the demands and expectations of those to whom he ministered. He admitted he was not perfect in living out what he believed to be true. But he pointed to the one servant who did live it perfectly. One has only to read the Gospel of Luke to discover how many times Jesus taught about the importance of prayer to his disciples and how many times his own habit of prayer is described. Jesus' primary relationship with God was the heartbeat of his mission. Everything he did was out of obedience to the One who loved him and sent him. Such a tightly knit relationship prevented Jesus from being distracted by the many opportunities around him that could have caused a deviation from his Father's plan. This relationship also prevented Jesus from giving in to the temptation to be what others wanted him to be instead of what his Father required. His disciples desired a liberator, a king, a revolutionary who would bring temporal

---

[164] Nouwen, *Way of the Heart*, 72.
[165] Ibid., 73.
[166] Nouwen, *In the Name of Jesus*, 30.

independence for their people. Jesus knew the plan was far beyond what they could imagine because he knew the heart of his Father. His relationship with God the Father was central to everything.

One can also see the influence of the Desert Fathers on Nouwen in regard to ministry and a relationship with God nurtured by prayer. The desert monks ministered to those who sought them and they also ministered to each other. They believed their relationship with God in prayer gave them the wisdom and discernment needed for their service to others. They were extreme in their commitment to place knowing God above all other desires or demands so that their lives might be truly fruitful when it came to ministering to others.[167]

Nouwen's instructions to professional ministers are intensely relevant for those ministering in the modern American churches. Ministers, like their flocks, tend to live according to the mores of their culture, which promote success, prestige, accomplishment, and a work ethic that has no time to waste time. Their own expectations and the expectations of others do not easily incorporate the disciplines of prayer and solitude and silence. Yet Christian leaders cannot lead others where they have not been. A Christian spirituality that is mature and has depth cannot develop within the American Christian community unless there are those who can fulfill the role of spiritual guides for the journey.

Conclusion

Nouwen obviously had a great deal to say about the spiritual relationship between a Christian and other human beings. Nouwen believed loving others was most assuredly the obligation and the privilege of the follower of Christ. In the discussion of every theme, Nouwen pointed back to the example and inspiration of Jesus as the one who demonstrated best how to love others.

Woven into every theme about loving others is the reminder that one's relationship with God and with self are intimately connected to the ability to love others well. Whether clergy or laity, all believers must base all other facets of the Christian life on a deep and abiding relationship with God. This brings the discussion of Nouwen's spirituality back to the place where we began. The circle is complete.

---

[167] See the stories contained in *The Desert Fathers*, trans. from the Latin with an introduction by Helen Waddell (New York: Vintage Books, 1998, originally published London: Constable, 1936).

CHAPTER SIX

◈

Nouwen's Legacy for Modern American Spirituality

M ichael Downey wrote in *Understanding Christian Spirituality*:

The history of Christian spirituality is less about neat development of truths and insights over the course of time, and more about the stumbling and sometimes erratic efforts of particular individuals who tried, sometimes by fits and starts in the mess of their own history, to live in Christ by the presence of the Spirit. Spirituality in history is a story of flesh and blood people who lived lives that only later generations came to see as smooth sailing down an easy street called the spiritual life.[1]

Henri Nouwen was by no means a perfect saint. As Philip Sheldrake wrote, "Saints belong to, and reflect, the societies which produce and honor them. . . . All models are relative and can never exhaust the possible forms of Christian holiness."[2] This study does reveal, however, one man who did try to live the Christian life with passion and who managed to write about his experiences in such a way that many Americans read his work and were influenced by it. After having explored a brief history of American spirituality as well as the life of Henri Nouwen and his thought concerning Christian spirituality, what conclusions can be drawn concerning his place and significance for Christian spirituality in America?

General Characteristics of Nouwen's Spirituality

First, Nouwen's spirituality was *relational* in that he focused on the relationships that make up the spiritual life of a human being: the rela-

[1] Downey, *Understanding Christian Spirituality*, 64.
[2] Sheldrake, *Spirituality and History*, 93.

tionship with God, with self, and with others. Nouwen consistently underscored the fact that one's relationship with God is the foundation for all other relationships. Nouwen did not dictate lists of ways in which his readers must change in order to be better Christians. Nouwen emphasized the necessity to allow one's relationship with God to transform one, which, in turn, transforms one's relationship with self and with others.

Nouwen's spirituality was *biblical* in that the primary authority to which he appealed for the support of his thought about Christian spirituality was the Bible. Nouwen used Scripture in a variety of ways to illustrate his thought and made application of the Scripture for the contemporary reader. The Bible was not his only source of support and illustration, but it was by far the most prominent one, especially in his later works. This leads to the next point in that Nouwen's spirituality was *christological*. Jesus was the primary role model to which he appealed again and again in order to illustrate his spirituality. Thus Nouwen's spirituality was *orthodox* in the sense that his teachings were in keeping with the teachings of Christ and the rest of Scripture. Nouwen's Roman Catholic background is evident in his writings, but he wrote from within the mainstream of Christianity.

Nouwen's spirituality was also *historical*, or *traditional*, in that he drew some of his thought not only from Scripture but also from the lives and writings of other Christian saints throughout the history of the church. His focus was especially strong on the Desert Fathers and Mothers.

Nouwen's spirituality was certainly *contemporary* in that he did not dwell on the "good old days" of long ago but tried to address the contemporary circumstances of contemporary Christians. His background in psychology made him especially able to communicate with a modern generation accustomed to speaking about life in psychological terms. Perhaps it could be said that psychological language is the vernacular of most modern Americans. Nouwen also spoke about the Christian life within the context of modern temptations and difficulties. Nouwen attempted to speak to current circumstances with practical implications about what it meant to be a Christian in the late twentieth century.

Nouwen's spirituality was definitely *integrated*, or *holistic*. Nouwen spoke to all aspects of daily life and all relationships. Life was not compartmentalized for Nouwen. To speak about the spiritual life was to speak about the whole of life. Nouwen's spirituality was also *balanced* in that he insisted the Christian life is a life that exercises spiritual disciplines for the purpose of allowing God's transforming power to work. Nouwen was not, however, ascetic or austere in his teachings about the disciplines of the Christian life. In fact, Nouwen did not have a great deal to say about those disciplines which might be perceived as particularly extreme, such as fasting and voluntary poverty.

Nouwen's spirituality was *ecumenical* in that people from all of the various traditions of the Christian faith could relate to his thought and glean useful insights from his perspectives on the spiritual journey. Nouwen was not universal in the sense that people from any religion could easily apply all of his thought to their own faith. Nouwen did try to be sensitive to those of other faiths and was not overtly critical of other faiths, but his writings are distinctively Christian in their orientation. Within the Christian faith, however, Nouwen was particularly adept at crossing the boundaries of traditions without diluting his own story and his own tradition. Although Nouwen was Roman Catholic, much of what he said is just as applicable to a Protestant who might disagree strongly with some of his theology. Nouwen had a knack for sharing to the fullest extent from the richness of his Roman Catholic heritage regarding spirituality, but he did not raise many red flags on the issues of possible controversy. After all, there is much held in common across the various traditions and all of them would agree with the need to emphasize loving God and loving others as much as oneself. Nouwen was also especially helpful in bringing together the common features between East and West. Nouwen helped many of his readers discover the rich diversity that is evident among the various Christian traditions, yet he never advocated a rootless spirituality that has no place to call home. Nouwen was Roman Catholic but he believed he had something to offer to Protestants, including evangelicals, and he believed they had something to offer him.

Nouwen's spirituality was *experiential* and *personal*. Nouwen used his own personal experiences to teach lessons about the spiritual journey. His was not a spirituality that was totally subjective. He based his appraisal of his experience on the life and teachings of Jesus and he certainly advocated certain truths that are applicable to all who are committed to the Christian way of life. Yet Nouwen recognized the personal and unique nature of every human being's experiences. He shared his own experiences in the hope that others could relate in some way and glean insights into their own journeys.

Nouwen's spirituality was both *idealistic* and *realistic*. Nouwen pointed to Jesus as the ideal model of the Christian life and he advocated certain characteristics of the Christian life that are to be pursued by all who claimed to follow Christ. Yet Nouwen was no pie-in-the-sky, ivory-tower prophet who ignored the real struggles of fallen human beings caught in the quagmire of a fallen and broken world. Nouwen, instead, often acknowledged the reality of suffering and encouraged his readers to face their struggles, even embrace them, for the purpose of knowing and understanding God more, and he insisted that Christians should speak out against the forces of evil at work in society.

Because of his insistence on both prayer and activism, Nouwen's spirituality was both *contemplative* and *active*. Nouwen was more of a contemplative in that he believed prayer must have priority and be the spring from which activity in the world draws its direction and strength. Nouwen admitted the difficult struggle in his own life to make prayer the priority but he continually challenged his readers to grow first and foremost in the discipline of communion with God in prayer. Another way to say it is that Nouwen's spirituality was apostolic, not monastic. He emphasized the importance of ministry in the world, but it was a ministry that had to be immersed in prayer so that the ministry accomplished would be a fruitful ministry that was in accordance with the will of God.

Finally, Nouwen's spirituality was both *communal* and *individualistic*. Nouwen emphasized the importance of community because American society tended toward individualism and isolation. Yet individualism was also present in Nouwen's spirituality in that every Christian is responsible for a personal relationship with God that has to be nurtured as well as the relationship to the community of believers. Every person's journey is unique and yet every believer has a responsibility for and a need for the community. Yet Nouwen's emphasis on community was conspicuously lacking in a specific focus on the role of the institutional church, Roman Catholic or otherwise.

Given a general sense of Nouwen's spirituality, how did his particular life, which was lived at a particular time in history, affect the particular circumstances surrounding American spirituality during the years when he lived and worked in North America? Is Nouwen significant for American spirituality? If so, why?

Nouwen's Significance for American Spirituality

Nouwen's significance is grounded first in the fact that many people, including family, friends, colleagues, students, and his remarkable and loving flock at Daybreak, loved him and were profoundly influenced by his life. In spite of his quirks and idiosyncrasies, his woundedness and his neediness, Nouwen was a human being who had a wondrous ability to love others and to help them see that they were loved even more by God. In light of the spirituality that Nouwen himself embraced, his love for God and his love for others is eternal and significant regardless of his successes as a professor, author, and internationally known speaker.

Yet Nouwen is also significant because he willingly recorded something of his own spiritual experiences and his thought on the spiritual life. In North America alone, Nouwen sold over one and one-half million copies of his books. This alone places Nouwen within a small circle of Christian leaders who have made an impact on American spirituality. But the final question remains as to why so many Americans responded to his message. What was it about Nouwen's spirituality that caused so many to desire his friendship, to be his students, to listen to his lectures, and to read his books?

As was described in chapter 1, American spirituality began to move in the 1960s from a "dwelling-oriented" spirituality to a "seeking-oriented" spirituality. Nouwen sensed the intense spiritual thirst of many Americans but he also sensed their rootlessness as many of them left the "dwelling" of the institutional church. Nouwen recognized that there was a need for Christian spiritual leaders who could be spiritual guides and help those on a spiritual quest to make sense of the Christian faith in light of the cultural convulsions of the late twentieth century. What made him so effective in fulfilling this role? I believe his effectiveness was founded in his ability both to challenge American culture and to accommodate it.

To begin with, one of Nouwen's distinct advantages by way of accommodation was his understanding of the psychology of religion. Late-twentieth-century Americans tend to understand life and relationships in psychological terms. This does not mean that Nouwen catered to their narcissistic tendencies but that Nouwen had the capability to help many Americans realign their worldview into one that was authentically Christian. He accomplished this by explaining the Christian life in relational terms and by asking the psychological questions that many Americans were asking, such as who am I? Who is God? What is my purpose for being?

Nouwen's significance is not in that he told Americans what they wanted to hear. He was not a self-help guru who used the principles of Christianity to help Americans indulge themselves in another self-centered quick fix of instant gratification. His significance is that he understood American culture and the way Americans think, and he managed to be a bridge, a translator of the authentic Christian life in the midst of their culture. Nouwen answered the major questions about the meaning and purpose of life from the perspective of the Christian faith. Annice Callahan wrote, "His prophetic voice speaks in a special way to North Americans. In our technological era when busyness and frenetic energy fill our lives, he invites us to attend to matters of the heart, namely our relationship with ourselves, God, and others."[3]

A second aspect that contributed to Nouwen's unique ability to relate to the American culture was his accessibility. Thomas Merton will remain perhaps the most influential voice of the twentieth century in the area of Christian spirituality. He was a literary and philosophical genius as well as a contemplative and a social critic. Nouwen's style of communication was more simple and direct. He never used long or complicated arguments and his books were short monographs for the most part. I do not mean to imply that he lacked depth or was rudimentary. On the contrary, Nouwen's messages were challenging and creative. Yet Nouwen's work appealed to a wide variety of readers because they could easily grasp his messages and find their own story in reading his.

Nouwen's accommodation is also seen in the fact that his work was well received by Christians from both the Roman Catholic and Protestant traditions. Nouwen managed to keep his messages directed towards the fundamental essence of what it meant to live the Christian life and refused to get caught up in controversial issues.

Yet Nouwen's significance for modern American spirituality lies not only in his accommodation to American culture but also in the fact that Nouwen challenged the very fabric of modern American culture by challenging its value system. In a time when most Americans defined themselves by what they did, what they possessed, and who they could impress, Nouwen reminded them that their innate value was based on the fact that they were God's creations, truly loved and truly valued simply because they were children of God. Nouwen cautioned Americans that self-identity based on the compulsions of the false self would never fulfill the desire of the human heart to be loved unconditionally. But the true self, confident and assured of God's love, is truly free to live an abundant and fruitful life that is not centered on self but on God and one's neighbor.

At a time when secularism wanted to eliminate the existence of God, Nouwen was writing and speaking about truly experiencing the reality of God in the stillness of prayer. Only in that deep and intimate relationship with God through Jesus Christ could one truly come to know the truth about the meaning and purpose of life. Nouwen was not an apologist for the existence of God, but he helped Americans to understand how to nurture their relationship with God in a time when many did not know how. Many of the churches were still attempting to relate to peo-

---

[3] Annice Callahan, *Spiritualities of the Heart* (New York: Paulist Press, 1990), 211.

ple as if they still operated within a "dwelling-oriented" paradigm of spirituality. When young people began to question everyone in authority, Nouwen pointed them inward and taught them to listen to their own hearts and to hear the voice of God speaking to them there. No amount of power or success or productivity could satisfy the desire to know God and be known by Him.

Nouwen also challenged the competitive and hostile nature of American society by teaching the way of compassion. Nouwen knew that people naturally react to one another out of fear because the compulsions of the false self are so strong. Yet if they could somehow begin to understand the first love of God and allow that love to transform them from the inside out, then they could learn to love others in a truly compassionate way.

Nouwen also called Christian churches in America to accountability by pointing out the disturbing reality that many American churches are just as much captives of their culture as those they are trying to reach. They are not transforming culture. Instead they are themselves being conformed by its worldly mold. Nouwen called the Christian community to be a catalyst for the transformation of society as they allowed God to transform them through prayer for the purpose of service. In an era when the flowering interest in spirituality could serve to distort or dilute Christianity, Nouwen called American Christians back to an authentic Christian worldview which has as its center the mandate to love God with all that we are and to love others with a love that has its source in God.

The last thirty years in America have produced a generation that chose to leave the status quo of religion behind and try to make its own way spiritually in a world that was all too quickly overwhelming the soul. Like the prodigal son, some Americans are wondering if they can ever come home, not home to a particular church, but home to the Father who is beyond all human machinations. In the cafeteria of spiritual options available to such seekers, Nouwen communicated an authentic and relevant expression of the Christian life without the attitude of an authoritarian. Nouwen did not threaten or manipulate. He invited those who would listen to understand the Christian life as he understood it. The Christian life is not about "shoulds" and "oughts." Nouwen gently and persuasively invited people to accept the simple yet profound gift of God's love and to allow that loving relationship to transform all other relationships.

At the death of Henri Nouwen, Americans, as well as the rest of the world, lost a significant spiritual guide. His loss is deeply felt by those who knew him and those who read him. Nouwen was not perfect. His transparency concerning his own struggles could make a person uncomfortable at times. But the value of a guide is found in his or her ability to meet you where you are, to understand how you got there, and to lead you to where you need to be. Nouwen was a spiritual guide who was well acquainted with the struggle of the spiritual journey but he had also glimpsed the hope of living in the light of God's love. Inasmuch as he longed deeply to know the love of God for himself, he longed for others to know this surpassing love as well. He spent the majority of his life trying to point the way and he continues to do so through his writings. This is Henri Nouwen's spiritual legacy.

Selected Bibliography

Primary Sources

Nouwen, Henri. Collection of papers, published and unpublished. Yale Divinity School Library, New Haven, Ct.

Books

Nouwen, Henri. *Intimacy: Essays in Pastoral Psychology*. San Francisco: HarperSanFrancisco, 1969.

———. *Creative Ministry*. New York: Doubleday Image Books, 1971.

———. *The Wounded Healer: Ministry in Contemporary Society*. New York: Doubleday Image Books, 1972.

———. *With Open Hands*. Notre Dame: Ave Maria Press, 1972. Rev. ed. 1995.

———. *Aging: The Fulfillment of Life*. New York: Doubleday Image Books, 1974.

———. *Out of Solitude: Three Meditations on the Christian Life*. Notre Dame: Ave Maria Press, 1974.

———. *Reaching Out: The Three Movements of the Spiritual Life*. New York: Doubleday, 1975.

———. *The Genesee Diary: Report from a Trappist Monastery*. New York: Doubleday, 1976.

———. *Clowning in Rome: Reflections on Solitude, Celibacy, Prayer and Contemplation*. Westminster, Md.: Christian Classics, 1979.

———. *In Memoriam*. Notre Dame: Ave Maria Press, 1980.

———. *A Cry for Mercy: Prayers from the Genesee*. Maryknoll, N.Y.: Orbis Books, 1981.

———. *The Living Reminder: Service and Prayer in Memory of Jesus Christ*. San Francisco: HarperSanFrancisco, 1981.

———. *Making All Things New: An Invitation to the Spiritual Life*. San Francisco: HarperSanFrancisco, 1981.

———. *Thomas Merton: Contemplative Critic*. Liguori, Mo.: Triumph Books, 1981.

———. *The Way of the Heart: Desert Spirituality and Contemporary Ministry*. New York: Ballantine Books, 1981.

Nouwen, Henri, Donald P. MacNeill, and Douglas A. Morrison. *Compassion: A Reflection on the Christian Life*. New York: Doubleday Image Books, 1982.

Nouwen, Henri. *A Letter of Consolation*. San Francisco: HarperSanFrancisco, 1982.

———. *¡Gracias!: A Latin American Journal*. San Francisco: Harper and Row, 1983.

———. *Love in a Fearful Land: A Guatemalan Story*. Notre Dame: Ave Maria Press, 1985.

155

————. *Lifesigns: Intimacy, Fecundity, and Ecstasy in Christian Perspective*. New York: Doubleday Image Books, 1986.

————. *Behold the Beauty of the Lord: Praying with Icons*. Notre Dame: Ave Maria Press, 1987.

————. *Letters to Marc About Jesus*. San Francisco: HarperSanFrancisco, 1988.

————. *The Road to Daybreak: A Spiritual Journey*. New York: Doubleday Image Books, 1988.

————. *Heart Speaks to Heart*. Notre Dame: Ave Maria Press, 1989.

————. *In the Name of Jesus: Reflections on Christian Leadership*. New York: Crossroad Publishing Company, 1989.

————. *Beyond the Mirror: Reflections on Death and Life*. New York: Crossroad Publishing Company, 1990.

————. *Walk with Jesus: Stations of the Cross*. Maryknoll, N.Y.: Orbis Books, 1990.

————. *Life of the Beloved: Spiritual Living in a Secular World*. New York: Crossroad Publishing Company, 1992.

————. *The Return of the Prodigal Son: A Story of Homecoming*. New York: Doubleday Image Books, 1992.

————. *Jesus and Mary: Finding Our Sacred Center*. Cincinnati: St. Anthony Messenger Press, 1993.

————. *Here and Now: Living in the Spirit*. New York: Crossroad Publishing Company, 1994.

————. *Our Greatest Gift: A Meditation on Dying and Caring*. San Francisco: HarperSanFrancisco, 1994.

————. *With Burning Hearts: A Meditation on the Eucharistic Life*. Maryknoll, N.Y.: Orbis Books, 1994.

————. *The Path of Freedom*. New York: Crossroad Publishing Company, 1995.

————. *The Path of Peace*. New York: Crossroad Publishing Company, 1995.

————. *The Path of Power*. New York: Crossroad Publishing Company, 1995.

————. *The Path of Waiting*. New York: Crossroad Publishing Company, 1995.

————. *Can You Drink the Cup?* Notre Dame: Ave Maria Press, 1996.

————. *The Inner Voice of Love: A Journey Through Anguish to Freedom*. New York: Doubleday, 1996.

————. *Ministry and Spirituality: Creative Ministry, The Wounded Healer, Reaching Out*. New York: Continuum, 1996.

————. *Spiritual Journals: Genesee Diary, ¡Gracias!, The Road to Daybreak*. New York: Continuum, 1997.

————. *Adam: God's Beloved*. Maryknoll, N.Y.: Orbis Books, 1997.

————. *Bread for the Journey: A Daybook of Wisdom and Faith*. San Francisco: HarperSanFrancisco, 1997.

————. *The Sabbatical Journey*. New York: Crossroad Publishing Company, 1998.

Collections (Readers)

Dear, John, ed. *The Road to Peace*. Maryknoll, N.Y.: Orbis Books, 1998.

Durback, Robert, ed. *Seeds of Hope: A Henri Nouwen Reader*. New York: Bantam Books, 1989. Rev. ed. 1997.

Garvey, John, ed. *Henri Nouwen*, The Modern Spirituality Series. Springfield, Ill.: Templegate Publishers, 1988.

Johna, F., ed. *Show Me the Way: Readings for Each Day of Lent.* New York: Crossroad Publishing Company, 1992.

Jonas, Robert A., ed. *Henri Nouwen: Writings Selected with an Introduction by Robert A. Jonas.* Maryknoll, N.Y.: Orbis Books, 1998.

Articles

Nouwen, Henri. "Training for Campus Ministry." *Pastoral Psychology* 18 (March 1969): 27–38.

———. "Finding the Friendly Space." *The Episcopalian* (June 1973): 8–10, 44.

———. "The Gift of Solitude." *Faith/At/Work* 89 (April 1976): 28–29.

———. "Drawing Closer to God and Man." *The Sign*, May 1976, 10–16.

———. "Solitude and Intimacy in the Family." *A.D. Correspondence* 13 (31 July 1976): 1–6.

———. "Called to Be Hosts." *Faith/At/Work* 89 (September 1976): 30–31.

———. "Living the Questions: The Spirituality of the Religious Teacher." *Union Seminary Quarterly Review* 32 (Fall 1976): 17–24.

———. "Reflections on Political Ministry." *Network Quarterly* 4 (Fall 1976): A1–2.

———. "Disappearing from the World." *The Sign*, November 1976, 5–7.

———. "Compassion: the Core of Spiritual Leadership." *Worship* 51 (January 1977): 11–23.

———. "What Do You Know By Heart?" *Sojourners* 6 (August 1977): 14–16.

———. "Compassion in a Callous World." *Sojourners* 6 (September 1977): 15–18.

———. "Not Without Confrontation." *Sojourners* 6 (October 1977): 9.

———. "The Authority of Suffering." *Sojourners* 6 (November 1977): 10.

———. "Five Faculty Views on the University's Mission." *Yale University Journal*, November 1977, 10–11.

———. "Voluntary Displacement." *Sojourners* 6 (December 1977): 15.

———. "The Poverty of 'No Control.'" *Sojourners* 7 (January 1978): 11.

———. "Solitude and the Community." *Worship* 52 (January 1978): 13–23.

———. "The Faces of Community." *The Catholic Worker*, March–April 1978, 3, 7.

Nouwen, Henri, with Donald MacNeill and Douglas Morrison. "The Parish As a Community of Compassion: A Style of Pastoral Leadership." *St. Luke's Journal of Theology* 21 (March 1978): 89–101.

Nouwen, Henri. "Anchored in God Through Prayer." *Sojourners* 7 (April 1978): 20–21.

———. "Contemplation and Ministry." *Sojourners* 7 (June 1978): 9–12.

———. "Celibacy." *Pastoral Psychology* 27 (Winter 1978): 79–90.

———. "The Hell of Mercy." *Sojourners* 7 (December 1978): 19.

———. "Solitude." *Sojourners* 8 (March 1979): 20–23.

———. "Letting Go of All Things." *Sojourners* 8 (May 1979): 5–6.

———. "The Monk and the Cripple: Toward a Spirituality of Ministry." *America* 142 (15 March 1980): 205–10.

———. "The Desert Counsel to Flee the World." *Sojourners* 9 (June 1980): 14–18.

———. "Silence, The Portable Cell." *Sojourners* 9 (July 1980): 22–26.

———. "Descend with the Mind into the Heart." *Sojourners* 9 (August 1980): 20–24.

———. "As I See It: Our God Is a God Who Cares." *Church Leaders Bulletin for Laity and Clergy* 25 (Fall 1980): 1–5.

———. "What Is the Goal of Spiritual Growth? Moving from Absurdity to Obedience." *Faith/At/Work* 93 (September–October 1980): 7.

———. "Spiritual Direction." *Reflection*, January 1981, 7–8.

———. "Encounter in Solitude." *Sign*, February 1981, 10–17.

———. "The Selfless Way of Christ." *Sojourners* 10 (June 1981): 12–15.

———. "Temptation." *Sojourners* 10 (July 1981): 25–27.

———. "A Self-Emptied Heart." *Sojourners* 10 (August 1981): 20–22.

———. "Spiritual Direction." *Worship* 55 (September 1981): 399–404.

———. "Where You Would Not Rather Go." *The Princeton Seminary Bulletin* 3 (1982): 237–39.

———. "Prayer and Peacemaking." *Catholic Agitator*, December 1982, 4–6.

———. "Reflections of Fr. Henri Nouwen After a Month in Nicaragua." *Mercy on Your People, Lord* newsletter, July 1983, 1–2.

———. "Henri Nouwen's Plea for Nicaragua." *National Catholic Reporter* 19 (August 26, 1983): 9–11.

———. "We Drink from Our Own Wells." *America* 149 (15 October 1983): 205–208.

———. "Christ of the Americas." *America* 150 (21 April 1984): 293–302.

———. "Prayer Embraces the World." *Maryknoll*, April 1985, 17–21.

———. "Creating True Intimacy." *Sojourners* 14 (June 1985): 14–18.

———. "Bearing the Fruit of the Spirit." *Sojourners* 14 (July 1985): 26–30.

———. "Living in Joyful Ecstasy" *Sojourners* 14 (August–September 1985): 27–31.

———. "Prayer and Resistance: A Spirituality of Peacemaking." *Harvard Divinity Bulletin* 16 (October–November 1985): 5–7, 10.

———. "Saying 'No' to Death in All Its Manifestations." *New Oxford Review* 52 (October 1985): 10–18.

———. "Saying a Humble, Compassionate, & Joyful 'Yes' to Life." *New Oxford Review* 52 (November 1985): 19–26.

———. "The Spirituality of Peacemaking." *The Lutheran* 1 (5 February 1986): 12–14.

———. "The Holy Obligation of Peacemaking." *The Lutheran* 1 (19 February 1986): 14–15.

———. "Working for Peace." *The Lutheran* 1 (5 March 1986): 10–11.

———. "The Fullness of Divine Love." *Sojourners* 15 (June 1986): 24–27.

———. "Running from What We Desire." *Partnership* (July–August 1986): 32–35.

———. "A New Life Among the Handicapped." *New Oxford Review* 53 (September 1986): 5–13.

———. "The Trusting Heart and the Primacy of the Mystical Life." *New Oxford Review* 53 (October 1986): 5–14.

————. "Orthodox Downward Mobility or Secularist Prosperity?" *New Oxford Review* 53 (November 1986): 7–15.

————. "Coping with Distractions." *New Oxford Review* 53 (December 1986): 5–9.

————. "Christ's Simultaneous Absence and Presence." *New Oxford Review* 54 (January–February 1987): 4–7.

————. "A Spirituality of Waiting." *Weavings* 2 (January–February 1987): 6–17.

————. "The Journey from Despair to Hope." *Praying*, no. 17 (March–April 1987): 4–7.

————. "The Most Profound Basis of All Human Flesh." *New Oxford Review* 54 (March 1987): 15–18.

————. "To Meet the Body is to Meet the Word." *New Oxford Review* 54 (April 1987): 3–7.

————. "The Extraordinary Witness of Marthe Robin." *New Oxford Review* 54 (May 1987): 4–10.

————. "Trying to Avoid Temptations When Among the Famous and Successful." *New Oxford Review* 54 (June 1987): 9–14.

————. "L'Arche and the World." *Letters of L'Arche*, nos. 53 and 54 (September–December 1987): 29–33.

————. "Spirituality and the Family." *Weavings* 3 (January–February 1988): 6–13.

————. "The Peace That Is Not of This World." *Weavings* 3 (March–April 1988): 23–34.

————. "Adam's Peace." *World Vision* (August–September 1988): 4–7.

————. "A Glimpse Behind the Mirror: Reflections on Death and Life." *Weavings* 4 (November–December 1989): 13–23.

————. "Acceptance of God's Will." *Dictionary of Pastoral Care and Counseling*, ed. Rodney J. Hunter (Nashville: Abingdon Press, 1990): 466–467.

————. "Finding Vocation in Downward Mobility." *Leadership* 11 (Summer 1990): 60–61.

————. "Living in the Center Enables Us to Care." *Health Progress*, July–August 1990, 52–54.

————. "A Sudden Trip to Lourdes." *New Oxford Review* 57 (September 1990): 7–13.

————. "Hidden Treasures in Our Lives." *Praying*, no. 39 (November/December 1990): 5–8.

————. "Tidings of Great Joy: Every Day is a Holy-Day." *News from Celebration* (December 1990): 1, 3–4.

————. "Story Demonstrates True Meaning of Compassion." *The Liberal*, 13 March 1991, B8.

————. "Unchanged by the World." *Sojourners* 20 (August–September 1991): 28–29.

————. "A Time to Mourn, A Time to Dance." *Catholic New Times* 16 (15 March 1992): 8–9.

————. "Forgiveness: The Name of Love in a Wounded World." *Weavings* 7 (March–April 1992): 7–15.

———. "The Freedom to Dance." *Catholic New Times* 16 (12 April 1992): 3.

———. "The Duet of the Holy Spirit: When Mourning and Dancing Are One." *New Oxford Review* 59 (June 1992): 5–12.

———. "The Beloved of God." *Sojourners* 21 (October 1992): 22–23.

———. "All Is Grace." *Weavings* 7 (November–December 1992): 38–41.

———. "Finding the Trapeze Artist in the Priest." *New Oxford Review* 60 (June 1993): 8–14.

———. "Living in Deep Gratitude." *The Lutheran* 6 (June 1993): 14, 16.

———. "The Vulnerable God." *Weavings* 8 (July–August 1993): 28–35.

———. "Touching Stone: The Sculpture of Steve Jenkinson." *Image*, no. 4 (Fall 1993): 14–22.

———. "Going Home." *Faith/At/Work* 106 (Winter 1993): 16–18.

———. "Power, Powerlessness and Power." *Letters of L'Arche*, no. 78 (December 1993): 2–5.

———. "A Picnic on a Tombstone and Other Reflections." *New Oxford Review* 61 (March 1994): 9–15.

———. "Reborn from Above." *St. Angela News*, 19 March 1994, 8.

———. "Pilgrimage to the Christian East." *New Oxford Review* 61 (April 1994): 11–17.

———. "Moving from Solitude to Community to Ministry." *Leadership* 16 (Spring 1995): 81–87.

———. "We the Beloved: On Accepting the Love of God." *Therefore . . .* , May 1997, 1–8.

Interview Articles

Nouwen, Henri. "Prayer and Ministry." *Sisters Today*, February 1977, 345–55.

———. "A Visit with Henri Nouwen." Interview by Todd Brennan. *The Critic*, Summer 1978, 42–49.

———. "The Spiritual Life." Interview by Charles Angell. *A.D. 1979*, March 1979, 16–18.

———. "Can You Be Intimate with More Than One Person?" Interview by Edward Wakin. *U.S. Catholic*, July 1979, 6, 8–10.

———. "Henri Nouwen." *Haelan*, Fall 1980, 16–19.

———. "The Parish . . . A Safe Place to Face Our Pain." *Alban Institute Action Information*, January–February 1981, 1–5.

———. "A Ministry of Presence." *Alban Institute Action Information*, March–April 1981, 8–11.

———. "A Quality of Heart." Interview by John Garvey. *Notre Dame Magazine*, December 1981, 29–32.

———. "A Conversation with Henri J. M. Nouwen." Interview in *Living with Apocalypse: Spiritual Resources for Social Compassion*, ed. Tilden H. Edwards. San Francisco: Harper and Row, 1984.

———. "Spirituality and Ministry." *pmc*, Spring 1987, 11–13.

———. "Father Henri Nouwen on Growing Spiritually." Interview by Mitch Finley, part 1. *Our Sunday Visitor*, 18 December 1988, 7.

————. "Father Henri Nouwen on Growing Spiritually." Interview by Mitch Finley, part 2. *Our Sunday Visitor,* 25 December 1988, 8–9.

————. "The Church and Its Ministry in the '90s." Interview by Gunar Kravalis. *The Presbyterian Record,* September 1991, 30–32.

————. "Gazing at Jesus." *Youthworker,* Spring 1993, 38–44.

————. "For Henri Nouwen, Death Not So Mortal." *National Catholic Reporter,* 1 April 1994, 11–12.

————. "On Death and Aging." *Cross Point,* Fall 1995, 1–8.

————. "Loneliness and Community." Interview by Darryl Tippens. *Wineskins* 2, no. 7: 14–19.

————. "Interview with Henri Nouwen." *Alive Now!,* November–December 1994, 36–43.

Introductions and Forewords to Books

Nouwen, Henri. Foreword to *The Practice of the Presence of God.* New York: Doubleday Image Books, 1977.

————. Introduction to *Soul Friend: The Practice of Christian Spirituality.* San Francisco: Harper and Row, 1977.

————. Introduction to *Desert Wisdom: Sayings From the Desert Fathers.* Garden City, NY: Doubleday & Company, 1982.

————. Foreword to *Man and Woman He Made Them.* London: Darton, Longman and Todd, 1984.

————. Foreword to *From Brokenness to Community.* Mahwah, N.J.: Paulist Press, 1992.

————. Introduction to *A Dry Roof and A Cow.* Akron, Pa.: Mennonite Central Committee Publication, 1994.

Pamphlets

Nouwen, Henri. "A Conversation with Henri Nouwen." *Harvard Divinity Bulletin,* April–May 1983, reprint in pamphlet form by The Wider Quaker Fellowship, 1984.

————. *Discovering Our Gifts Through Service to Others: A FADICA Conversation with Rev. Henri J. M. Nouwen.* Washington, D.C.: FADICA, November 1994.

————. *The Peace That Is Not of This World.* Stafford, Va.: American Life League, n.d.

Chapters in Books

Nouwen, Henri. "Celibacy and the Holy." Essay in *Celibate Loving: Encounter in Three Dimensions,* ed. Mary Anne Huddleston. New York: Paulist Press, 1984.

Nouwen, Henri, Donald P. MacNeill, and Douglas A. Morrison. "Action." In *Modern Spirituality: An Anthology.* Templegate: Templegate Publishers, 1986.

Nouwen, Henri. "Christ of the Americas." In *Border Religions of Faith.* Maryknoll, N.Y.: Orbis Books, 1987.

Nouwen, Henri, and Richard Foster. "The Spiritual Leader's Vitality." In *Leaders: Learning Leadership from Some of Christianity's Best*, ed. Harold Myra. Waco: Word Books, 1987.

Nouwen, Henri. "Theology as Doxology: Reflections on Theological Education." Essay in *Caring for the Commonweal: Education for Religious and Public Life*, ed. Parker J. Palmer, Barbara G. Wheeler, and James W. Fowler. Macon: Mercer University Press, 1990.

———. "Our Story, Our Wisdom." In *HIV/AIDS: The Second Decade*. San Francisco: National Catholic AIDS Network and Communication Ministry, 1995.

Papers Presented at Professional Meetings

Nouwen, Henri. "Integrating the Disciplines in Theological Education." Paper presented at the twelfth biennial meeting of the Association for Professional Education for Ministry, Macalester College, St. Paul, Minn., 15–18 June 1972.

———. "From Resentment to Gratitude." Paper presented at the National Conference of Catholic Seminarians, Chicago, Ill., 28 April 1973.

Unpublished Manuscripts

Nouwen, Henri. "The Death of Martin Luther King."

———. "Education to the Ministry."

———. "From Opaqueness to Transparency: Reflections on the Prayerful Life."

———. "Marriage as Ministry."

———. "On the Possibility and Desirability of Love."

———. "The Self-Availability of the Homosexual."

———. "Spiritual Direction."

Speeches, Addresses, Homilies

Nouwen, Henri. "Contemplation and Action." Sermon preached at St. Paul's Church, Columbia University, 10 December 1978, for the tenth anniversary of Thomas Merton's death.

———. "The Spirituality of the Religion Teacher." Homily given at St. Patrick's Cathedral, 22 April 1981, for the NCEA Religious Education Congress.

———. "A Call to Peacemaking." Adapted from a talk entitled "A Journey Interrupted" delivered in Washington, D.C., 27 July 1983, at a worship service arranged by the U.S. Catholic Mission Association.

———. "The Spirituality of Peacemaking." Speech made for the celebration of the anniversary of the Nobertine Foundation in Peoli, 1983.

———. "The Power of Love and the Power of Fear." Address made at the Presbyterian Peace Fellowship Breakfast, 197th General Assembly, Presbyterian Church (U.S.A.), Indianapolis, Ind., June 1985.

———. "Mary, Mother of Priests." Address for the Feast of the Visitation of the Blessed Virgin Mary, Cathedral Church of St. Michael, Toronto, Marian Year 1988.

Videocassette

————. *Angels Over the Net*. Prod. Isabelle Steyart and dir. Bart Gavigan. 30 min. Spark Productions, 1995.

Miscellaneous Unpublished Papers

Nouwen, Henri. Syllabus for Communion, Community, Ministry course at Regis College, Toronto, September 1994. Nouwen Archives, Yale Divinity School Library.

Secondary Sources

Books

Ahlstrom, Sydney E. *A Religious History of the American People*. New Haven: Yale University Press, 1972.

Bellah, Robert N., Richard Madsen, William M. Sullivan, Ann Swidler, and Steven M. Tipton. *Habits of the Heart*. New York: Harper and Row Perennial Library, 1985.

Beumer, Jurjen. *Henri Nouwen: A Restless Seeking for God*. Trans. David E. Schlaver and Nancy Forest-Flier. New York: Crossroad Publishing Company, 1997. Originally published in Dutch as *Onrustig zoeken naar God: spiritualiteit van Henri Nouwen* (Tielt, Belgium: Uitgeverij Lannoo, 1996).

Bouyer, Louis. *The Spirituality of the New Testament and the Fathers*. London: Burns and Oates, 1913.

Callahan, Annice. *Spiritual Guides for Today*. New York: Crossroad Publishing Company, 1992.

————. *Spiritualities of the Heart*. New York: Paulist Press, 1990.

Carroll, Jackson W., Douglas W. Johnson, and Martin E. Marty. *Religion in America: 1950–Present*. San Francisco: Harper and Row, 1979.

Conn, Joann Wolski. *Spirituality and Personal Maturity*. Lanham, Md.: University Press of America, 1989.

Cunningham, Lawrence S., and Keith J. Egan. *Christian Spirituality: Themes from the Tradition*. New York: Paulist Press, 1996.

Desert Fathers, The. Trans. from the Latin with an introduction by Helen Waddell. New York: Vintage Books, 1998. Originally published in 1936.

Douglas, Mary, and Steven Tipton, eds. *Religion and America: Spiritual Life in a Secular Age*. Boston: Beacon Press, 1983.

Downey, Michael. *Understanding Christian Spirituality*. New York: Paulist Press, 1997.

Elder, E. Rozanne, ed. *The Spirituality of Western Christendom*. Kalamazoo: Cistercian Publications, 1976.

————. *The Spirituality of Western Christendom, II: The Roots of the Modern Christian Tradition*. Kalamazoo: Cistercian Publications, 1984.

Ellwood, Robert S. *The Fifties Spiritual Marketplace: American Religion in a Decade of Conflict*. New Brunswick: Rutgers University Press, 1997.

Flowers, Ronald B. *Religion in Strange Times: The 1960s and 1970s*. Macon: Mercer University Press, 1984.

Foster, Richard. *Celebration of Discipline*. Rev. ed. San Francisco: HarperSan-Francisco, 1988.

————. *Streams of Living Water*. San Francisco: HarperSanFrancisco, 1998.

Gallup, George, Jr., and Jim Castelli. *The People's Religion: American Faith in the 90s*. New York: Macmillan Publishing Company, 1989.

George, Carol. *God's Salesman: Norman Vincent Peale and the Power of Positive Thinking*. New York: Oxford University Press, 1993.

Hanson, Bradley C., ed. *Modern Christian Spirituality*. Atlanta: Scholars Press, 1990.

Henderson, Kyle L. "The Reformation of Pastoral Theology in the Life of Henri J. M. Nouwen." Ph.D. diss., Southwestern Baptist Theological Seminary, 1994.

Holmes, Urban T. *A History of Christian Spirituality*. New York: The Seabury Press, 1981.

Holt, Bradley P. *Thirsty for God: A Brief History of Christian Spirituality*. Minneapolis: Augsburg Fortress, 1993.

Hudson, Winthrop S. *Religion in America*. 3d ed. New York: Charles Scribner's Sons, 1981.

Jaszczak, Sandra, ed. *Encyclopedia of Associations*. 32d ed. Detroit: Gale Research, 1997.

Jones, Cheslyn, Geoffrey Wainwright, and Edward Yarnold, eds. *The Study of Spirituality*. Cambridge: University Press, 1986.

Jorstad, Erling. *Holding Fast/Pressing On: Religion in America in the 1980s*. New York: Greenwood Press, 1990.

Kelly, Thomas R. *A Testament of Devotion*. San Francisco: HarperSanFrancisco, 1996.

Lawrence, Brother. *The Practice of the Presence of God*. Mount Vernon, N.Y.: Peter Pauper Press, 1973.

Martin, William. *Prophet with Honor*. New York: William Morrow and Company, Inc., 1991.

McBrien, Richard P. *Catholicism*. Rev. ed. San Francisco: HarperSanFrancisco, 1994.

McGinn, Bernard. Introduction to *Christian Spirituality*, Vol. 16 of *World Spirituality: An Encyclopedic History of the Religious Quest*. New York: Crossroad Publishing Company, 1992.

Miller, Craig Kennet. *Baby Boomer Spirituality: Ten Essential Values of a Generation*. Nashville: Discipleship Resources, 1992.

Noll, Mark A. *A History of Christianity in the United States and Canada*. Grand Rapids: Wm. B. Eerdmans Publishing Company, 1992.

Noonan, D. P. *Missionary with a Mike: The Bishop Sheen Story*. New York: Pageant Press, 1968.

Plato. *Dialogues of Plato*. Vol. 7 of *Great Books of the Western World*, ed. Robert M. Hutchins. Chicago: Encyclopedia Britannica, 1952.

Roof, Wade Clark. *A Generation of Seekers: The Spiritual Journeys of the Baby Boom Generation.* San Francisco: HarperSanFrancisco, 1993.

Saliers, Don E. "Christian Spirituality in an Ecumenical Age." *Christian Spirituality: Post-Reformation and Modern,* ed. Bernard McGinn. New York: Crossroad Publishing Company, 1991.

Sheldrake, Philip. *Images of Holiness.* London: Darton, Longman and Todd, 1987.

———. *Spirituality and History: Questions of Interpretation and Method.* London: SPCK, 1995.

Smith, Hannah Whitall. *The Christian's Secret of a Happy Life.* Uhrichsville, Ohio: Barbour Publishing, 1998.

Tickle, Phyllis A. *Re-Discovering the Sacred: Spirituality in America.* New York: Crossroad Publishing Company, 1995.

Willard, Dallas. *The Divine Conspiracy.* San Francisco: HarperSanFrancisco, 1998.

Wuthnow, Robert. *After Heaven: Spirituality in America Since the 1950s.* Berkeley: University of California Press, 1998.

———. *The Restructuring of American Religion.* Princeton: Princeton University Press, 1988.

Journal Articles

Alexander, Jon. "What Do Recent Writers Mean by Spirituality?" *Spirituality Today* 32 (1980): 247–56.)

Ashley, J. Matthew. "The Turn to Spirituality? The Relationship Between Theology and Spirituality." *Christian Spirituality Bulletin* 3 (Fall 1995): 13–18.

Astell, Ann W. "Postmodern Christian Spirituality: A *Coincidentia Oppositorum*?" *Christian Spirituality Bulletin* 4 (Summer 1996): 1, 3–5.

Becker, William H. "Spiritual Struggle in Contemporary America." *Theology Today* 51 (July 1994): 256–69.

Belshaw, G. P. Mellick. "The Issue of Christian Spirituality." *Anglican Theological Review* 49 (April 1967): 204–14.

Boers, Arthur. "Abide in Me." *The Other Side* 27 (January–February 1991): 13.

———. "Henri Nouwen: A Conversation with a Friend." *The Other Side* 25 (September–October 1989): 14–19.

———. "A Spiritual Feast for Nouwen Aficionados." *Compass,* May–June 1995, 41.

Brussat, Frederic A. "27 Ways to Live a Spiritual Life Every Day." *Utne Reader,* no. 64 (July–August 1994): 91–95.

Cenkner, William. "Theme and Counter-Theme in Contemporary Spirituality." *Horizons* 9 (Spring 1982): 87–95.

Coleman, John A. "Exploding Spiritualities: Their Social Causes, Social Location and Social Divide." *Christian Spirituality Bulletin* 5 (Spring 1997): 9–15.

Conn, Joann Wolski. "Horizons on Contemporary Spirituality." *Horizons* 9 (Spring 1982): 60–73.

Cooper, David A. "Invitation to the Soul." *Parabola,* Spring 1994, 6–11.

Cousins, Ewert. "A Spirituality for the New Axial Period." *Christian Spirituality Bulletin* 2 (Fall 1994): 12–15.

Cunningham, Lawrence S. *"Extra Arcam Noe*: Criteria for Christian Spirituality." *Christian Spirituality Bulletin* 3 (Spring 1995): 6–9.

Emeth, Elaine V. "A Change of Heart." *Sojourners* 22 (January 1993): 43–44.

Grainger, Brett. "Henri: A Heart's Desire." *Sojourners* 25 (November–December 1996): 26–30.

Hanson, Bradley C. "Theological Approaches to Spirituality: A Lutheran Perspective." *Christian Spirituality Bulletin* 2 (Spring 1994): 5–8.

Hardy, Richard P. "Christian Spirituality Today: Notes On Its Meaning." *Spiritual Life* 28 (1982): 151–59.

Hiltner, Seward. "Henri J.M. Nouwen: Pastoral Theologian of the Year." *Pastoral Psychology* 27 (Fall 1978): 4–7.

Jones, Timothy. "Book Review: Three Books on Spiritual Life." *Quarterly Review* 7 (Summer 1987): 101–8.

Kelly, Philip. "Living the Second Loneliness: Henri Nouwen at Daybreak." *Companion*, January 1990, 4–12.

Kerr, Hugh T. "Spiritual Discipline." *Theology Today* 49 (January 1993): 449–53.

Kinerk, Edward. "Toward a Method for the Study of Spirituality." *Review for Religious* 40 (1981): 3–19.

King, Anna S. "Spirituality: Transformation and Metamorphosis." *Religion* 26 (1996): 343–51.

Leitner, Gloria J. "The Skeptical Eye: Spirituality From a Skeptical Believer's Point of View." *The Humanist*, May–June 1996, 32–33.

Leonard, William J. "Contemporary Spirituality in Historical Perspective." *Review and Expositor* 76 (Spring 1979): 241–55.

Lewis, Albert Micah. "The Middle Aging of America: Spiritual and Educational Dilemmas for Clergy Education." *Journal of Religious Gerontology* 7:4 (1991): 47–53.

Lynch, Joe. "Way Stations on the Journey." *Sojourners* 18 (May 1989): 36–37.

Marty, Martin E. "American Religious History in the Eighties: A Decade of Achievement." *Church History* 62 (September 1993): 335–77.

———. "The Spirit's Holy Errand: The Search for a Spiritual Style in Secular America." *Daedalus* 96 (Winter 1967): 99–115.

McGinn, Bernard. "The Letter and the Spirit: Spirituality as an Academic Discipline." *Christian Spirituality Bulletin* 1 (Fall 1993): 1, 3–9.

McGuire, Meredith B. "Mapping Contemporary American Spirituality: A Sociological Perspective." *Christian Spirituality Bulletin* 5 (Spring 1997):1, 3–8.

Mogabgab, John S. "The Spiritual Pedagogy of Henri Nouwen." *Reflection*, January 1981, 4–6.

Moore, Thomas. "Does America Have a Soul?" *Mother Jones*, September–October 1996, 26–32.

Mouw, Richard J. "Busy." *The Reformed Journal* (May 1987): 3–4.

Principe, Walter. "Toward Defining Spirituality." *Studies in Religion* 12 (Spring 1983): 127–41.

Principe, Walter H. "Broadening the Focus: Context as a Corrective Lens in Reading Historical Works in Spirituality." *Christian Spirituality Bulletin* 2 (Spring 1994): 1, 3.

Schneiders, Sandra. "Contemporary Religious Life: Death or Transformation?" *Cross Currents*, Winter 1996–97, 510–535.

———. "A Hermeneutical Approach to the Study of Christian Spirituality." *Christian Spirituality Bulletin* 2 (Spring 1994): 9–14.

———. "Spirituality as an Academic Discipline: Reflections from Experience." *Christian Spirituality Bulletin* 1 (Fall 1993): 10–15.

———. "Spirituality in the Academy." *Theological Studies* 150 (December 1989): 676–697.

———. "The Study of Christian Spirituality: Contours and Dynamics of a Discipline." *Christian Spirituality Bulletin* 6 (Spring 1998): 1, 3–12.

———. "Theology and Spirituality: Strangers, Rivals, or Partners?" *Horizons* 13 (Fall 1986): 253–74.

Sheldrake, Philip. "Some Continuing Questions: The Relationship Between Spirituality and Theology." *Christian Spirituality Bulletin* 2 (Spring 1994): 15–17.

———. "The Crisis of Postmodernity." *Christian Spirituality Bulletin* 4 (Summer 1996): 6–10.

Talbert, Betty. "Contemplation in the Spirituality of Henri Nouwen." *Mission Journal* 16 (August 1982): 3–6.

Talbert, Betty W. "The Way of the Heart." *Mission Journal* 16 (August 1982): 19–21.

Toolan, David S. "Harmonic Convergences and All That: New Age Spirituality." *Cross Currents* (Fall 1996): 369–78.

Uomoto, Jay M. "Human Suffering, Psychotherapy and Soul Care: The Spirituality of Henri J. M. Nouwen at the Nexus." *Journal of Psychology and Christianity* 14: 4 (1995): 342–54.

Vanier, Jean. "The Healing Community." *Compass*, September 1989, 6–8.

Van Ness, Peter H. "Philosophy as Spiritual Catalyst: Spirituality in a Secular Age" *Christian Spirituality Bulletin* 5 (Spring 1997): 16–18.

Wallis, Jim. "The Deepest Questions of Life and Faith." *Sojourners* 25 (November–December 1996): 29.

Whitney-Brown, Carolyn. "Safe in God's Heart." *Sojourners* 25 (November–December 1996): 30–32.

Winter, Gibson. "America in Search of Its Soul." *Theology Today* 53 (January 1996): 466–75.

Wiseman, James A. "Teaching Spiritual Theology: Methodological Reflections." *Spirituality Today*, 1989, 143–54.

Dailies and Weeklies Articles

Argan, Glen. "Nouwen Finds a Home." *Western Catholic Reporter*, 21 March 1994, 6.

Armbruster, Carl J. "Creative Ministry." Book review in *Commonweal*, 3 March 1972, 528.

Begley, Sharon. "Science of the Sacred." *Newsweek*, 28 November 1994, 58–59.

Bickel, Bob. "Priest's Prolific Prose 'An Afterthought.' " *Rochester* (N.Y.) *Democrat and Chronicle*, 2 February 1983, B5.

Bloesch, Donald G. "Lost in the Mystical Myths." *Christianity Today* 35 (19 August 1991): 22–24.

Boers, Arthur. "A Feast of Nouwen." *Christianity Today* 33 (16 June 1989): 38–42.

———. "Spiritual Retreat Unites People and Traditions." *Mennonite Reporter*, 1 November 1993, 8–9.

———. "What Henri Nouwen Found at Daybreak." *Christianity Today* 38 (3 October 1994): 28–31.

Byron, William J. "Spirituality on the Road to Re-employment." *America* 161 (20 May 1995): 15–16.

Carr, Neil J. "Liberation Spirituality: 60 Years of A.A." *America* 161 (17 June 1995): 20–22.

Coady, Mary Frances. "Nouwen Finds Rest at Daybreak." *Catholic New Times*, 23 November 1986, 3.

Crean, Martha. "L'Arche Celebrates 25 Years in Canada." *Catholic New Times*, 22 January 1995, 18.

Crosby, Harriet E. "Where to Start Reading Contemporary Christian Spirituality." *The Christian Century* 109 (3–10 June 1992): 584–87.

Culligan, Kevin. "Are We Wired for God?" *America* 163 (22 March 1997): 23–24.

———. "Spirituality and Healing in Medicine." *America* 162 (31 August 1996): 17–21.

Dart, John. "Protesters Mark Atomic Bombings at Nevada Test Site." *Los Angeles Times*, 10 August 1985, 4.

Desiato, Tonia. "Writing a Reflection of Life." *The Catholic Register*, 1 October 1994, 9.

Doyle, Dennis M. "Traffic Jam on the Spiritual Superhighway." *Commonweal*, 9 September 1994, 18–22.

Durback, Robert. "Ministry and Friendship." *Christian Century* 113 (16 October 1996): 957.

"Dutch Theologian Nouwen to Teach at Divinity School." *Harvard Gazette*, 28 January 1983, 3.

Erb, Maureen. "Thoughts on a Course Taught by Henri Nouwen." *For All the Saints*, newsletter published by All Saints Parish, Brookline, Mass., XLII, no. 22: 12–13.

Frawley, Joan. "A Physician of the Heart, Himself Healed." *National Catholic Register*, 21 December 1986, 9.

Galen, Michele, and Karen West. "Companies Hit the Road Less Traveled: Can Spirituality Enlighten the Bottom Line?" *Business Week*, 5 June 1995, 82–84.

Garvey, John. "Henri Nouwen: Restless No More." *Commonweal*, 8 November 1996, 6–7.

Gergen, David. "A Pilgrimage for Spirituality." *U.S. News and World Report*, 23 December 1996, 80.

Glaser, Chris. "Nouwen's Journey." *Christian Century* 114 (19–26 March 1997): 302–3, 305–6.

Goulet, Yvonne. "Father Nouwen on Nicaragua." *The Church World*, 29 September 1983, 3, 12–13.

Greene, Amy. "An Interview with Catholic Priest Writer Henri Nouwen." *SBC Today*, September 1990, 10–11.

Groves, Richard. "A Living Word." *Christian Century* 113 (16 October 1996): 956–57.

Hamma, Robert M. "The Changing State of Spirituality: 1968–1993." *America* 159 (27 November 1993): 8–10.

"Henri Nouwen Receives Appointment at HDS." *Harvard Divinity Bulletin*, February–March 1983, 2.

Johnston, Jerry. " 'Here and Now' Is Full of Spiritual Lessons." *Desert News*, 15 January 1995, E6.

Jones, Timothy. "The Whole Prayer Catalog." *Christianity Today* 36 (5 October 1992): 72–74.

Kantrowitz, Barbara. "In Search of the Sacred." *Newsweek*, 28 November 1994, 53–55.

Kelley, Ralph. "Nouwen Puts Busy-Ness of Life in Perspective." *The Catholic Transcript*, 3 September 1982, A4.

Kendrick, Stephen. "In Touch with the Blessing: An Interview with Henri Nouwen." *Christian Century* 110 (24–31 March 1993): 318–20.

Kravalis, Gunar. "At Home with Henri Nouwen—A Visit to Daybreak." *The Presbyterian Record*, April 1989, 23–25.

———. "Witness to Parched and Barren Spirits." *Christian Week*, 23 January 1990, 14.

Laabs, Jennifer J. "Balancing Spirituality and Work." *Personnel Journal*, September 1995, 60–76.

Legge, Gordon. "Theologian Reveals Struggles of Heart." *Calgary Herald*, 11 February 1989, E11.

Lusson, Dave. "Guesss Who's Coming to Dinner?" *Newsletter*, published by The School of Divinity, St. John's University, Collegeville, Minn., 1.

Lyall, Sarah. "The Post-New-Age Reader." *The New York Times*, 13 April 1994, C19, c.2.

McDonald, Marci. "The New Spirituality." *Maclean's* 107 (10 October 1994): 44–48.

Meehan, Francis X. "He Pleads, Knowing the Charge to Come." *The Philadelphia Inquirer*, 13 August 1983, A9.

Mullen, Conal. "A Lesson in Love." *The Edmonton Journal*, 26 March 1994, B4.

Odell, Catherine. "Father Nouwen Sees the Light at Daybreak." *Our Sunday Visitor*, 12 July 1992, 5.

Oden, Thomas C. "Blinded by the 'Lite.' " *Christianity Today* 30 (12 September 1994): 14–15.

O'Laughlin, Michael. "Henri Nouwen in Life and in Death." *America* 163 (10 May 1997): 18–20.

Old, Huges Oliphant. "Rescuing Spirituality from the Cloister." *Christianity Today* 38 (20 June 1994): 27–29.

Ortberg, John. "What Makes Spirituality Christian?" *Christianity Today* 39 (6 March 1995): 16–17.

Parachini, Patricia. "Life of the Beloved." *The Catholic World*, March–April 1995, 89.

Parise, Michael. "Catholic-Evangelical Relations Take Historic Step at Congress '85." *The Pilot*, 1 February 1985, 5.

Peterson, Eugene H. "Spirit Quest." *Christianity Today* 37 (8 November 1993): 27–30.

Poundstone, Pat. "The Importance of Prayer." *North Texas Catholic*, 1 April 1994, 14, 16.

"Priest Sees Love, Not Fear, As Basis for Peacemaking." *Catholic Chronicle*, 17 May 1985, 7.

Raspberry, William. "The Desire for a Life That Makes Sense." *Washington Post* 117 (10 December 1993): A, 31, c. 1.

Renner, Gerald. "Modern-day 'Saint' Reflects on Works, Life." *The Hartford Courant*, 14 October 1993, Connecticut page, B11.

Roberts, Mark D. "Read All About It: But Fast, Meditate and Pray for Yourself." *Christianity Today* 29 (20 September 1985): 17.

Rossman, Parker. "Why Are You Going to the Trappists?" *Christian Century* 91 (2 October 1974): 906–9.

Salmon-Heyneman, Jana. "Dutch Priest Advises Spending More Time with God." *Macon Telegraph and News*, 4 January 1989, D1–2.

Sheler, Jeffery L. "Spiritual America." *U.S. News and World Report*, 4 April 1994, 48–59.

Spring, Beth. "A Gallup Poll Finds a Rising Tide of Interest in Religion." *Christianity Today* 27 (21 October 1983): 41.

Steele, Lee. "Priest Says That Peace Must Be Based On Love." *The Blade: Toledo Ohio*, 6 May 1985, 11.

Todd, Douglas. "In Weakness There Is Strength." *The Weekend Sun*, 16 April 1994, D15.

Uhler, Mary C. "From Harvard to l'Arche: Henri Nouwen Shares His Journey." *Catholic Herald*, 23 July 1987, 1, 3.

Vesey, John E. "Nouwen's Difficult Journey." *The Tablet*, 19 May 1983, 3.

Wakefield, Dan. "Spiritual Impact: Encounters with Henri Nouwen." *Christian Century* 114 (19–26 March 1997): 301–3.

Wallis, Claudia. "Faith and Healing." *Time*, 24 June 1996, 59–68.

Walsh, Catherine. "Perspectives." *America* 162 (26 October 1996): 8.

White, Cecile H. "Finding God Within and Without." *Houston Chronicle*, 16 April 1994, E1, 3.

Willard, Dallas. "What Makes Spirituality Christian?" *Christianity Today* 39 (6 March 1995): 16–17.

Witvoet, Bert. "Profile." *Calvinist Contact*, 23 October 1987, 10–11.

Wojcicki, Ed. "Confronted by My Own Words." *Catholic Times*, 27 November 1988, 4.

———. "Dear Henri: About Those Feelings." *Catholic Times*, 30 November 1986, 4.

———. "Dear Henri: Of Hope and Passion in '91." *Catholic Times*, 1 December 1991, 4.

———. "Dear Henri: A Reflection on Power." *Catholic Times*, 3 December 1989, 4.

Woodard, Kenneth L. "Born Again!" *Newsweek*, 25 October 1976, 68–70, 75–76, 78.

———. "On the Road Again." *Newsweek*, 28 November 1994, 61–62.

Yancey, Philip. "Confessions of a Spiritual Amnesiac." *Christianity Today* 40 (15 July 1996): 72.

———. "The Holy Inefficiency of Henri Nouwen." *Christianity Today* 40 (9 December 1996): 80.

Interviews

Christie, Kathy. Interview by author. Tape Recording. Richmond Hill, Ontario. 10 March 1998.

Mosteller, Sue. Interviews by author. Tape Recordings. Richmond Hill, Ontario. 9, 10, and 11 March 1998.

Unpublished Work

Boers, Arthur. "From the House of Fear to the House of Love: An Encounter with Henri Nouwen." Unpublished, n.d. Henri Nouwen Archives, Yale Divinity School Library.

Scripture Index of Nouwen's Books

173

Index